To Sally

Enjoy the
book with a
great glass of
wine

A Mateson

Women of Wine

Women of Wine

*The Rise of Women
in the Global Wine Industry*

Ann B. Matasar

UNIVERSITY OF CALIFORNIA PRESS

Berkeley   Los Angeles   London

University of California Press, one of the most distinguished
university presses in the United States, enriches lives around the
world by advancing scholarship in the humanities, social sciences,
and natural sciences. Its activities are supported by the UC Press
Foundation and by philanthropic contributions from individuals
and institutions. For more information, visit www.ucpress.edu.

University of California Press
Berkeley and Los Angeles, California

University of California Press, Ltd.
London, England

Library of Congress Cataloging-in-Publication Data

Matasar, Ann B., 1940–
    Women of wine : the rise of women in the global wine
industry / Ann B. Matasar.
        p.   cm.
    Includes bibliographical references and index.
    ISBN 0-520-24051-0 (cloth : alk. paper)
    1. Women in the wine industry.   I. Title.

    HD9370.5. M37 2006
    331.4'86632—dc22   2005023244

Manufactured in the United States of America

15 14 13 12 11 10 09 08 07 06
10 9 8 7 6 5 4 3 2 1

The paper used in this publication meets the minimum
requirements of ANSI/NISO Z39.48–1992 (R 1997) (*Permanence
of Paper*).

CONTENTS

LIST OF ILLUSTRATIONS

ACKNOWLEDGMENTS

Winemaking has inspired thousands of books over the years. Few, if any, however, have been devoted solely to women's contributions to the world of wine. This book is intended to fill that void, to highlight those contributions, and to create greater visibility for the remarkable women who are influencing today's wine industry.

Although I have relied heavily on primary and secondary resources for background material, this book would not have been possible without the women and men who granted me interviews. To those individuals with whom I met, my thanks for your insights, thoughtfulness, honesty, inspiration, time, and hospitality. Your experiences and knowledge have given life to this work. I also want to thank the many women throughout the world who responded to my lengthy questionnaire. Although I was unable to interview all of these women, many of their responses are included in the text.

One of the most striking things I discovered in the course of my work was the large number of influential women in the wine industry worldwide. Few days went by without someone telling me about another woman they considered worthy of mention. Unfortunately, it was simply not possible to contact, meet, and include them all in this work, despite their significant contributions. I would like to extend my apologies for such omissions.

Many people provided assistance in producing this book. I am indebted to librarians at Roosevelt University, who expeditiously and pleasantly handled seemingly endless interlibrary loans. Axel Borg at the University of California at Davis guided me through the university's extensive holdings and treated me with exceptional professional courtesy. The reference librarians at the Northbrook, Illinois, Public Library obtained a plethora of resources from a vast number of libraries throughout the United States. The Internet notwithstanding, there is still no substitute for a skilled and caring librarian prepared to assist with interminable interlibrary loans, to chase down obscure articles, and to help locate archival materials.

I have been blessed with several talented friends who have assisted me in this work. To my former student and good friend Muriel Blanchier, a profound *merci* for compensating for my inferior command of French. Barry and Susan Feinberg proved themselves to be picture-perfect friends in helping me assemble the photographs. As we delved into the accuracy of each footnote and quotation, Deborah Pavelka, my colleague, friend, and co-author on many other projects, demonstrated her skills as a forensic accountant. And to Gary Wolfe, who took the time to review the entire manuscript and provide valuable editorial advice, I am eternally grateful. After all this support, any errors that remain are solely mine.

My ability to travel extensively for interviews and research was underwritten by funding from my named professorship at Roosevelt University. The university also granted me a research leave for the spring 2004 semester to complete my work on the Southern Hemisphere. I wish to thank all members of the Roosevelt University administration for their support and encouragement.

To my children, Seth and Toby, whose interest in wine helped inspire this project and whose encouragement kept my spirits up when progress was slow, my love. Last, but hardly least, my love and gratitude to my husband, Bob, without whom this work would not have been possible. He suffered through it all on a daily basis as a counselor, constructive critic, wine enthusiast, and companion waiting patiently for me to complete interviews. More than a chauffeur who drove on both sides of the road, he kept me on track and challenged me to be my best. He deserved every great glass of wine he was offered. It is to Bob that I dedicate this book.

Introduction

Throughout recorded history, wine has been a common thread running through innumerable cultures, religions, and nations. No business or industry reaches further back in history or is more global in scope than the wine industry. And no other industry has so resolutely excluded women from positions of influence for so long.

Despite the overwhelming male dominance of the wine industry, one hears repeatedly about individual women who have broken the barriers. Everyone seems astonished to discover a unique woman who has conquered age-old prejudices in order to become an exemplary winemaker, a winery owner, or a sommelier. But we have lacked an evaluation of the cumulative implications of women's advancement in the world of wine—in other words, scholarship has focused on the trees but ignored the forest.

Individual women, like the separate tiles of a mosaic, do not reflect the whole scene. Standing back to look at the completed mosaic, one discovers a new and exciting phenomenon: a substantial and growing number of women who now influence the wine industry and hold positions of power within it. Although the industry remains male dominated, it is no longer able to exclude women or prohibit their advancement across the board. No list of today's premier winery owners and winemakers is complete without the names of women. Any discussion of those in authority who shape the industry—from educators, writers, and critics to executives and sommeliers—must now include both genders. In the Old World as well as the New World, women are represented all the way up the power structure.

Within the experiences of individual women, the gender bias they have encountered is an inescapable theme, but the degree to which it has impeded their progress varies greatly. Men appear in their narratives not only as obstacles and naysayers but also as mentors, partners, and friends. The most striking common characteristic of all these accomplished women is that they are a gutsy group of supreme achievers who refused to be diverted from their path.

Some, such as Corinne Mentzelopoulos (Château Margaux), Baroness Philippine de Rothschild (Château Mouton Rothschild), May-Eliane de Lencquesaing (Château Pichon Longueville Comtesse de Lalande), Laura Bianchi (Castello di Monsanto), Lorenza Sebasti (Castello di Ama), or Chiara Lungarotti and Teresa Severini (Cantine Lungarotti), are proprietors of legendary estates. Others, such as Sandra MacIver (Matanzas Creek Winery), Cathy Corison (Corison Winery), Susana Balbo (Susana Balbo), and Diana Cullen (Cullen Wines), founded new estates. Some represent the present and future generations of well-established wine families: Gina Gallo (Gallo of Sonoma), Albiera Antinori (Cantine Marchesi Antinori), Laura Catena (Bodega Catena Zapata).

Some are winemakers whose name on a wine label imparts a guaranteed cachet—Lalou Bize-Leroy (Domaine Leroy), Heidi Peterson Barrett (La Sirena), and Vanya Cullen (Cullen), for example. Others, such as Serena Sutcliffe, MW (Sotheby's), and Jancis Robinson, MW, OBE, are writers and critics who have extraordinary influence over consumers' tastes, the demand for particular wines, and the prices those wines command. Some, including Madeline Triffon, MS, and Alpana Singh, MS, are sommeliers who oversee the selection of wines and match wines with food for the world's finest restaurants. Others—such as professors Ann Noble, Carole Meredith, and Linda Bisson (all of the University of California at Davis)—provide the knowledge needed to improve the industry.

What one sees is the emergence of an industry that is changing in a multitude of ways, from vineyard management to winemaking to international sales. No matter where you look, women are participating in and leading these changes. Their collective experience provides an instructive paradigm for women seeking advancement throughout the business world.

This book begins by establishing a historical context for appreciating women's contributions to the modern wine industry. Chapter 1 discusses the hurdles placed in the path of women historically. Chapter 2 reviews the changes in the global wine industry during the last twenty-five years of the twentieth century that opened the gates for substantial numbers of women. This chapter also provides a general overview of the wine industry, particularly those aspects most relevant to understanding women's influence. Chapter 3 is a historical tribute to four nineteenth-century women pioneers who left an indelible mark on the industry and their name on some of the world's greatest wines.

The four chapters that follow are devoted to women winemakers and proprietors. The discussion corresponds to the geographic division of the wine world, namely, the Old World, defined as European winegrowing nations (chapters 4 and 5), and the New World, defined as winegrowing nations originally colonized by Europeans (chapters 6 and 7).

Chapters 8 and 9 present portraits of professional women who influence the wine industry by virtue of specialized expertise. Chapter 8 focuses on women who add to the body of knowledge on which the industry and consumers of wine depend. Those involved with unique aspects of wine marketing are the subject of chapter 9. Finally, chapter 10 offers an overview and a look toward the future of women in the world of wine.

Throughout, the chapters draw insights from the women and men who were interviewed for this work. A complete list of the interviewees is found in appendix 1. In addition, many others responded to a detailed questionnaire; their quoted responses appear in italic type. No citations accompany these comments, nor is there a list of respondents, because these individuals were promised anonymity.

CHAPTER ONE

Women Need Not Apply

For centuries, biases, traditions, religious practices, superstitions, physical characteristics, and social stereotypes have conspired to keep women from achieving positions of influence in the world of wine. As the wine industry advanced and spread from the Old World to the New World, one theme remained constant: "Women need not apply."

NICE GIRLS DON'T DRINK

In the aftermath of the Great Flood, Noah planted grapes, made wine, and became intoxicated on Mount Ararat.[1] He's lucky he wasn't a woman, because he would have been remembered more for his inebriation than for his ark. Throughout history, gender distinctions have permeated all aspects of wine—its production, its consumption, its distribution, and its appreciation.

Wine has been "perhaps the most historically charged and culturally symbolic of the foods and beverages with which we regularly have contact."[2] Inextricably linked with religious worship, revelry, camaraderie, and upper-class entitlement, wine has often been a beverage reserved for men of privilege. Women, regardless of social standing, were associated with wine's excesses rather than its benefits: inebriated women were frequently linked to indiscriminate sexuality, promiscuity, and adultery. The Roman poet and satirist Juvenal asked, "When she is drunk, what matters to the Goddess of Love? She cannot tell her groin from her head."[3]

Wine, known as "the gift of the gods," helped the ancient Egyptians attain a heightened spirituality. It also was the aspirin of its day, used medicinally to relieve daily stress and alleviate a host of physical ailments. Jars of wine were among the items placed in the tombs of Egyptian upper-class men so that life after death would continue to be comfortable. The social status of the deceased determined the amount of wine used for anointing bodies and entombments. Egyptian women, however, were not entitled to similar benefits for fear they would become intoxicated and act promiscuously in the afterlife.[4]

In ancient Greece, all men were able to experience the reduced inhibitions, greater relaxation, and enhanced social interactions (including sexual relations) that accompanied wine drinking. But the Greeks, like the Egyptians, believed that women had a predilection for drunkenness and excess and therefore frowned on female drinking. Upper-class Greek men also considered women who did drink barbaric because, unlike men, women did not dilute their wine or use additives such as seawater.[5]

The Greeks established the first great male drinking clubs, called symposia, in which wealthy men came together to converse and consume wine. Greek women were allowed to participate only as accessories, as musicians, servers, or prostitutes.[6] The Greeks understood that such informal social interaction provided the basis for formal political and commercial relationships—and when respectable women were excluded from these interactions and conversations, they were also excluded from political and economic activities. Fraternization in a single-sex environment intended for drinking remains a major hindrance to the advancement of women in all professions to this day.

The Romans replaced the Greek symposia with male gatherings known as convivia, centered on fellowship and wine drinking. In early Rome, prohibitions on female drinking were more severe than those imposed by the Greeks: women were not even permitted to serve wine, and until 194 B.C.E. any woman found drinking could be put to death or divorced. Over the years, this unambiguous opposition eased, as wine became a dietary staple. On occasion, women were even permitted to participate in the convivia. But Roman men, fearful of female adultery, continued to bar married women from social settings where wine was consumed, establishing a precedent for gender discrimination based on marital status.[7]

Prejudices regarding women and wine continued through the centuries. In seventeenth- and eighteenth-century Europe, prostitutes were the only women admitted to male-only drinking establishments such as French cabarets and taverns. Married women were not allowed to cross the thresholds even when they needed to speak with their husbands.[8]

Nothing changed as wine drinking spread to the New World. Private gentlemen's clubs and all-male dinner parties were the direct descendants of the earlier symposia and convivia. The collegiality, intellectual sophistication, and learning long associated with wine consumption remained identified with male-only environments.[9] Additional, more "modern" biases were added to the longstanding concerns regarding female wine consumption. The ability to appreciate wine's nuances became associated with masculinity. Some assumed that women would spoil tastings by wearing perfume that detracted from the wine's bouquet.[10]

It is not a great leap from all-male private clubs to male-only winegrowers' associations. Not until the year 2000 did the oldest and most prestigious of the Bordeaux *confréries* (brotherhoods), the Jurade of Saint-Emilion, finally admit its first two women, after eight hundred years of exclusion. It was self-interest that eventually opened up the membership rolls of the Jurade: the organization recognized that its significance was being undermined because it did not include some of the most important wine personalities in Saint-Emilion—who happened to be women. This change is a great affirmation of the achievements of women in the wine world. It is notable, however, that the two female inductees, Beatrice Ondet and Françoise de Wilde, declined to be labeled as feminists. Ondet remarked, "I am not by any means a feminist. . . . It isn't a question of sex, but of competence and devotion to the profession. A woman is just as likely to be able to do certain things as well as a man." Not acknowledging the inconsistency between her disclaimer of feminism and her assertion of equality, she also denied "that she and other formidable women in Bordeaux may have exerted pressure on the gentlemen of the Jurade." Both women agreed to dress in the same ceremonial robes as the men and to be called *jurat*, a masculine term.[11]

WINE IN RELIGIOUS RITUALS

Both Jewish and Christian religious traditions incorporate wine into festivities and rituals.[12] Wine drinking has a long history in Jewish tradition: Noah planted grapes and made wine on Mount Ararat, and the two spies sent by Moses to scout the Land of Canaan returned bearing grapes.[13] Judaism associates wine with consecration and sacraments, including wine drinking in the celebration of the Sabbath and all religious events and holidays. Both men and women are expected to consume four glasses of wine at the seder and prescribed amounts at other rituals such as weddings. Women have a special role at the bris (circumcision) of eight-day-old boys: the mother consumes the wine used as an anesthetic when saying prayers for her child.[14]

Specifically, Judaism requires kosher wine for all religious functions and for the recitation of the Kiddush, the prayer thanking God for the fruit of the vine. Written by the rabbi, philosopher, and physician Maimonides (Moses ben Maimon), the rules defining kosher wine represent the first legal code governing wine production. They provide a clear example that "patterns of wine use . . . typically reveal a great deal about how religious groups go about incorporating new members and, in turn, separating these members from 'outsiders.'"[15]

Unlike the Egyptian, Greek, and Roman traditions, Jewish law does not preclude women's participation in the winemaking process or denigrate female wine drinking. Rather, the central stipulation governing the production of kosher wine is that "the grapes and wine can be handled only by Sabbath observant Jews from grape crushing to consumption, unless the wine is Mevushal (pasteurized)."[16] Because women as well as men can qualify as Sabbath observant, gender is not a requisite factor in the making of kosher wine or in serving as the *mashgiach,* the supervisor who ensures that the wine is made in a kosher manner.[17]

Historical practice, however, has strayed from gender neutrality. Kosher wine is made exclusively by Orthodox Jews, who have strict rules regarding gender separation. Because women cannot be rabbis within Orthodox Judaism, only men are able to serve as a *rav hamachshir,* the person who determines whether a wine is kosher. Orthodox practice also requires a Jewish man to lead the Kiddush. In practice, then, kosher winemaking is virtually an exclusively male preserve.

Like Jews, Christians also include wine in their rituals. The great Christian theologian Paul Tillich explained the sacramental importance of wine by comparing it to the life cycle: "Only wine of all drinks continues to live and grow in the bottle. First, it is a baby, then it is a child, then it enters puberty and becomes a teenager, then it becomes a young adult, then wine reaches its full maturity, and slowly it enters old age—some wines gracefully, some harshly, and then it dies. Of all drinks, wine alone recapitulates life. That is why wine is a sacrament."[18]

Christianity attributes symbolic importance to wine for the commemoration of Jesus's first miracle at Cana, where he converted water to wine at a wedding. The inclusion of wine at the Last Supper led to the incorporation of wine into the Eucharist as the embodiment of Jesus's blood.[19]

It is wine's ritualistic importance to Catholicism, in particular, that caused vineyards and winemaking to be protected after the fall of Rome and eventually introduced to all corners of the earth. The importance of the Catholic Church in the spread of winemaking can be seen throughout the Old World. Great European vineyards on the sites of former monasteries such as Graacher Himmelreich (Germany), Badia a Coltibuono

(Italy), and Châteauneuf-du-Pape (France) bear ongoing testament to this tradition. Much of the New World owes its winemaking industry to Catholic missionaries, primarily male priests, who planted grapes and made wine for ritual use as well as for daily consumption.[20]

The association of wine with Catholic rituals and the dominance of Catholic missionaries in wine production by definition excluded women, who were not allowed to conduct Mass and who were either absent from the missions or in subservient roles. In California, for example, this legacy continued to adversely affect women's participation in the wine industry until the early 1970s, when the demand for California wine and for workers to produce it made the continued exclusion of women impractical. Other New World nations experienced similar phenomena.

FEMININE WINES AND OTHER FICTIONS

As more women entered the wine world, gender distinctions were sometimes transferred to the wines themselves. Enophiles describe wines as either "feminine" or "masculine," with the latter often considered superior. Feminization of wine is intended as a left-handed compliment that conjures up old social and cultural stereotypes and reinstates the unflattering relationship of women, wine, and sexuality: "Wine itself has many feminine qualities. It is graceful, it pleases, it needs great care and attention . . . and, during its variable lifetime, you never know what it will do next."[21] The attributes assigned to "feminine" wines abound: soft, elegant, charming, seductive, buxom, sensual, voluptuous, lively, bewitching, fine, delicate, subtle, restrained, showing breed and finesse.[22]

Winemaking itself has long maintained a gender-based division of labor. In many instances, only men were permitted to harvest grapes and handle the crush. Women were not allowed to stomp the grapes, in the belief that their physical structure and lack of height would foul the extract. They were, however, permitted to pick and sort grapes, tasks that required patience, delicate hands, and almost maternal caring. Vin

Santo, an Italian dessert wine made in small quantities, actually came to be know as "the women's wine."[23] Still, some proprietors did bar women from picking grapes, considering females too chatty and inefficient.[24]

The most serious handicap encountered by women was lack of access to cellar work, an essential area of experience for anyone seeking to be a winemaker. Women were considered too weak to do cellar work, which involved handling barrels, racking, and working with other equipment. Even with the advent of modern technology that substantially reduced the need for physical strength, this "protection" of women became a subterfuge for discrimination. Rather than being assessed as individuals, women as a class were written off.[25]

Persistent superstition compounded the problem. In some French wineries to this day, women are not allowed near fermenting wine because of the belief that if they are menstruating the wine might turn to vinegar or referment monthly.[26] One French woman winemaker vividly remembers this biased treatment: *"When I started, there wasn't a field more sexist than vine-growing and enology! At that time, it was said that a woman shouldn't get into a wine cellar, because if she did, her 'petticoat' would make the wine turn sour."*

Ironically, there is at least one physical distinction that should have worked to the benefit of women: the sense of taste, including the sense of smell. In two olfactory sensitivity studies, one conducted at the Clinical Smell and Taste Research Center of the University of Pennsylvania and the other at the Social Issues Research Centre of the University of Cardiff in Wales, women consistently outperformed men in odor identification and sensitivity on the Smell Identification Test, regardless of age, ethnicity, or cultural background.[27] Additional research on taste perceptions conducted by Dr. Linda Bartoshuk, professor of neuroscience in the ear, nose, and throat section of the Yale School of Medicine's Surgery Department, established three categories of tasters: nontasters (a projected 25 percent of the population), medium tasters (50 percent), and supertasters (25 percent). The group of supertasters, who had the most taste buds and the greatest sensitivity to taste differences, was made up predominantly of women.[28]

Wine tasting, of course, is a subjective experience, a skill that is honed over time. Women may have a natural ability to be better tasters, with more sensitive palates, but their social exclusion from tastings and judging panels prevented them from developing their skills to the fullest. Opportunity, practice, and training have allowed men to dominate a field in which women held a natural advantage. In Australia, for example, women were excluded as judges on the panels of wine shows until 1983. Judging at the wine shows "was the last bastion of male domination in the Australian wine industry guided in principle and deed by an agricultural society rooted in rural conservativism."[29]

SOCIAL AND PSYCHOLOGICAL FACTORS

Women continue to face obstacles arising from social stereotypes, psychological factors, and role conflicts. Conventional wisdom, for example, holds that women are more averse to risk-taking than men and thus will be less likely to succeed in the uncertain and competitive enterprises of grape growing and winemaking.[30] Another damaging assumption is that women cannot manage effectively because men will refuse to work for them. In fact, the large Medoc (Bordeaux) estates do not hire women as managers, in order to avoid these sorts of power struggles.[31] Even in some areas of the New World, fewer women are found in viticulture, for fear that male migrant workers will not accept them as supervisors. As this book will show, however, the women of today's wine industry have given the lie to such generalizations—they courageously take the risks necessary for success, they manage large enterprises, and they skillfully supervise both male and female employees.

Although many male-dominated wine groups have become substantially more hospitable to women in recent years, there remains an underlying current of discomfort and a sense of social isolation for many women in the wine world: *"Being a female, I have been underpaid and over-*

worked. My opinion has not been readily accepted by men with seniority over me. I cannot socially join the men winemakers' network." "Social situations are still difficult to comfortably infiltrate." "I often feel I am overlooked or forgotten about when the 'boys' plan an event or a marketing trip."

Women's responses to this lingering discrimination are varied. Some women sulk and become embittered; others feel compelled to deny or downplay their gender ("I am not a woman winemaker; I am a wine-maker"), believing that this is the only way they can gain full recognition for their accomplishments and acceptance on an equal footing with their male colleagues. Many others fight back, both by resisting discrimination and by pushing themselves to higher levels of achievement; the vast majority of women interviewed for this book acknowledge that women must be better at their jobs than men in order to be deemed equal. Some seek to establish women's networks such as La Donne del Vino (Italy) or Vinissima (Germany) to promote equality and provide support for female wine professionals.

Women's unease in the industry is apparent in one striking way: the frequent hesitation of many female winemakers and proprietors to put their own names on their labels. This may stem from a lack of self-confidence or from a reluctance to seem self-promoting or conceited. Most men have no such qualms; they expect to be recognized for their accomplishments from the outset. For women, however, putting their own name on their label is a sign of increased confidence and pride. In fact, one can follow the personal growth of some women by following the changes in their labels. Sometimes it is a case of overcoming an attitude like the one expressed by an Old World proprietor: *"To reach a high position as a professional remains, in our culture, a male prerogative. One day I heard a neighbor saying, 'Be careful not to become a man.'"*

As is the case in every profession, ambitious women sometimes find that their roles as wives and mothers can conflict with their career goals. Family obligations can still be a major obstacle for women's advancement. Although some have successfully resolved these competing pressures, many women connected to the wine world express great reservations about combining a career with motherhood. As the following comment of a female British journalist reveals, motherhood and its demands can create difficulties between women as well as with male employers: *"I suppose there may be women who encounter problems because of their sex. I think I might tend to say it's because they 'opt out'— 'My child is crying,' 'I've got to take little Willy to school'—all that stuff. As I never had children, I don't know [about those pressures], but I do know that several of the women colleagues here hide behind their brats."*

"WHERE ARE THE WOMEN?"

Given this long history of exclusion and discrimination, it is not surprising that women remain a distinct minority throughout the world of wine. Fortunately for the wine lovers of the world, women's talent, skill, and dedication more than compensate for their lack of numbers. But even the numbers are changing.

The headline of a 1999 article in *Wine Spectator* by executive editor Thomas Matthews asked, "Where Are the Women?" Matthews bemoaned the lack of women in tasting groups (including his own), their low rates of participation in *Wine Spectator*'s annual Wine Experience, and their underrepresentation on that publication's subscriber list. He did acknowledge that financial concerns could be a cause.[32]

But a better way to view the situation would be to applaud the enormously increased presence of women, compared to their numbers thirty years ago when *Wine Spectator* was founded. The Wine Experience, in particular, exemplifies women's interest in wine. It is a two-and-a-half-day extravaganza of wine and food costing at least fifteen hundred dollars per person, excluding hotel and travel expenses. Given the substantial earnings gap that still exists between men and women, the fact that women make up almost one-third of the attendees at the Wine Experience is extraordinary. Additionally, although only about 20 percent of *Wine Spectator*'s subscribers are women, the magazine believes that approximately 40 percent of both the readership and the Web site sub-scribers are female.[33]

During the last quarter of the twentieth century, and now into the twenty-first, women have risen to unexpected heights throughout the wine world. The real answer to the question "Where are the women?"—as this book hopes to show—is "everywhere."

CHAPTER TWO

The Changing Face
of the Wine Business

To wine lovers, "complex" is a sensory term conjuring up myriad aromas and flavors associated with great wines. But it also is an apt description of the wine industry itself. The wine business is one of the world's largest, most intricate, and most intriguing commercial ventures: focused on an exponentially diverse product whose appeal and value change with production conditions, age, and vineyard location;[1] influenced by a dizzying array of social, political, and economic forces; and engaged in a trade maze encompassing global markets with prices ranging from inexpensive to exorbitant. Its vast economic reach employs 1 percent of the world's labor force, with vineyards covering approximately 19.5 million acres and production of more than 7.25 billion gallons.[2] By any measure, wine is not your typical agricultural product.

GLOBALIZATION

Produced in only a limited number of countries blessed with the temperate climate and soil characteristics essential for growing wine-producing grapes, *Vitis vinifera,* wine has always relied on international trade for its global reach.[3] Old World nations, consumers and producers of a majority of the world's wine, dominated the wine trade without serious competitors until the last quarter of the twentieth century. Bound to tradition and straitjacketed by protective regulations, Old World producers at that time were the unchallenged global arbiters of quality—exporting, along with their wine, the mystique of a site *(terroir),* the unpredictable romance of each new vintage, and the glamorous pursuit of the "perfect wine," their enological equivalent of the Holy Grail.

To New World producers, who were often bogged down within their own borders and were ill prepared to rise to the Europeans' challenge, the Old World's advantage appeared insurmountable. Reeling from the havoc caused by Prohibition, Americans were busy re-creating their indigenous wine industry. Isolated geographically, Australia and New Zealand were well-kept secrets "down under." Under the shadow of dictatorships, unstable economics, and the Andes, Argentina and Chile were producing few quality wines. And apartheid had made South Africa an international pariah.

In the mid-1970s, however, New World producers, led by the United States and Australia, began to be significantly more than a blip on the global wine trade's radar screen. Eschewing Old World practice and preaching, they placed their faith in education and modernization to produce consistently high-quality wines at lower cost.[4] They championed agricultural innovations such as drip irrigation, canopy management, and green harvesting (cluster thinning); technological advances such as temperature-controlled fermentation tanks; and the use of science as well as art in winemaking. They not only developed a new style of wine; they created a clash of cultures aimed at the hearts, minds, and pocketbooks of the world's wine consumers.

The balance of power between Old World and New World wines was unexpectedly and permanently upset in 1976 in Paris by a blind-tasting panel of French wine judges, who selected California wines as superior to the French competitors.[5] No longer would New World wine consumers apologize for drinking domestic wines; no longer would Old World wines be the only ones flowing through the arteries of international trade. The floodgates opened for New World wines to compete internationally with Old World wines for global dominance. Trade became bidirectional as all producing nations found themselves suddenly, to some degree, on both sides of the export/import equation.

The struggle between the Old World and the New World quickly gained immediacy, intensity, and economic significance. Intercontinental air travel introduced New World consumers to the Old World lifestyle, in which wine was a normal part of a meal rather than a beverage for special occasions. Wine consumption in the United States alone rose from 267 million gallons in 1970 to 595 million gallons by 2002. During this period, U.S. per capita wine consumption rose from 1.31 to approximately 2 gallons per year.[6]

Television made culinary celebrities such as Julia Child into icons who touted the pleasures of wine and expanded its popularity. Specialized publications, including *Wine Spectator, Decanter,* and *The Wine Advocate,* and syndicated wine columns written by such luminaries as Frank Prial in the *New York Times* and Jancis Robinson in the *Financial Times* (London) introduced wider audiences to wine and guided readers in selecting wines from the seemingly endless assortment being offered.[7] Consumers gained sophistication and confidence in selecting wines and matching them with foods, often gathering information from the Internet, where a plethora of Web sites covered every wine-related topic from Amarone to Zinfandel. Globalization, ordinarily credited with making the world smaller, conversely made the wine world larger, more interconnected, and competitive. In the words of Robert M. Parker Jr., the world's most influential wine critic, "In less than 25 years, there has been nothing less than a complete reorganization of the wine universe."[8]

Modern medicine was also a major force in promoting wine drinking and expanding the industry's consumer base. Following in the footsteps of Hippocrates, who considered moderate amounts of wine to have health benefits,[9] recent scientific research has extolled the virtues of wine, especially red wine, consumed in moderation. Studies of the "French paradox"[10] theorize that red wine consumption may be one of the factors responsible for the low incidence of heart disease among the French despite their penchant for cheese and cigarettes, while other studies consider wine a source of antioxidants that may prevent or alleviate a host of ailments associated with the aging process.[11] In a professional version of "a glass a day keeps the doctor away," one physician has asserted: "In summary, if there is no contra-indication, consuming wine in moderation is the single most important preventative health measure one can do other than giving up smoking."[12]

In addition to increasing wine's worldwide audience, augmented trade created two distinct market segments: a mass consumer market for wines of reliable quality at reasonable prices at local supermarkets; and an elite market for fine wines among connoisseurs, collectors, and social climbers hunting for rare wines at specialty stores, boutique wineries, and auction houses. In different ways, both markets provided new opportunities for women to influence the wine industry.

SUPERMARKETS AND BOUTIQUES

The introduction of New World wines onto the international scene coincided with the global expansion of liquor and beer companies into the wine business, the consolidation of firms within the wine industry, and the increased importance of supermarkets as outlets for wine sales. Confronted with stagnation and decline in the sales of their traditional products, liquor and beer companies transformed themselves into alcoholic beverage firms by buying wineries throughout the world. Diversifying their products, they moved into new market segments and took advantage of the new and burgeoning popularity of wine. As they extended their reach globally, they also conformed to consumer preferences for consistent quality, availability, variety, and reasonable prices. The alcoholic beverage firms benefited immensely from these moves. They increased market share, reduced agricultural and political risk, guaranteed a steady supply of quality wines, circumvented outdated local regulations, gained access to local expertise as well as international distribution networks, and thwarted consumer parochialism that had favored domestic wines over imported ones.[13]

Despite concerns that they might dilute their brand image through expansion, certain large, well-known wineries also entered the moderately priced sector and built their international presence. Relying on a "halo effect," premier wineries such as Mouton Rothschild and Mondavi capitalized on their highly regarded names to expand their product line, foster global partnerships, and utilize economies of scale and scope through mergers and acquisitions.[14] Large firms starting at the lower end of the quality and price spectrum, such as Gallo, also sought to gain advantage in the new market segments, although they experienced more difficulty than the upscale firms. As one observer noted, "It is much harder to build a brand from the bottom up, starting with relatively humble stuff and then trying to convince consumers that you can also make top-of-the-range wines."[15] Although the fragmented labyrinth of small, individual wineries did not disappear,[16] their importance diminished as the new wine conglomerates collectively replaced them as the preferred suppliers of supermarket chains.

Women, who were a majority of supermarket customers, became the core group of wine buyers targeted by corporate advertising campaigns, particularly women who were newly independent, health conscious, better educated, and career oriented. Capitalizing on wine's medicinal benefits, its symbolic status and cachet, and its growing public acceptance, wine ads created brand recognition to assist uninitiated consumers in selecting products, to gain customer loyalty, and to differentiate products on crowded grocery shelves. Still excluded from male-only social and drinking clubs, women appeared in wine ads to attract female consumers and to project a fresh, upscale image that appealed to both sexes. A classic example is the appearance of Gina Gallo in ads for Gallo of Sonoma. In addition to creating a brand image for these new wines, her appearance distanced them from the more humble wines for which her family's company was famous.[17] Ironically, "macho" alcoholic beverage firms and premium wine companies had to broaden their appeal to women in order to rescue the wine industry.[18]

Women's collective influence on the mass market, however, pales in comparison to their individual and collective impact on production at the high end of the business. In the late twentieth century, Old World and New World female proprietors and winemakers migrated to the premium wine sector, the best place to be because "growth [was] fastest and margins [were] fattest."[19] Some ended up there by chance, following the vagaries of birth or inheritance; others gravitated there as part of the influx of highly qualified winemakers from university enology programs such as the University of California at Davis, which graduated its first female enology student, MaryAnn Graf, in 1965; and Australia's Roseworthy Agricultural College, now part of the University of Adelaide, which admitted its first female student, Pam Dunsford, in 1972.[20]

Profitability was only one lure that drew women proprietors and winemakers to the premium wine sector. This sector had the greatest need for educated, skilled, and capable people, regardless of gender, to help meet skyrocketing demand. It also provided an alternative to the alcoholic beverage companies, most of whom came from a hard liquor, anti-female tradition that made it difficult for women to advance. In truth, women had few options other than the premium wine sector to gain recognition, a stellar reputation, and riches. With society still skeptical of their business savvy and still ambivalent about the propriety of women drinking, female wine professionals associated themselves with fine wine because they could depend on the quality of their wines to set them apart and give them status. As Parker put it, "They had no wiggle room."

Women thrived in the premium wine sector. Those who inherited or were in line to inherit prestigious Old World estates in select regions, such as Corinne Mentzelopoulos at Château Margaux, gained automatic admission to this sector. Through association with their high-quality, expensive wines, they attained instantaneous celebrity status with buyers, predominantly male, who linked a wine's quality and desirability with its scarcity and price.[21] Initially reliant on their excellent wines to make them famous, their names and personal marketing appeal eventually grew to enhance the fame of their wines.

Some women in the New World also inherited wineries of distinction. Unlike the Old World, however, the New World afforded opportunities for women entrepreneurs, such as Sandra MacIver at Matanzas Creek, to establish their own wineries. Male and female owners of boutique wineries hired women as consultants and winemakers. These wineries avoided the normal retail distribution channels still dominated by hard liquor firms. Instead, by skillfully limiting supply (artificial scarcity) and using sales-restrictive subscription lists to sell their highly rated "cult" or "trophy" wines[22] at sometimes absurdly stratospheric prices, they created a demand frenzy, especially during the economic boom of the 1990s. Their wines became luxury goods that turned elasticity of demand on its ear—limited supply drove demand upward, along with prices. Women boutique winery owners became richer; and women winemakers, particularly the high-profile consultants associated with wines from several boutiques, became so famous that "now when some aficionados select wine, they look at the consultants involved as well [as] the vintage and the winery."[23]

The wine world was certainly changing: it now had a more scientific bent; it had become global; it had developed a mass market, which required branding and differentiation; and wine had become a collectible commodity. These changes combined with advancements in society at large, such as legislation supporting women's rights and greater educational opportunities, to benefit women who were in professions outside the wine industry but were nonetheless positioned to influence it. In the wine revolution after the mid-1970s, female academics received professional appointments in enology departments, where they conducted important research and helped to train and mentor a new generation of winemakers.

Often educated in the liberal arts, women learned to adapt their knowledge and talents to the needs of the global wine community. Combining linguistic skills with marketing acumen, many women were able to bridge the gap between the Old World and the New World to sell wines globally. Journalists, critics, and experts with superb professional wine credentials as well as exceptional writing skills educated global consumers with newspaper and magazine columns and with books such as *Wine for Dummies,* by Mary Ewing-Mulligan and her husband, Ed McCarthy; and *The Wine Bible,* by Karen MacNeil.

Wealthy wine collectors and connoisseurs, mostly male, bought rare wines for the pleasure of consumption, ego gratification, or snob appeal. Collectors hoping to recoup their costs by reselling wine that had appreciated[24] spurred the growth of auction markets for older or rare vintages. Such events became a popular way to raise money for charities. They simultaneously helped to underwrite the careers and enhance the influence of several women such as Serena Sutcliffe and Ursula Hermacinski.

Parker states that the revolution in wine was accompanied by a concurrent revolution in restaurants.[25] Realizing that great wine lists attracted customers and also added considerably to the cost of the average meal, restaurants upgraded their lists and hired sommeliers to help diners select the wine that best matched their meal. Upscale restaurants that once hired only male waiters soon realized that women could also effectively sell wine to customers (and that female customers might even appreciate having the wine list offered to them instead of to their male companions).

· · ·

The June 25, 2004, Master of Wine (MW) examination contained the following compulsory essay topic as part of "Paper 4," Contemporary Issues: "In wine, women are more influential than men. Discuss."[26] A topic that would have been unthinkable twenty-five years earlier could be addressed in 2004 in a multitude of ways. Women are a force to be reckoned with as consumers, the backbone of supermarket sales worldwide. They are on the global wine map in virtually every profession related to the wine industry. Women are proprietors of great wineries. They make phenomenal wines. They consult domestically and are in the international ranks of the "flying winemakers," university-trained consultants who export state-of-the-art knowledge and set trends throughout the world.[27] They are distinguished educators, researchers, writers, and critics. They are successful marketers, auctioneers, and sommeliers. The wine industry's growth at the end of the twentieth century not only opened new avenues for women; it forever altered the relationship of women and wine.

CHAPTER THREE

A Toast to the Past

At first glance, women's influence in the wine industry seems to be of recent vintage. Hindered by nineteenth-century traditions that excluded them from the world of commerce, women did not achieve worldwide visibility in the wine business until the middle of the twentieth century, most notably during the past thirty years. Women who worked in the industry before that time did so behind the scenes in family businesses and received little, if any, recognition for their efforts.

But a few women did succeed in establishing independent reputations. Veuve Clicquot, Pommery, A. A. Ferreira, and Penfolds are not just names on the labels of great wines. They are the names of women who left an indelible mark on the wine industry in earlier years. These women were remarkably similar: strong, self-reliant risk-takers with demonstrable business acumen. Committed to quality and willing to venture overseas, they had an uncanny understanding of marketing, which enabled them not only to recognize new opportunities but also to capitalize on them. Although some historians have unjustly attributed their success to excellent male personnel, these women deserve to be remembered as skilled employers with an eye for good talent and as consummate entrepreneurs who led their firms from modest beginnings to international prominence. Their stories provide the historical backdrop for the women who influence the wine industry today.

Overcoming personal tragedy and simultaneously breaking free of societal restrictions are themes in the experience of all four of these matriarchs. It is a tragic irony that they had to be widowed in order to demonstrate their entrepreneurial and commercial talents, sparking the observation that "far from being half a woman, a widow is the only complete example of her sex. In fact, the finished article."[1]

No region of the world has exemplified this better than Champagne. It has been said that "no business in the world can have been as much influenced by the female sex as that of champagne."[2] Even if it is not true that "something in the air of Champagne . . . kills the men off early, and then infuses the women with this androgynous potency,"[3] there is no doubt that modern Champagne owes an enormous debt to the women known collectively as the "Champagne Widows."

The development of modern Champagne is most often attributed to the blind monk Dom Perignon, whose heightened tasting sensibilities helped him blend different grapes to enhance the flavor of the wine. But the clarified bubbly liquid we think of as Champagne owes just as much to two of the fabled Champagne Widows: Nicole-Barbe Clicquot-Ponsardin, known as Veuve (Widow) Clicquot; and Jeanne-Alexandrine Melin Pommery, known as Madame Pommery. Their innovations transformed Champagne from a pale, flat red wine to a clear, sparkling white; and their sales instincts, public relations flair, and courage made Champagne the most recognizable and celebrated wine in the world.

VEUVE CLICQUOT

Born in Reims in 1777 to a politically influential family (her father was the mayor), Nicole-Barbe Ponsardin seemed destined for domesticity. At twenty, she married François-Marie Clicquot, the heir of the House of Clicquot, which had been founded in 1772. She became a widow with a three-year-old daughter in October 1806, when her husband died at the age of thirty after a brief illness. Her father-in-law, Philip Clicquot Muiron, was prepared to abandon the business, which had been experiencing financial difficulties. Her first achievement was convincing him to allow her to continue the House of Clicquot.[4]

From that time until her death on July 29, 1866, Veuve Clicquot headed the House of Clicquot. She is credited with three major contributions to the improvement of her firm and the Champagne industry: developing the process of *remuage sûr pupitre;* internationalizing the Champagne market; and establishing brand identification.

The making of Champagne involves several stages of production, including two stages of fermentation in order to create its unique effervescence. During the second fermentation, sediment builds on the side of the bottle that can diminish the clarity and, ultimately, the pleasure of the wine. The winemaker must remove this sediment before the final corkage. Veuve Clicquot became concerned about the decanting method used to accomplish this, believing that it was time consuming and endangered the wine's effervescence. In 1816, in conjunction with her cellar master *(chef de caves),* Antoine-Aloys de Muller, she developed what is known as *remuage,* or riddling.

In this process, the Champagne bottles are placed neck first *(sûr pointe)* into two racks *(pupitre)* united at an acute angle to form an A or upside-down V. Each rack contains sixty holes cut to allow the bottles to be angled slowly upward from their original horizontal position to rest at a 45-degree angle. Daily over the course of six to eight weeks, the bottles are given a succession of quarter turns that force the sediment to loosen and move slowly toward the cork. Then the neck of the bottle is frozen, allowing the ice pellet containing the sediment to be disgorged *(dégorgement).* Subsequently, a combination of sugar and wine or brandy *(dosage)* is added to the remaining clarified wine before corkage, to create modern Champagne.[5]

There is disagreement regarding the degree of Veuve Clicquot's personal involvement in developing this process. Her detractors, including her male winemaking contemporaries who dismissed her experimentation on the basis of her gender, give all the credit to Muller.[6] Some, however, view her as the sole inventive genius. She surely instigated the research, encouraged and participated in developing the process, and can lay claim to it as the firm's owner.

The internationalization of the Champagne trade, especially its spread to the Russian market, involved the combined genius of Veuve Clicquot and her dedicated overseas sales representative, Louis Bohne. Stories abound regarding Bohne's endeavors on her behalf and the instinctively good advice he gave her. Her willingness to heed his advice and accept its inherent risks, which could have jeopardized her only source of revenue, provides insight into the steely mentality of the woman who later came to be known as "La Grande Dame." Her decisions were rewarded when the name Veuve Clicquot became synonymous with Champagne in Russia. Legend has it that she opened her cellars to the thirsty Russian troops who invaded Reims, winning their devotion to her Champagne, which had been banned in Russia during the Napoleonic Wars, along with other French wines.[7]

Veuve Clicquot and Bohne arranged to have her Champagne readily available for the Russian market when hostilities ceased and thus gained early and permanent entry into the land of the czar. Bohne's strategy required placing ten thousand bottles aboard a ship stationed in Konigsberg, to be moved into Russia immediately after the fighting stopped. Veuve Clicquot transported her fragile product over bad roads on horse carts and across closed borders to the boat.[8] By selecting a Dutch vessel, the *Gebroeder,* with a foreign flag, she bypassed political problems on the high seas and in port. She also gained a competitive advantage by demanding that no other wines be aboard. This shipment and two subsequent ones in quick succession enabled her to make Russia (along with the central and eastern European markets opened by her husband) the cornerstone of her business and to turn around the firm's fortunes, which had suffered during the political upheavals.[9] Her Champagne, which she blended to satisfy the Russian preference for sweetness, held a virtual monopoly in Russia until the fall of the czars almost a century later and accounted for up to 70 percent of her production.

Veuve Clicquot also understood the need to differentiate her product and safeguard its brand distinction. Her yellow-orange labels, which helped average consumers immediately identify her bottles then and now, matched the distinctive color of the egg yolks of the famous corn-fed hens of Bresse.[10] Taking vigorous legal action against anyone who sullied her name or sought to use it fraudulently, she established the primacy of her brand. One unfortunate recipient of her wrath, Marc Robin, another Champagne producer, had used her initials, V.C.P., on corks in the bottles of Champagne he sent to Russia. She made a merciless example of him by having him tried in absentia while he was in hiding. He was sentenced to ten years imprisonment at hard labor, branded with an F for fugitive on his right shoulder, and fined.[11] This iron-willed and courageous woman was not to be taken lightly. Even greedy suitors who hoped to marry her daughter learned this lesson when she capped the amount of the dowry rather than allow her rapidly expanding fortune to be diminished.[12]

Despite her career and her successes, Veuve Clicquot was a woman of her times. Although she never remarried, she was surrounded by male colleagues, one of whom, Mathieu-Edouard Werle, became her partner when he relinquished his German citizenship in 1831. Hired originally as a clerk in 1821, Werle helped Veuve Clicquot extricate herself from unwise decisions to diversify into textiles and banking and reduced the firm's dependence on the Russian market by expanding into new overseas markets. At her death, Veuve Clicquot bequeathed the firm and most of the vineyards to Werle. Her daughter inherited only the remaining vineyards and played no role in the firm's operation.[13] Ahead of her time as a businesswoman of extraordinary ability, Veuve Clicquot's vision of women in business did not extend beyond herself.

MADAME POMMERY

Jeanne-Alexandrine Melin Pommery also played an important role in the Champagne industry. Born on April 13, 1819, she was the self-confident product of a predominantly female household that included her widowed mother and two aunts, one widowed with two children and the other unmarried. By the time she married Louis Alexandre Pommery in 1840, Madame Pommery was an unusually worldly and educated woman, having attended private schools in England and France. Nonetheless, during her married years, she took no part in her husband's Champagne business and assumed the customary role of wife and mother.[14]

Despite years of domesticity, she emerged as an independent figure when she was widowed in 1858. She is said to have declared: "I have decided to carry on with the business and take the place of my husband."[15] Committed to high quality (her motto was *qualité d'abord*—quality first), Madame Pommery, like Veuve Clicquot, expanded her market internationally and developed brand distinction. Her domination of the English market was the result of a multidimensional plan for targeting her clientele. In 1860, she hired an export manager, Adolph Hubinet, to develop the British market; the following year, she set up an agency in London to support his efforts. Having lived in England, she was familiar with the British preference for dry rather than sweet wines and accommodated this by ceasing to make still wines and producing only sparkling Champagne. Additionally, she revolutionized Champagne in 1870 by developing brut, or dry, Champagne. In 1875, Pommery Nature appeared, the first vintage brut Champagne that became synonymous with the Pommery style or image.[16] Today, brut and extra brut, the driest forms of Champagne, account for almost all Champagne sales.

Her English strategy also included her most spectacular legacy, the winery in Reims and its cellars. In order to flatter her British clients, she built her home and winery to resemble the homes of two of her most prominent English customers. Beneath these structures, she converted the natural chalk pits *(crayères)* into a two-hundred-mile-long wine cellar. With a capacity of 250 million bottles, this cellar could store dry Champagne for the longer period it required.[17] As with everything she did, Madame Pommery built the cellars and the winery with panache and an eye toward luxury, distinctiveness, and public relations. A visit to her winery allows one to appreciate not only its enormity but also the art she commissioned to decorate it and set it apart from others. The cellars are adorned with decorative bas-reliefs chiseled into the chalk by the sculptors Gustave Navlet and Jean Barat, and a hundred-thousand-bottle Pommery cask carved by Emile Galle sits at the entrance.[18]

Madame Pommery's command of marketing transcended her British strategy. She developed a direct marketing program, which required her to sign thousands of letters destined for potential customers in Belgium. Additionally, she understood the need for consistency in projecting her product's image, refusing to reduce the price of her Champagne to gain market entry and market share. Rather, she kept her prices high to identify her wine as a luxury item prized by members of the elite, whom she wished to attract as her clientele.[19]

Madame Pommery's contemporaries recognized her intellect and hard work and reluctantly "complimented" her for having a cerebral "organization" (way of thinking) that they considered more masculine than feminine. Nonetheless, as in the case of Veuve Clicquot, many have denied her credit for her accomplishments and awarded it to the men who worked for her. In particular, her success is often attributed to her associate Henry Vasnier, the brother of a friend from her days in Paris.[20] Those skeptical of her ability or her active participation in the firm, however, are perhaps unaware that in 1870, when war broke out, Vasnier and half of her workers were conscripted, thus leaving her to run the company alone, a task she was fully capable of performing.[21]

Madame Pommery was determined to retain close supervision of her firm. Unlike Veuve Clicquot, who checked ledgers every day but built her home in the countryside away from her business and eventually delegated substantial control to her partner, Werle, Madame Pommery built her home adjacent to her winery so that she could balance her business obligations with her familial ones, a problem not unfamiliar to today's working women.[22]

When she died in 1890, Madame Pommery's firm had grown from the 45,000 bottles produced in 1858 to 2.25 million bottles per year.[23] Nonetheless, she too proved to be a woman of her times, bequeathing control of the firm to Vasnier and her son, Louis. To her married daughter, she left only shares but no part in management.

Although the great Champagne Widows of the nineteenth century are not always remembered as innovative entrepreneurs, they helped to redefine an important part of the wine industry. If imitation is the most sincere form of flattery, the contemporaries of the widows of Champagne gave them indirect praise by using fictional or fantasy widows on their labels, such as Veuves Damas, de la Pleyne, Monnier, Sillery, and Fonteyne.[24] Nonetheless, the widows' reluctance to capitalize on their entrepreneurship and independence and extend them to their daughters "paradoxically defied and reconfirmed established notions about women's function in French society. By the turn of the century, these women came to serve as symbols, not of the burgeoning women's emancipation movement, but of the 'genuine mother, attentive and devoted' to both family and firm, thus shaping a unique definition of women's entrepreneurship in modern France."[25]

DONA ANTÓNIA ADELAIDE FERREIRA

The experience of the Champagne Widows was replicated in several other parts of the wine world, most notably in Portugal, where Dona António Adelaide Ferreira was a major force in the Port wine industry from 1844 to 1896. Her legacy continues to cast a glow over her firm, A. A. Ferreira, the largest seller of Port within Portugal to this day.

The ability of Dona António to dominate the Douro, the central region of the Port wine industry, is particularly amazing in light of Portugal's treatment of women, who had long been forced into backward and servile conditions. That she eventually controlled a significant portion of the total Portuguese economy, which until 1930 depended on Port wine as the nation's primary export (at three times the value of the next largest export, cork),[26] almost defies belief.

Portuguese women struggled to enter the twentieth century as the rest of western Europe approached the twenty-first. Subjugated to traditionally dictatorial men, Portuguese women, like their counterparts in other Mediterranean countries, had a literacy rate that was barely more than 75 percent in 1911.[27] Until receiving full equality in the Constitution of 1976, women had for centuries been "obliged by law and custom to be subservient to men. . . . [They] had few rights of either a legal or a financial nature and were forced to rely on the benevolence of their male relatives." The 1933 Constitution proclaimed everyone equal before the law "except for women, the differences resulting from their nature and for the good of the family." Married women were particularly handicapped; they could not obtain a passport or leave the country without their husband's consent until 1969.[28] Despite this situation, no figure looms larger in the nineteenth-century Port wine trade than the twice-widowed Dona Antónia Adelaide Ferreira.

The firm with which Dona Antónia was associated and to which she dedicated most of her adult life had been founded by her great-grandfather in 1751.[29] Like Veuve Clicquot and Madame Pommery, with whom she is often compared, she initially was not expected to participate in the firm. After marrying her first cousin, Antonio Bernardo Ferreira II, in 1834, she allowed him to run the estates while she bore two children, Antonio Bernardo III in 1837 and Maria da Assuncao in 1842.[30] While her husband administered the wine estates *(quintas)* from Oporto, where he led a rather wild life and spent lavishly, Dona Antónia remained in the Douro, close to the land, and rarely left her property. When she was widowed in 1844 at age thirty-three, she began to actively participate in running the firm, with her father's blessing, and became sole proprietor when he died.[31]

Dona Antónia ran her firm during the Port trade's greatest, most eventful, and turbulent period, which included foreign invasions, civil war, revolution, and twenty years of an infestation of phylloxera, the root louse that destroys grapevines.[32] But the woman who would be unofficially crowned "Queen Victoria of the Douro" was dedicated, tough, and determined. She successfully competed with the British Port traders who systematically took over the vineyards as well as the trade. She also capitalized on the natural and economic disasters that devastated others. Dwindling production that put many vintners out of business led to her crowning achievement: buying the land of her less fortunate competitors and thus creating the largest quintas of the Douro. Eventually, she increased her holdings from three quintas to more than thirty and became the single largest landowner in the Douro. By the time of her death on March 26, 1896, she was the richest woman in Portugal, with a fortune exceeding 3.5 million British pounds.[33] Even today, the quintas she established allow the firm named after her to supply 40 percent of its grape requirements from its own vineyards, the highest percentage in the trade.

Dona Antónia differed from her contemporaries in Champagne in two important ways: her relationship with her daughter, and her willingness to remarry. She was prepared to defy the norms of her day to protect her daughter and displayed great courage in doing so. In 1854, while still widowed, she was approached by Prime Minister Duque de Saldanha, Marechal of Portugal, who wanted her twelve-year-old daughter to marry his son. The prime minister offered to let the girl remain with Dona Antónia until she reached the legal age for marriage. Dona Antónia refused the overture, despite threats to her safety and a subsequent offer that would have made her Condessa de Vesuvio. She insisted that the marriage could wait until her daughter was the proper age to make her own decisions. Fearing that the prime minister would abduct her daughter, Dona Antónia disguised herself as a peasant, hid with her children in a convent, and then escaped with them to England by trekking over the mountains to reach an embarkation point. The person who helped her in this venture was her agent, Francisco Jose da Silva

Torres, an old friend of her husband, who would later become her second husband. When he died, she continued to devote all her attention to running her estates.[34]

In addition to her strength of character and excellent business acumen, Dona Antónia was extremely charitable and is remembered for her benevolence. The affectionate, diminutive term "Ferreirinha" was bestowed on her and even today remains synonymous with her company in local usage and on wine labels. The firm itself added the "A. A." to its name to honor her when she died. Although her family sold the company in 1987, it is still run by her great-great-grandson, Francisco Olazabal, a descendant of her daughter.[35]

MARY PENFOLD

On the other side of the world, the story of Mary Penfold parallels that of Dona Antónia. Dr. Christopher Rawson Penfold arrived in Australia from England on August 8, 1844, at age thirty-three with his wife, Mary, and daughter, Georgina. They were accompanied by Ellen (Elise) Timbrell, who served as Mrs. Penfold's personal maid, Georgina's nurse, and, until her death in 1858, Dr. Penfold's assistant winemaker.[36] After his arrival, Dr. Penfold practiced medicine. Believing in the medicinal value of wine, especially for treating anemia, he had brought with him fifty grenache vines from southern France and showed an early interest in planting a vineyard and creating a wine business. Although he eventually relinquished his medical practice to devote himself full time to his wine business, women assisted him with the business until his death in March 1870 at age fifty-nine. At that point, Mary Penfold, who had been the farm manager and winemaker before her husband's death, took control of the firm.[37]

Under her management, Penfolds grew in size and stature to become Australia's most prominent wine producer.[38] Mary Penfold ran the company with two men in a manner reminiscent of her European counterparts. In the beginning, she worked with her son-in-law, Thomas Francis Hyland, who lived in Melbourne. Hyland handled sales and initially assumed that Mary would be helpless and unfit to sustain the business. In 1881, she hired John Gillard, whose vineyard and cellars she had previously acquired so that she could avoid selling wines younger than four years old.[39] When she retired in 1884, she handed over managerial responsibilities to Gillard. The firm she developed accounted for approximately one-third of the wine gallons produced in South Australia, had vineyards that had grown from the eighty hectares (nearly 198 acres) planted by her husband to more than four hundred hectares (slightly more than 988 acres), and had a substantial international presence.[40]

Mary Penfold continued to live at the family house, called The Grange (named after her home in England), until her death in 1895 at age seventy-nine. Her descendants, both male and female, continued to run the firm. Because of her expansion of the company through acquisitions, her strong hands-on management, her cultivation of international markets, and her famous home adjacent to her vineyards, Mary Penfold can be compared with Veuve Clicquot and other famous wine widows. Given the opportunities of the New World and the current prominence of women there today, however, it is interesting to note there are few early role models like Mary Penfold.

· · ·

Collectively and individually, the female luminaries of the nineteenth-century wine industry demonstrated that gender need not be a factor in making great wine, that the wine industry was not destined to be an all-male preserve, and that "some leaders were born women." Despite a hiatus of a half-century or more, women throughout the wine world can look to these early pioneers as a source of inspiration and build on their legacy. Women today, however, also would be wise to note that the influence of the nineteenth-century widows waned as their companies moved from family-owned enterprises to corporate status.

CHAPTER FOUR

Viticultrices et Propriétaires

To call wine fermented grapes is like calling paté chopped liver—accurate on paper but not on the palate. Wines have individuality and personality. They embody regional differences and the distinctiveness of a particular vineyard: its soil, topography, and climate; the sun, the wind, and the rain—its *terroir*. And, like terroir, that elusive French term, the French women of wine, the *viticultrices* (winemakers) and *propriétaires* (owners), also provide individuality and personality to their wines.

THE REGIONS

Centuries of deep-seated prejudices and superstitions that kept French women out of the wine cellars, excluded them from male-only wine fraternities, or relegated them to insignificant and menial tasks are not easily overcome. History notwithstanding, women today can be found in wineries throughout all regions of France. Their presence and influence are most notable in several of the nation's, and the world's, most prestigious wine regions: Alsace, Bordeaux, Burgundy, Champagne, and the Loire.

Long a focal point of conflict between the French and the Germans, Alsace is a compact, picturesque region of storybook villages filled with beamed houses that overflow with hanging floral pots each summer. This area provides the terroir for several great wines: Riesling, Gewürztraminer, Pinot Gris, Muscat, and Pinot Blanc. It is also home to the local delicacies that accompany the wines, including *charcuterie* (cured and smoked meats), *kougelhopf*, quiche lorraine, *tarte a l'oignon* (onion tart), and Muenster cheese.

In this setting one finds Domaine Weinbach, whose grounds, Clos de Capucins, formerly a walled monastery, now serve as the primary vineyard for Colette Faller and her two daughters, Catherine and Laurence. Since the death of her husband, Théo, in 1979, Colette has managed the business. Catherine has handled marketing for the past several years; and Laurence, who holds degrees in chemical engineering and enology along with an MBA, has been the winemaker since 1993. Just down the road in the town of Bergheim is Domaine Spielmann, managed by Sylvie Spielmann, who turned her family's small, relatively insignificant winery into one of the finest in Alsace.

Divided by the Gironde River and its tributary, the Dordogne, into a Right Bank on the east and a Left Bank on the west, Bordeaux is the largest winegrowing area in the world for fine wines. In this region, several women hold prominent positions in the wine world, thanks to a combination of history, circumstance, and individual determination.

History played a more pronounced role on the Left Bank. During the Paris Exposition of 1855, the Chamber of Wine-Brokers of Bordeaux classified sixty-one of the region's Left Bank wines into five categories of quality, or growths. The first growths *(premier grand crus classés)*, the most prestigious classification, originally included only four châteaux: Haut-Brion, Lafite-Rothschild, Latour, and Margaux. A fifth château, Mouton Rothschild, was elevated from a second to a first growth in 1973.[1] Significantly, in Bordeaux today, women own three of the five first growths: Château Margaux is owned by Corinne Mentzelopoulos, Château Mouton Rothschild by Baroness Philippine de Rothschild, and Château Haut-Brion by Joan Dillon, Duchesse de Mouchy.[2] One of the most prestigious second growths, often referred to as a "super second," Pichon

1. *Left to right:* Catherine, Colette, and Laurence Faller, a team of mother and daughters, own, operate, and make the wines for Domaine Weinbach, a preeminent Alsatian winery.

Longueville Comtesse de Lalande is owned by May-Eliane de Lenc-quesaing. In addition, Françoise Levêque owns one of the better-known unclassified growths, Château de Chantegrive in Graves.

The Right Bank also boasts a number of women at prestigious châteaux. Château Petrus, which makes perhaps the world's most famous wine, was under the sole control of Madame Loubat from 1925 to 1961. At her death, her niece, Lily Paul Lacoste, inherited 50 percent of the château, although she sold it in 1969.[3] Other women in the region include Christine Valette, the owner of Château Troplong Mondot, a grand cru classé estate in Saint-Emilion; Claire Laval, a trained agronomist who owns Château Gombaude-Guillot; and Catherine Pére-Vergé, Château Montviel's owner.

As the twentieth century was drawing to a close, some of these Bordeaux women were making history by receiving invitations to join formerly all-male wine brotherhoods. In 1991, Claire Laval and Catherine Pére-Vergé were the first women inducted into the Confrérie des Hospitaliers de Pomerol. Françoise Levêque served as president of the Syndicat Viticole des Graves from 1992 to 1997, becoming one of the few women in France ever to direct a winegrowers' association.[4]

Burgundy competes with Bordeaux for the devotion of many of the world's red wine lovers. History and the French legal system, however, have conspired to create significant differences in the wine industries of these two regions. According to Serena Sutcliffe, "The history of the vine in Burgundy is unalterably linked with the Church." Burgundy's fragmented vineyard structure originated after the French Revolution of 1789, when the holdings of the nobility, including those of the Catholic Church, were divided because they were on the losing side of the conflict.[5] (Bordeaux's vineyards, on the other hand, remained unaffected by the revolution because they were largely under British ownership and therefore disassociated from the fighting.)[6]

The Napoleonic Code that governs French society has influenced the size and ownership of all estates in France, but most notably those in Burgundy. Ironically, the inheritance rules of this male-dominated society do not include primogeniture, nor do they exclude women. Rather, they require equal division of property among all legitimate heirs regardless of gender.[7] This legal mandate resulted in splintering some estates and spawning others, "usually in a welter of hyphens," causing Sutcliffe to note, "One of the keys to the whole enigma that is Burgundy is the multifarious ownership of the vineyards."[8]

Burgundy, like Bordeaux, has a hierarchy that affects women's position within its winemaking community. It is divided into five districts: Chablis; Côte d'Or, whose northern part is the Côte de Nuits and whose southern part is the Côte de Beaune; Côte Chalonnaise; Mâconnais; and Beaujolais,[9] which has one of the only all-female confréries in France, Les Demoiselles de Chiroubles. The wine produced in the region is classified by the Appellation d'Origine Contrôlée (AOC) designations and the labels on wine bottles.

Because property in the region is so segmented, resulting in substantial differences in terroir, specificity of site has heightened importance. Single-vineyard wines are believed to have more distinctive character than those blended from grapes grown in several locations. The vast majority of wines reflect their lesser designation by including their region and district in their labeling. Wines of Burgundy's second highest classification, premier cru, some 11 percent of the region's wines, are produced in approximately 560 wineries. Their labels denote the name of their village and commune as well as their vineyard. Only 1 percent of the wines of Burgundy are designated grand cru, the highest classification, and are allowed to have labels reflecting only their vineyard.[10] Simply put, when reading Burgundian labels, less is more—the less information on the label, the more prestigious and valuable the wine inside the bottle. Like their counterparts in Bordeaux, the women who excel in Burgundy, such as Marcelle Marie Elise (Lalou) Bize-Leroy at Domaine Leroy,[11] Anne-Claude Leflaive at Domaine Leflaive, Anne Gros at Domaine Anne Gros, and Jacqueline Mugneret and her two daughters, Marie-Christine and Marie Andrée, at Domaine Mugneret-Gibourg and Domaine Georges Mugneret, produce grand cru wines.

A substantial number of the finer wines from Burgundy are produced by an elite group of *négociants,* wine merchants who buy grapes, wines, or juices and then age and blend them for sale under their own label. Here, too, women such as Nadine Gublin, head winemaker at Antonin Rodet and the first woman selected as Best Enologist of the Year by the *Revue du Vins de France* in 1997, are playing an increasingly important role as winemakers. (Three American sisters—Sue Mueller, Patricia Colagiuri, and Brenda Helies—are sole owners of the prominent négociant house Louis Jadot, a wholly owned subsidiary of Kobrand, which they inherited from their father. But the three played no role in management during their father's lifetime or subsequent to his death.)[12]

Continuing the legacy of the Champagne Widows (described in chapter 3), widows remained prominent in Champagne wineries in the twentieth century. Representing a substantial number of prestigious wines *(grandes marques)* and with lengthy ownership tenures, the twentieth-century widows of Champagne collectively maintained the region's traditions and the cachet of its sparkling beverage, despite the introduction of similar products elsewhere in the world. There remains only one place that can call its sparkling wine Champagne.

Most prominent among the twentieth-century widows to whom the Champagne industry is indebted for retaining its quality, reputation, and market domination was Elizabeth (Lily) Bollinger, who was also called Madame Jacques in honor of her late husband. A colorful figure known for riding her bike around her property to conserve gasoline during World War II and for protecting her workers and her winery from the Nazis, she managed the firm full time for thirty years, from 1941 to 1971. She required strict adherence to traditional methods to preserve excellence and historical blending (she never made Blanc de Blancs), refused to participate in trends that reduced the purity of Champagne (she never made pink Champagne), and nonetheless succeeded in doubling her production and sales.[13]

No widow in modern Champagne ever attained the prominence of Veuve Clicquot or Madame Pommery, however. In keeping with the sweeping consolidation of the wine industry worldwide, it is not surprising that one of the most prominent women in Champagne today is a corporate executive. Cécile Bonnefond is president and CEO of Veuve Clicquot, which is now a wholly owned subsidiary of LVMH Moët Hennessey Louis Vuitton and includes Veuve Clicquot Ponsardin, Krug, and Canard-Duchene.[14]

Among the fairy-tale châteaux and lush orchards in the Loire Valley, from Orleans in the east to Nantes in the west, are intertwined some of the finest white wine areas of the world: Sancerre; Vouvray; and Savennières, a region in which women play an extremely important role. In the 1960s, Denise Joly restored to preeminence an entire appellation— her family's seven-hectare vineyard, Clos Coulée de Serrant—and produced a wine that the Prince of Gastronomy, Curnonsky, declared one of the five greatest white wines in France.[15] Just down the road is Domaine du Closel, a château owned and operated by three generations of women since 1900. Madame du Closel, the widow of the founder, ran the château from 1900 to 1975. She was succeeded by her niece, Michele de Jessey, who, with her daughter, Evelyne de Jessey-Pontbriand, operates the Domaine today. Madame de Jessey also has the distinction of being the first woman elected president of her appellation.

THE BURDEN OF TRADITION LIVES ON

Adjustment to new social patterns does not come easily in the Old World, and France is no exception. Despite the increased presence of women in the French labor force, they are not encouraged to work, particularly if they are married and have children. Female workers are considered to have jobs rather than careers, and the assumption is that if they do not need to be employed, they should not and will not be. This attitude is reinforced by the general unwillingness of men to share in housework and other responsibilities such as child raising. Consequently, women in France often feel pressured to choose between a family and a job. One winery owner notes that her husband is *"terrified of me being too independent."* She believes that *"very few women in France with . . . children and a husband . . . are making a career."* She resents the fact that her husband *"still considers that a lot of domestic tasks are to be my tasks, because I am a woman."*

The superstar women of the French wine industry have all had to make significant personal sacrifices in order to be successful. Married with one son, Nadine Gublin estimates that 90 percent of her time is spent away from her family because wine is her "addiction." During harvest (crush), Nadine rarely sees her son, who is cared for largely by her mother. Though she rues this situation and wishes for more balance in her life, Nadine accepts that such balance is impossible if she is to maintain her winemaking status. Her fear is that she might be forced to choose between her family and her passion for winemaking.

Other French women profiled here have managed to marry and have children, but they all have struggled with the issue of balance. For example, the Mugnerets close their doors on Wednesday to coincide with the French school schedule so that they can be with their children.[16] Unlike many of their contemporaries such as Nadine Gublin and Anne Gros, Marie-Christine and Marie Andrée cannot look to their mother, Jacqueline, for child care assistance because she continues to play an active administrative role in the winery. Colette Faller "solved" the problem by bringing daughters Catherine and Laurence into the business, erasing the separation between the personal and the professional. Still, tensions exist in some households because these French women are rarely at home and are forced at times to neglect their traditional duties as wives and mothers.

Corinne Mentzelopoulos, the sole owner of Château Margaux, concurs.[17] Sitting in her office on the Avenue Montaigne, using a magnifying glass to review photos for a new marketing brochure, she is the picture of an intensely hands-on owner. Subscribing to the motto "TGIM" (Thank God, It's Monday) because she looks forward to starting her work week, she has made Château Margaux her career. Along with her family, it is also her passion and, she would add, her responsibility to the memory of her father, André, who died in 1980.

With the exception of the time she devotes to her family, Corinne is at work. She has little, if any, time for herself. She believes that a woman's work carries over to her home in a way that is not expected of men, including her husband. Obsessed with details and a stickler for perfection, she puts in a full work week when in Paris and goes far beyond "normal" working hours when in Bordeaux or on the road representing her wine. In order to spend sufficient time at home and not shortchange her family, she refuses most social engagements.

She asserts that if she had to choose between family and work, she would choose the former, but it is difficult to imagine her not working. A woman who has told her daughters never to depend on men for financial support and who believes that work leads to personal enrichment is not a homebody. She admits that the burdens of family and work are

2. Corinne Mentzelopoulos, the sole owner of Château Margaux, is credited with returning this great Bordeaux first growth estate to its historical prestige and quality. Photo by Govin Sorel.

greater for women than for men and that she would probably travel more if she did not have family responsibilities. Unable to imagine spending all her time going to the hairdresser or shopping, she believes that men have fuller lives than the unemployed women of her generation and therefore are more interesting.

Other than the well-known widows, many married women who have played a significant role in their family's wineries have toiled out of public view, working in the back office or handling marketing duties. Some ran the entire business while receiving little or no recognition. Marie An- toinette Spielmann ran her family's eight-hectare vineyard in Alsace and made all the wine in order to earn additional income for her large family. She never saw her name on a bottle of wine; the labels reflected only the name of her husband, Jean-Martins, who played no part in running the winery. It was her daughter, Sylvie, who finally gained long over-due recognition for women at Domaine Spielmann by replacing her father's name on the label with her own.

It is not surprising that French women get little credit for their work because, generally, expectations for them are often low. Baroness Philippine de Rothschild notes that her father, Baron Philippe de Rothschild, who described himself as a "woman lover" rather than a "womanizer" and claimed never to have spent a full night with any one lover,[18] believed that women, particularly attractive ones, were stupid and incompetent in business and politics.

A unique handicap affecting women winemakers has been their exclusion from wine cellars because of superstitions that menstruation could contaminate fermenting wine or because of assumptions regarding their physical abilities. Many French female enologists confronted this situation by turning to lab work rather than winemaking. This tradition retains its impact today. In recent years, 40 percent of the students passing the enology course at the University of Bordeaux have been women. The vast majority end up working in labs, in sales positions, or as quality controllers for négociants. For example, most people in the industry have heard of Michel Rolland, one of France's most famous and influential wine consultants. But not many realize that his wife, Dany, is also an enologist, who graduated in the same year with a higher class rank. Although she participates in their consulting firm and helps to manage the family vineyards, she remains largely out of the spotlight, working in their lab in Libourne.[19]

INHERITANCE

Inheritance, too, has had an enormous impact on women in winemaking families. Some French women who inherited wineries simply lacked male siblings (Corinne Mentzelopoulos, Baroness Philippine de Roth-schild, Lalou Bize-Leroy, Anne Gros). Others had brothers who proved incapable of running the family business (May-Eliane de Lencquesaing, Anne-Claude Leflaive) or who were uninterested (Sylvie Spielmann). In many different ways, these women received the message that a woman inheriting a winery was "unnatural" and that if a brother had been available, there would have been no question about who would be running the family business. As a result, they often feel, unconsciously perhaps, a much greater need than men to justify their inheritance.

Corinne Mentzelopoulos and Baroness Philippine de Rothschild have more than first growth châteaux in common. They both had brothers who died prematurely, leaving them as the only surviving descendants at the time of their fathers' deaths. Each in her own way seeks to prove herself worthy of her inheritance. Corinne refuses to take credit for restoring the glory and the value of Château Margaux. She claims that her accomplishments are merely the culmination of her father's plans, that he was the "genius" and the "visionary." Additionally, she credits her all-male team for her winery's prosperity. Inheritance, for her, is a burden as well as an opportunity, a responsibility as well as a privilege. She believes that people who are self-made, like her father, can take more credit for their accomplishments than those who inherit what they have, regardless of how much value and prestige they add.

Corinne Mentzelopoulos is not simply a brilliant businesswoman seeking money or cognitive challenges. She lives and breathes Château Margaux. It is not surprising that she beat out all competitors to become the sole owner of the estate. Even when it was one of her least significant holdings, it was her "most significant emotional asset."[20] Her 2003 acqui-sition of 100 percent of Château Margaux should go a long way toward alleviating her uncertainties.[21] Corinne exercised her family's right of first refusal in the transaction, stating that she could not have coped with losing the estate.

Baroness Philippine de Rothschild has no such angst. Her relation-ship with her father was entirely different from Corinne's. Baron Philippe took control of second growth Château Mouton Rothschild in 1922 and elevated it to first growth status, making it the only château to accomplish this feat since 1855. He revolutionized quality-control methods in Bordeaux by introducing estate bottling and expanded the region's sales by introducing less expensive, high-quality blended brand wines.

His wine instincts were as strong as his attitudes toward women were weak. Baroness Philippine says, "He would be as surprised to know of women's advancement as Marie Antoinette would have been seeing a motor car." Although he had a good relationship with his daughter, he never considered her capable of leading the business and never prepared her for it. Her background in no way approximated that of Corinne Mentzelopoulos, who holds the equivalent of an MBA and had been the chief financial officer of her father's grocery and finance conglomerate, Félix-Potin. For Baroness Philippine, it was not an easy or natural transition from being an actress in the Comédie Française to being head of the board of Château Mouton Rothschild. Rather than blaming her father's sexism for her initial lack of business training, however, Baroness Philippine believes that he was too egocentric to think that anyone could replace him. She says that her father subscribed to the philosophy of King Louis XV: *"Après moi le déluge"* (After me, the flood).

Baroness Philippine capitalizes on the aura of her name and her legendary château. She is royalty and projects it. She is used to getting her way and can be intimidating if necessary. At the same time, she is a highly cultured woman who has tremendous grace and presence. No one should underestimate her understanding of power—she knows that she signs the checks. She also has an excellent grasp of marketing and the importance of labels. It is not coincidental that among the 2000 Bordeaux vintage, one of the greatest of all time, the golden-etched black bottles of Mouton Rothschild are the most distinctive.[22] She has earned the right to use her father's motto: "First, I am; second, I was; Mouton does not change."

Lalou Bize-Leroy has a personality like her wines—bold and unforgettable. She is one of Henri Leroy's two children, both daughters. In

1955, at her father's insistence, Lalou abandoned her plans to settle in Switzerland, where she intended to pursue her passion for mountain climbing. Instead, she agreed to revive the "Great Wines" that had been created by her grandfather, François Leroy, but had become somewhat neglected by her father, who was preoccupied with other business matters.

Unlike her wines, which are adored by wine lovers the world over, she is a woman surrounded by controversy, particularly in regard to her family history and her ownership of some of the greatest properties in Burgundy. Lalou is now exclusively associated with Domaine Leroy, the estate originally called Domaine Charles Noëllat, which she purchased in 1988 with financial backing from the Japanese importer Takashimaya; and with Domaine d'Auvenay, an estate that she owns with her husband, Marcel Bize (now deceased).[23] She also runs the family négociant business, Leroy S.A. Through Domaine Leroy, she owns vineyards in numerous areas of Burgundy, including nine that produce grand cru and seven that produce premier cru. Lalou's reputation as a winemaker, however, developed originally at Domaine de la Romanée-Conti (DRC), where she still owns 25 percent.

The involvement of the Leroy family in DRC began in 1942, when Henri Leroy, Lalou's father, purchased 50 percent of it. The other 50 percent became the property of Edmond Gaudin de Villaine, who had been associated with DRC since 1911. From 1942 until 1950, the two families worked together to make DRC the finest estate in Burgundy. In 1973, Henri Leroy's négociant business, Société Leroy, received the exclusive rights to distribute DRC in all markets other than the United States and the United Kingdom.

In that same year, Henri de Villaine's son, Aubert, and Lalou were appointed co-directors of DRC. When Henri Leroy died in 1980, Lalou and her sister, Pauline Roch, each inherited 50 percent of their father's interest in DRC, thus giving them each 25 percent of DRC and equal ownership of Société Leroy. Ten members of the de Villaine family retained the other 50 percent of DRC. Unlike her sister, who had moved to Geneva and owned a construction firm, Lalou had worked in the négociant house with her father since 1955; and therefore she became the manager of Société Leroy.[24]

Jealousies and animosities grew steadily over the years between Lalou and the shareholders of DRC, who raised concerns about possible conflicts of interest related to her dual roles in production at DRC and sales at Société Leroy. Suspicions grew after she founded Domaine Leroy on property adjacent to DRC in 1988 and truly became a competitor.[25] In 1992, the problem finally came to a head when Lalou's sister, Pauline, joined the de Villaine family in dealing Lalou a major financial and emotional blow. They stripped her of the exclusive rights to represent DRC overseas and removed her as co-director of DRC in order to give the position to Pauline's thirty-five-year-old son, Charles.[26]

Lalou's attempts to have the courts redress her grievances by reinstating her as co-director and by renewing the special business arrangement of Société Leroy were unsuccessful. Given the 75 percent vote controlled by the de Villaine family and Pauline Roch, the courts determined that they were well within their ownership rights to make these decisions.[27] Not having any brothers guaranteed Lalou's inheritance but not control.

Lalou Bize-Leroy was able to withstand this setback because of the passion she has displayed since she was a "cellar rat alone in the cave" in her quest to create the perfect wine. A vintner of extraordinary ability and a strict adherent to biodynamic agricultural practices since 1988,[28] Lalou is focused on seeking ever better wines and creating a "purer" technique of growing and harvesting grapes that is not only ecologically correct but positively spiritual in its practice. While some people might look askance at biodynamics, Lalou preaches it with Sunday morning conviction, knowing that it will bring her closer to the perfect wine. If anyone can reach the elusive goal of perfection, it is probably Lalou, whose father believed that his daughter was so fiercely committed to her goals "that she could swim upstream."

The fourth of five children (two sons and three daughters), Sylvie Spielmann grew up in a traditional, male-dominated French family. The

3. Lalou Bize-Leroy, winemaker and owner of Burgundy's Domaine Leroy, initially attained fame as the winemaker at Domaine de la Romanée Conti, where she remains a co-owner.

major source of income was the family's building supply company, specializing in gypsum and plaster. Their eight-hectare winery was a sideline for Sylvie's mother, Marie Antoinette. Sylvie's older brother entered the family's primary business. But the building supply company could not absorb everyone, and the family grew concerned about the future of Sylvie's younger brother. To assure him of a career with sufficient income to support a family, the family decided that he would inherit the winery. No one except Sylvie gave any consideration to her economic future or her interest in the wine business. Her opportunity to inherit the winery arose only after her younger brother graduated from business school and chose to pursue other career options. Even then, Sylvie's parents were disinclined to give her the winery because they believed that winemaking was not a "female" profession.

The family's reluctance forced Sylvie to leave home to pursue her dream. She attained a baccalaureate degree and then studied for an additional two years in Bordeaux to earn her enology degree. Unable to gain experience as a winemaker in France because of her gender, she went overseas and worked at Bonny Doon in California and then at Hickenbotham in Tasmania (Australia). She finally returned to Alsace in 1988 to claim the family winery as her own.

When May-Eliane de Lencquesaing's father died in 1959, the Napoleonic Code guaranteed her a stake in Pichon Longueville Comtesse de Lalande (Pichon Lalande) and the other properties owned by her family, but it did not grant her the right to manage a property. That was the prerogative of her brother, who was assumed to be more capable because he was a man. By 1978, however, the properties had gone bankrupt under his direction. (Madame de Lencquesaing says, tongue in cheek, that he did not have the genes for running the winery, which had a legacy of female control.)[29] The family then decided to strip him of his position and conduct a drawing to divide the holdings. Madame de Lencquesaing's "inheritance" and ownership of Pichon Lalande truly resulted from the luck of the draw—she plucked the name out of a hat.[30]

May-Eliane de Lencquesaing has great style and has used it to her wine's advantage. A tremendously warm and generous person, she has overcome gender prejudice with honey rather than vinegar. She considers each new vintage akin to the birth of a child and talks about the need to give it special attention as it matures. She exudes a nurturing quality, both for her own wine and for the wines of Bordeaux in general. She has launched many wine education programs as well as projects that aim to integrate wine culturally with music and art. With her sincerity and warmth, she has become a spokesperson not only for her wine but also for the entire industry. This prominent position has no doubt contributed to her success.

SELF-RELIANCE AND NETWORKING

It is no coincidence that so many of the top women in the French wine industry are resolutely self-reliant—not to mention stubborn, tough, and competitive. Most lacked female role models and mentors. Additionally, a lack of networking opportunities for women forced them to draw on their own resources. Certainly their self-reliance has been positive; the resulting assertiveness and independence have been crucial to their success. In another sense, however, self-reliance has meant loneliness and isolation. Even for some of the married women with families, there was an inwardness and reticence that made them seem aloof.

While networking has become a key tool for women's success in other countries, it has not been part of French culture, at least not for women. Confréries—literally, "brotherhoods," though it might be better translated as "old boys' networks"—traditionally excluded women from wine-related rituals and tastings. Just as significantly, this exclusion prevented women from interacting with the people who serve on the local, regional, and national boards that govern the wine industry. Psychologically, too, networking remains foreign to most French women. A formal association of women in Bordeaux, Les Aliénor du Vin de Bordeaux, for instance, is a network in name only. Each of the twelve women in the group manages a wine estate in a different appellation of Bordeaux. A well-informed observer has described them as representing *"twelve crus, twelve appellations, twelve* femmes."

Although networking has increased in recent years, it still rubs many of these women the wrong way. Lalou Bize-Leroy has no need for networks and refuses to participate in wine organizations. Catherine and Laurence Faller reject networking because of the time it consumes and the lack of payback; Laurence refers to networking as an American concept.

May-Eliane de Lencquesaing, for one, has demonstrated her intense self-reliance by forming her own network when traditional ones rejected her. When she returned to Bordeaux after living in the United States, she found that no one would help her and that men would not allow her to join their professional organizations. Out of necessity, she leveraged her linguistic skills and understanding of foreign nations and cobbled together a network by strategically volunteering for tasks that others did not want to do and then fulfilling her obligations. In the early 1980s, she led her Bordelaise "network" in opening up the California market for Bordeaux wines.

RISK-TAKING

Everyone in the wine business takes risks. From the vagaries of viticulture to the uncertain aspects of fermentation and barrel aging, winery owners and winemakers must have a bit of the gambler in them. One of the myths about women—particularly in France—is that they are risk-averse. In reality, women owners and winemakers have taken tremendous chances in order to be successful. In 1984, Colette Faller, for instance, took the serious gamble of waiting until very late fall to harvest her grapes because cool, rainy weather had not ripened them sufficiently for the customary early fall harvest. While her male competitors in Alsace panicked and harvested at the usual time, Colette waited and chanced losing her entire vintage. Her gamble paid off when the grapes benefited from the many sunny days in late September, October, and November. The wines made from these late harvest grapes were named after St. Catherine, whose saint day is November 25, the date the harvest was completed. The St. Catherine wines proved infinitely superior to the largely mediocre wines produced by others in the region that year. For Colette Faller and most of the other women profiled here, mediocrity that tarnishes their reputation poses a greater risk than the loss of a vintage.

Domaine Leflaive, which has been a Société Civil d'Exploitation (SCE), or operating company, since 1973, is Burgundy's largest family-owned winery, by virtue of having thirty shareholders. Anne-Claude

Leflaive became general manager by combining luck, natural leadership ability, and a willingness to confront risk. In June 1990, Anne-Claude and her cousin, Olivier Leflaive, were appointed joint managers of the domaine, replacing their respective fathers, Vincent and Joseph-Régis. Despite his ownership of a négociant business, Olivier's position was assured. Anne-Claude, however, was appointed because her brother was not able to handle the responsibility.

By October 1990, Anne-Claude had become convinced that a radically different approach to viticulture and vinification was necessary for the long-term well-being of the domaine (and her extended family). Despite her father's skepticism and Olivier's opposition, she began to experiment with biodynamics by planting one hectare that incorporated village, premier, and grand cru properties. When the wines produced from the biodynamic sections proved better than others produced from the same terroirs, she extended the experiment to three hectares in 1991, six hectares in 1996, and to the entire domaine in 1997. The success of her experiments and her steadfast support of biodynamics caused Olivier to quit his managerial position and sell his shares in the SCE in 1994, leaving Anne-Claude completely in charge of the winery, which was making some of the world's finest white wines.

It also is interesting to note that many of these French winery owners and winemakers take risks routinely in their personal lives. Indeed, there is a tradition of such risk-taking among these women. Madame Joseph Krug, one of the twentieth-century widows of Champagne, turned her cellar into a dispensary during World War I. Later, she helped downed Allied airmen escape the Gestapo during World War II.[31] May-Eliane de Lencquesaing and her father, Edouard Miaihle, "hid two Italian Jewish families at . . . [one] of their properties, Château Palmer, with only a wall separating them from the German soldiers who occupied the main part of the building."[32] Lalou Bize-Leroy is an Alpine climber and was the first woman to conquer the Bonati passage of Mont Blanc.

Of course, men can also have this quality, which, like the concept of terroir, is both special and difficult to define. But all the women profiled here also have a distinctive style that has a great deal to do with their femininity—their charm, empathy, instinctiveness, and warmth. This style has helped them form critical relationships, sometimes with men who were prejudiced against women. It has helped them become brilliant marketers, convincing everyone from importers to owners of first-class restaurants to take on their labels. The fierce pride and assertiveness of Corinne Mentzelopoulos, for example, have allowed her to deal with all manner of people from a position of strength. She has a strong belief in herself and her wine, and this allows her to ignore prejudice and demand her due because of the quality of her wine.

. . .

The jury is still out on whether the current crop of female leaders of the French wine industry will prove more inclined than the nineteenth-century Champagne Widows to encourage greater participation by women. It also remains to be seen how strong a force they will continue to be as the wine industry becomes increasingly dominated by large public corporations. There is no doubt, however, that the women profiled here and their contemporaries have changed the face of the French wine industry permanently by altering the perception of women's abilities and associating themselves exclusively with excellence. Women in the French wine industry, present and especially future, owe them a debt of gratitude for throwing open the doors of opportunity.

As the educational system has expanded to include women in winemaking programs, the number of female winemakers has substantially increased in both family-owned and corporate wineries in France. With rare exceptions, however, women are excluded from executive positions within the corporate wine community and gain influence over a wine business only in family enterprises. Although inheritance laws, the presence of male heirs, and tradition continue to favor men within family businesses, those women fortunate enough to have no male competition within the family are more likely to become influential in their family's firms than in the general business community. Given the continued dominance of family operations within the French wine industry, there is reason to believe that women will continue to make their mark, not only as winemakers but also as business leaders.

CHAPTER FIVE

Le Donne del Vino

Transformations abound in today's Italian wine industry. Sophisticated, elegant, world-class wines are replacing the traditional straw-clad bottles of Chianti. Imported grape varietals are sharing the stage with traditional vines. Long-overlooked indigenous varietals are resurgent. A new generation of winemakers is discarding old production methods. And *le donne del vino*—the women of wine—are individually and collectively challenging the male dominance of the industry.

RISORGIMÉNTO: THE MODERN ITALIAN WINE RENAISSANCE

For years, Italians took their wines for granted—and so did the rest of the world. Italian wines were considered barely suitable for pizza, lacking the cachet and quality of their fine-dining French counterparts. While French producers were identifying their wine with a particular terroir, tightly controlling all aspects of viticulture and vinification, and watching the reputation, sales, and prices of their wines rise, Italian wineries were fostering an image of mediocrity by producing and marketing their wines in ever-greater amounts, emphasizing quantity over quality. Bottles of Italian wine gained more distinction for their appearance (in those ever-present straw baskets) than for their contents.

In 1963, Italy developed a set of national wine laws, patterned after the French AOC rules, in order to improve the image of Italian wines and attract a larger segment of the international market. Detailed rules governed everything from the vineyard to the bottling. Initially, there were two designated categories: Denominazione di Origine Controllata (DOC) and Denominazione di Origine Controllata e Garantita (DOCG). DOC "created legally defined production zones" and sought "to classify and regulate the production of wines from specific geographic areas, not only to authenticate these wines but to help them develop commercial identities."[1] The rules for DOCG zones, which encompass most of the more historic wines of Italy or especially esteemed ones,[2] are more rigorous. The term "Garantita" signifies that the wines from these zones are guaranteed for authenticity, not quality, which remains the responsibility of the individual producer.[3] In 1992, a third certified classification, Indicazione Geografica Tipica (IGT), was added to recognize "typical" wines representing a particular geographic area and to build consumer confidence in a greater number of Italian wines.[4] Wines that do not qualify for any of the governmental designations retain the generic label Vino da Tavola (VdT), table wine.[5]

Classifications proved to be both a blessing and a curse. The rules did improve standards and increase the recognition accorded Italian wines, but quality remained uneven. Additionally, rigid application of the rules often emphasized safeguarding traditions, even outdated ones, at the expense of innovation, creativity, and modernization.[6] While taking two steps forward, the Italians managed to take one step back in promoting their wines.

The modern Italian wine renaissance began when Piero Antinori, whose family had been making wine for more than six hundred years, challenged the DOC regulations by producing Tignanello, a sangiovese-based wine. Because it ignored the DOC rules regarding grape varietals, blending, and aging that were required for a designation as Chianti, Tignanello was officially unclassified and labeled VdT.[7] Consumers, however, knew the truth. Tignanello was far superior to ordinary Chianti.

On a par with great French wines,[8] it became known as a Super Tuscan, an unclassified wine of international distinction. Visionaries such as Antinori and his like-minded competitors, with the help of wine writers and consumers (and without the help of regulators), reinvented Italian wine and created the modern Italian wine renaissance.

Another dimension of this renaissance involves generational change and departure from tradition. Unlike their fathers, who had insulated themselves from external influences and new ideas, a younger generation of producers and winemakers, both sons and daughters, traveled throughout the world, gaining exposure to alternative techniques of vineyard management such as new trellising styles, irrigation methods, and green harvesting. They adopted vinification procedures that used stainless steel tanks and malolactic fermentation. They became familiar with New World wines such as California Chardonnay, Australian Shiraz, New Zealand Sauvignon Blanc, and Argentine Malbec as well as Old World wines from Bordeaux and Burgundy. As the world grew smaller and more accessible, their vision for Italian wine and their understanding of their international competition expanded. Like Marco Polo returning from the Far East, the new wine generation introduced dramatically different ideas that were greeted with varying degrees of acceptance.

Contemporary, avant-garde viticulture and production techniques, such as aging wine in small French oak *barriques* that are rotated or replaced frequently, openly challenged the older, traditional methods such as the use of large, infrequently changed oaken casks. Producers began to add nonnative grape varietals—cabernet sauvignon, merlot, cabernet franc, chardonnay—to their product mix alongside indigenous varietals such as nebbiolo, sangiovese, trebbiano, pinot grigio, and grechetto. Modern viticulture and vinification methods brought new or renewed prestige to teroldego, sagrantino, barbera, and many other indigenous grape varietals that had been traditionally ignored or used only to make Vino da Tavola. Trying to sort out the continually growing variety of Italian wines, consumers came to rely more on the producer's name or the brand recognition than on any government-decreed classifications.

The main features of the modern Italian wine renaissance—the quest for quality, modernization, name recognition, and international markets—along with a little bit of luck, provided the framework for women's entrance and expanded presence in the Italian wine industry, a phenomenon of the past ten to fifteen years.

REGIONS

From the alpine reaches of Trentino-Alto Adige in the north to the sultry heel of the boot in the Mezzogiorno in the south, grapevines carpet the Italian landscape. Making sense out of twenty regions, hundreds of grape varieties, a seemingly infinite assortment of wines from nine hundred thousand registered vineyards, and an ever-changing number of classified zones—more than 300 DOC, 20 DOCG, and 120 IGT—is no small accomplishment.[9] As in France, however, not all regions are created equal. To gain an understanding of Italian wines, it is sufficient to know Tuscany, Piedmont, Umbria, and Trentino-Alto Adige.[10]

In Tuscany, the region of the Medicis and the leading cities of the original Renaissance—Florence, Siena, and Pisa—history is in a sense repeating itself. Tuscany today is the fount of Italy's modern wine resurgence. Because of its size, commercialism, marketing prowess, and worldliness, some refer to it as the Bordeaux of Italy, while others call it the "center of the Italian wine universe." Tuscany is home to the first DOC zone, Vernaccia di San Gimignano; the first DOCG zone, Brunello di Montalcino; the Super Tuscans such as Tignanello, Sassacaia, Solaia, Ornellaia, and Cepparello;[11] and some of the country's most famous traditional wines, including Chianti Classico, Brunello di Montalcino, and Vino Nobile di Montepulciano. And, like Bordeaux, it can boast a who's who of women who operate, own, or are poised to inherit preeminent wineries: Albiera, Allegra, and Allessia Antinori at Marchesi L.&P. Antinori SRL; Laura Bianchi at Castello di Monsanto; Paola Gloder at

Poggio Antico; Giovannella Stianti Mascheroni at Castello di Volpaia; Emanuela Stucchi Prinetti at Badia a Coltibuono; and Lorenza Sebasti at Castello di Ama. The symbolic Black Rooster of Chianti certainly has a lot to crow about.

If Tuscany is the Bordeaux of Italy, Piedmont is the equivalent of Burgundy.[12] And just as Burgundy is distinct from Bordeaux, Piedmont's character, including its attitude toward women in the wine industry, varies considerably from that of Tuscany. Situated on a plain extending from the foothills of the Maritime Alps, Piedmont is as famous for its food delicacies (white truffles discovered by sniffing pigs and dogs) and its effervescent Asti Spumante as it is for its great nebbiolo-based wines such as Barolo and Barbaresco, which some consider the country's finest. Turin, the largest city in the region, an industrial center and home to Fiat, is almost an anomaly in this insular, landlocked, agricultural region. Asti and Alba, the smaller, stodgier, and less worldly wine centers, better reflect the region's traditional environment, which remains largely inhospitable to women in the wine industry. Nonetheless, here too women are running and will inherit well-regarded wineries: Bruna Giacosa at Casa Vinicola Bruno Giacosa, and Raffaella Bologna at Azienda Braida SRL. And if Chiara Boschis, owner of E. Pira & Figli, is an example of what the future holds, the Piedmontese are in for a big shock. Among the first Barolo producers to adopt modern techniques such as malolactic fermentation and to use entirely new barriques, she replaced the fiercely traditional Gigi Pira, the last man in Piedmont to tread his grapes.[13]

Made famous by St. Francis of Assisi, the ornate ceramics of Deruta, Luisa Spagnoli's exquisite Perugina chocolates, and the white wines of Orvieto, Umbria has lived in Tuscany's shadow, both physically and in terms of its wine reputation. The fine wines of Giorgio Lungarotti of Cantine Giorgio Lungarotti altered this regional imbalance and put Umbria on the world's wine map. Cantine Giorgio Lungarotti also transformed the tiny, undistinguished town of Torgiano into the hub of a multifaceted business empire, now containing two world-class museums and

4. Teresa Severini, winemaker and director of the great Umbrian winery Cantine Giorgio Lungarotti, was the first female enology graduate of the University of Perugia.

a five-star hotel. Today, this regional behemoth thrives under the ownership and operation of three women—Giorgio's widow, Maria Grazia, the inspiration for the wine and olive oil museums; his daughter and heiress, Chiara Lungarotti, a university-trained viticulturist and managing director of Cantine Giorgio Lungarotti; and his stepdaughter, Teresa Severini. Known throughout most of her professional life as Teresa Lungarotti, she was the first woman enology graduate of the University of Perugia and is a winemaker, the head of marketing, and a director of Cantine Giorgio Lungarotti.

Frequently grouped with Friuli-Venezia-Giulia and Veneto into an area referred to as Tre Venezie, Trentino-Alto Adige is located in northeastern Italy. It is separated physically, if not spiritually, from Austria, where few women vintners are found. For women, the climate of the region is cold in many ways. Rarely acclaimed for its wines, which are largely VdT, few producers in this region are given recognition. Standing out from the crowd, however, is Elisabetta Foradori at Foradori, an advocate of modern viticulture and vinification methods as well as a defender of traditional Italian grape varietals for making excellent wines. She has consistently received the highest recognition—Tre Bicchieri (Three Glasses)—awarded to Italian wines by *Gambero Rosso,* the prestigious Italian wine magazine and guide.

TRADITION

In Italy, "women winemakers have always been viewed with something between suspicion and amusement."[14] Inheritance through the "luck of the draw" was their key for opening the winery door (or the crowbar for prying it off its hinges). Talent, hard work, and ambition were no substitute for widowhood, brothers who were uninterested in the wine business, or the absence of male siblings. The Antinori sisters, Albiera, Allegra, and Allessia, are not simply the twenty-sixth generation of their family's winemaking dynasty; they are the first women to participate in the family business in more than six hundred years. Laura Bianchi, an attorney, preferred working at the family winery to practicing law. Her opportunity for a career change occurred when her older brother opted for the textile industry and city living after only six months at the rural winery. Chiara Lungarotti's father was "a conservative and rather prejudiced"[15] and required time to grudgingly accept her and her sister, Teresa, as winemakers. Having no sons, however, he had to bequeath Chiara his winery.

The vagaries of inheritance were not limited to women whose families had been in the wine business for generations. Women from families whose wealth was not traditionally associated with wine, such as

Paola Gloder and Lorenza Sebasti, had similar experiences. They were admitted to the wine world when their families purchased wineries as investments, diversions, or places in the country, in the wake of post–World War II land reforms and the subsequent rural exodus. Finally, women with neither great wealth nor distinguished wineries, such as Elisabetta Foradori, had to revive their properties and virtually start anew to compete successfully in the modern age of Italian wines. Advancement for all these women depended on one ingredient—no brothers with whom to compete.

Inheritance, however, does not equate to a guaranteed birthright; success has to be earned. Entrenched male prejudices required women to be tested to prove their worth. Paola Gloder's father, Giancarlo, a Milanese investment banker, challenged her to make a long-term career commitment at Poggio Antico. Since she had neither a university degree nor a head for investment banking, he considered it a good fit for her self-motivated, independent personality. Undeterred by her lack of management or winery experience, she picked up the gauntlet. Later, she asked her husband to relinquish his marketing position with Club Med and move to the country a year before they married, to be sure that he would be happy living at Poggio Antico. Having lived like a hilltop hermit at the winery in Montalcino since she was twenty, Paola had no intention of leaving the winery with which she was inextricably linked emotionally and professionally; it was more than her home—it was her *raison d'être*.

Piero Antinori may have been a visionary in the wine world, but he was a traditional, conservative Italian male in dealing with his eldest daughter, Albiera. At eighteen, when other women her age were embarking on their university education, she began picking grapes and cleaning wine barrels because her father believed that university education was not important for women. (Albiera concedes that her father would have sent a son to the university, and eventually he did send her youngest sister.) In 1995, when she was twenty-nine, Albiera was appointed president of Prunotto, a previously well-regarded but financially troubled Piedmont estate that her father had acquired six years earlier. Even though she could barely read a balance sheet, Piero gave her the keys and told her to turn it around—sink or swim.

She lived apart from her husband and two small children two days a week for four years, in the extraordinarily hostile, anti-female Piedmontese environment. Initially, Albiera was ignored or treated with contempt by local men and, occasionally, women. They spoke in Italian to her male staff but addressed her only in local dialect, a sign of disrespect. She stoically adopted the philosophy "Life is tough—so what?" and did not attempt to alter their attitude. She simply made it apparent that she was in charge and that if they wanted to do business with Antinori, they had to deal with her directly: "I'm not going anywhere, so you'll just have to do business with me," she explained.[16] Albiera increased the size of Prunotto's vineyard acreage, modernized and upgraded its production methods, underwrote the expansion of its product line, and was solely responsible for creating a new wine, Costamiole. Production and sales increased from 250,000 bottles to more than 1 million, and the estate became profitable.

Gender was not the only hurdle some of these Italian women had to overcome. In some cases, youth and inexperience compounded their difficulties. Albiera Antinori, Laura Bianchi, Paola Gloder, and Lorenza Sebasti were born in 1966, a poor vintage in Italy for wine but obviously not for women. Teresa Severini recalls, "At my first harvest in 1979, I had to confront male workers at the winery who had a consolidated experience and tradition and for whom the presence of a woman, and a young one at that, was almost a threat." Her younger sister, Chiara, concurs: "It's not easy explaining to the winery workers, some who have been here for years, that a 'young girl' is going to change things."[17] Out of deference to her father's memory and sensitivity to those around her, Chiara assumed his mantle gradually—it was a year before she moved into his corner office.

These Italian women are realists but retain the optimism of youth—their wine goblet is half full, not half empty. They are energized rather than defeated by their uphill battles. By using a variety of management styles, getting their hands dirty, listening respectfully to other people's ideas, using a team approach, and explaining rather than dictating ideas, they have deflected a substantial amount of resentment and doubt regarding their ability and dedication. Making *limoncello* from the lemon, they also dwell on the advantages rather than the disadvantages of their "secret weapons," gender and age: expectations are low, people can be caught off guard, and they are seen as curiosities, which can gain publicity for their wines and can prevent people who are intrigued with them from slamming doors in their faces.

Linguistic talent—particularly fluency in English and French—is another "secret weapon" many women credit for their early success. Paola Gloder gained her wine knowledge on the job at Poggio Antico, but her command of English was obtained at Cornell University, and her excellent French came from a privileged upbringing that included extensive travel in France. Teresa Severini remembers being excluded from wine tastings and treated as a "mascot" by the Italian Trade Commission in the United States. But such treatment ended when she was able to assist her male colleagues in answering technical questions posed to them in English.

Risk also is a part of these women's reality, and they do not shrink from it. *"As an entrepreneur, there is no doubt that you have to take your risks every day, and any decision is on your shoulders."* Teresa Severini says, "If creating a new wine is a risk, then I am a risk-taker. If obstinately carrying on a type of production which respects tradition and is a counter-current to the rest of the market, and believing firmly in this, is taking a risk, then I am again a risk-taker." Elisabetta Foradori sees her entire life as a risk—replanting her vineyards, relying on an ancient and unheralded grape, and supporting her children.

Some women were so young that they did not even recognize the risks they took—"what you don't know can't hurt you." Paola Gloder filled her car trunk with wine and delivered samples to potential buyers. On her first trip to England, she was detained while going through customs—

confused by driving on the "wrong" side of the road, she had incorrectly selected the lane labeled "Nothing to Declare." She had other equally unique and naïve marketing strategies. Knowing that great wines were identified by being part of the wine lists at top restaurants, she decided that such lists should include Poggio Antico. Targeting England, France, and Germany, she dined at elegant restaurants, paid her bill, and then asked to speak with the person in charge of wine to learn the name of their distributor. She then made cold calls to the distributor to introduce her wines. If the phone charges from her hotel room were too high, she armed herself with coins and made the calls from a local phone booth— definitely a pre-cellular marketing strategy.

For Lorenza Sebasti, CEO of Castello di Ama, and her winemaker husband, Marco Pallanti, risk-taking is a family activity. Despite their success in using merlot, a nonindigenous grape, to compete internationally, they changed their focus and committed themselves to making great Chianti Classico, "the signature wine of their territory." They replanted vineyards and blended grapes that had previously gone into single-vineyard wines to make their new Chianti. The Tre Bicchiere received by their Chianti Classico Castello di Ama '99 demonstrated that their risk was well calculated.[18]

THE GLASS IS HALF FULL, NOT HALF EMPTY

Equality may no longer be pure illusion, but many Italian women believe that they must continue to pursue it, acknowledging that they have to work harder than men to achieve success: *"It is more difficult for a woman. Now women have the same possibilities, but not in the past." "If a woman wants to be taken into consideration, [she has] to show one hundred times more [talent and determination] than a man." "I had to push and still have to, but it is improving."*

According to Teresa Severini, "This industry has always been run by men, and their machismo attitude makes it even worse for women in the business. . . . [In the beginning, it] was tough. . . . I started in a technical capacity, and workers—men who for years had been working under the direction of other men—were not used to taking orders from a woman. It was equally difficult when, as head of exporting, I traveled the world competing with men who are regarded as icons in the international world of wine."[19] Today, however, "the situation has changed: there are many women enologists, so many of the discriminations have disappeared." Chiara notes, "It was not nearly as difficult [for me] as it had been twenty years ago for Teresa. But it still is a male-dominated industry where machismo is the rule rather than the exception."[20]

Elisabetta Foradori testifies to the residual hostility faced by women at small wineries. In her region, Trentino, the local cooperative, made up exclusively of men, produced Vino da Tavola from teroldego, an ancient, indigenous grape with a reputation for mediocrity. Elisabetta, an enologist who had traveled through several of France's finer wine regions, believed that teroldego could be used to make something other than lackluster wines. When she inherited her property from her widowed mother, she gambled, replanted with teroldego, and used more modern production techniques—new barriques and extended aging—to make her award-winning wines. With limited financial resources and production facilities, she had to find a way to increase supply to meet the skyrocketing demand for her wine. She approached the local cooperative, asking the members to use the excess capacity in their storage tanks. They refused to help—competition from a woman was not appreciated.

Women have benefited from the fact that most Italian wineries are family businesses, not corporate subsidiaries. Although sometimes challenging and traditional, the family environment could be comfortable and supportive, particularly when the only heir apparent was an heiress. Family members or staff—most often male—provided the guidance and mentoring necessary to translate passion for wine into knowledge, self-confidence, and success. Two generations of Antinori men mentored Albiera: her paternal grandfather, who encouraged her; and her father, who moved her along in the business. Paola Gloder's father plans with her and discusses finance, but her mentors came from her professional staff.

Without disparaging her, they helped her to get her hands dirty and patiently taught her to run the winery from the bottom up. When he decided to get out of management and return full time to winemaking, Laura Bianchi's father put her in charge of the winery and gave her the support she needed. It was Laura's paternal grandmother, however, who developed Laura's palate and taught her tasting skills—as she had done for her son, Laura's father, a generation earlier.

In an industry that has been predominantly male for so long, it is hardly surprising that both role models and mentors were invariably male. In particular, women who represented their family's first generation in the business had to find industry leaders to emulate. Completely focused on her own winery, Paola Gloder hopes to model herself after Paolo di Marchi at Isole é Olena, who works the land, makes the wine, and is the public persona of his winery. Lorenza Sebasti's business education and her dedication to the quality of her traditional wines are apparent in her desire to fashion herself after visionaries such as Angelo Gaja and Piero Antinori, hoping to serve as an international ambassador for Italian wines, not only for her own.

Whatever role women choose to play, they are confronted by the difficulties of mixing career and family responsibilities, particularly children. These problems are exacerbated by demands for extensive international travel to promote and market their wines and to taste other wines and interact with other producers and winemakers. Having served as director of marketing for Lungarotti, Teresa Severini, mother of three, says, "Besides the occasional and temporary difficulties posed by the fact that I am a woman in a field which initially was male dominated, the greatest drawback is my total lack of free time, because my life is divided between my family and my work." She has bitter memories of losing her membership in the Academie Internationale du Vin in 1990 because her pregnancy made it impossible for her to attend a third consecutive meeting and thus automatically disqualified her—no excuses were allowed. Other women also struggle to find a solution to the family/career equation: *"In Italy, if a woman wants to remain in the family and raise a healthy child as the main part of her life, her advancement will always be hindered. But this is a personal choice." "My weakness is to be a woman, so that after my work I have to think of my house, to cook, to plan for my children, and I cannot delegate."*

Without hesitation, however, women with children put their family responsibilities above their business interests—a choice they do not often have to make in a family business. When Lorenza Sebasti and her family reside at Castello di Ama, work and family are blended. Her staff provides day care assistance for her while she works. At lunchtime, she joins her family and staff for a meal. Even in a small winery, Elisabetta Foradori sees no conflict between the winery and her family. For her, the winery provides the means for her to support her children. She says that you must know who you are, organize yourself, and ration your energy.

THE PATH FORWARD: FILLING THE GLASS

Unlike French women, who rarely network among themselves, Italian women have established a formal national network, called Le Donne del Vino (the women of wine), to foster greater equity for women in the wine industry. Founded in 1988 by two enologists—Elisabetta Tognana, a rally car racer in her first career incarnation, and Wanda Gradnik[21]—the association has more than five hundred members representing wine-related professions: producers, winemakers, viticulturists, restaurateurs, wine merchants, sommeliers, and journalists. Through special events such as seminars, tastings, roundtables, courses, and panels at Vinitaly (the annual trade fair), the organization promotes better understanding of wine, provides current information relevant to women in wine-related businesses, and offers a support system for women in the industry.[22] Laura Bianchi, who has served as president of the organization's Tuscany region, believes that Le Donne del Vino established a "new reality" in which women are able to help one another.

Despite enduring inequities in the Italian wine industry, particularly for women in smaller wineries, Le Donne del Vino's success in attracting and retaining members is uneven, shedding light on the difficulties encountered in developing a formal single-sex network. Women give a variety of reasons for not joining: lack of time for outside activities; a desire not to be simply a name on a membership roster; disagreement with the organization's structure or goals; a lack of educational substance in the group's programs; a belief that the network avoids addressing industrywide problems; a feeling that it fosters too much whining and bemoaning of women's fate rather than advancing women's causes in a positive manner and celebrating their accomplishments.

Laura Bianchi, one of a handful of women from prestigious wineries who has contributed considerable time as well as her name to the organization, believes that the primary reason that many women remain aloof is to avoid being labeled a "feminist" or, even worse, a "woman winemaker or owner." It is unclear to what extent she is correct. But this view does resonate throughout both the Old World and the New World of wine—some women want to be "one of the boys" or have bought into many of society's stereotypes and biases. Acknowledging that men remain overwhelmingly in charge, other women fear that joining a women's network will translate into further loss of influence and competitiveness through alienation, segregation, or isolation.

Despite membership problems at home, Le Donne del Vino's importance now extends beyond Italy's borders. It has become a role model for similar women's organizations throughout Europe. In 2003, the group joined with the prestigious International Wine and Spirits Competition to create the first Women in Wine Award.[23] Vinissima, Frauen und Wein e.V., the German women's wine network, founded in 1991 with the stated goal "More women should know more about wine!,"[24] has more than two hundred members, a regional structure, and a set of activities reminiscent of Le Donne del Vino. Le Donne del Vino also has developed its outreach by accepting non-Italian members. An informal club of Austrian winemakers called 11 Women and Their Wines includes Heidi Schröck, a consummate networker and member of Le Donne del Vino. Credited with resuscitating Ruster Ausbruch, the traditional Aus-

5. Heidi Schröck, winemaker and proprietor of Heidi Schröck Vineyards, helped to revitalize Austria's traditional sweet wine, Ruster Ausbruch.

trian sweet wine, Heidi serves as president of the Cercle Ruster Ausbruch and in 2004 was selected as Vintner of the Year by Austria's most influential food and wine magazine, *Falstaff*.[25]

For pioneering women such as Heidi Schröck; Mechthild Hammel, who attended the Fachhochschule Geisenheim in Wiesbaden and became the first female university-trained enologist in Germany in 1970;[26] and Annegret Reh-Gartner, who became the successful managing director of Weingut Reichsgraf von Kesselstatt, the largest estate in the Mosel, despite those who deemed her too young, slow, and incapable, women's networks came after they had achieved success rather than before. For the majority of women, however, these networks are more than an opportunity to commiserate—they are a place to find encouragement and guidance and to exchange ideas with other professional women in a non-threatening setting.

The following statements testify to the depth of the remaining bias and uphill fight for recognition, acceptance, and respectability faced by many European women and to the need for women's support groups: *"During my training, a man bluntly told me that women were ignorant and had no ideas. Today, I believe that that remark was an incentive to prove the opposite." "If you are working in a male-dominated job, men are not used to working with a woman. And they don't allow the women to get a step into the network of men." "People still have in mind that only men are good wine-makers." "Mainly, the male journalists cannot believe that a woman makes real wine."*

. . .

The problems confronting women in Europe—inheritance, youth, balancing families with careers—are the same in all nations. What differs is the extent, not the nature, of the biases. In recognition of this and because in numbers there is strength, several national women's networks created the International Federation of Women of Wine, which met for the first time in February 2003 in Mainz, Germany.[27] The glass may be half full today, but women hope to toast tomorrow with a full one.

During the late twentieth century, the Italian wine industry opened its doors to women. Through inheritance, Italian women, like their French counterparts, have become or will become proprietors of legendary wineries, while others are gaining stature as university-educated winemakers. Given their relative youth, these women individually are likely to exert influence within the wine industry for years to come. Collectively, through Le Donne del Vino, they also may promote women's advancement in the wine industry in other parts of the Old World.

CHAPTER SIX

The New World: California

Marching, demonstrating, rallying, and praying—but not yet voting—the Women's Christian Temperance Union (WCTU) campaigned early in the twentieth century to abolish all liquor-related industry in the United States. Associating alcohol consumption with immorality, marital infidelity, family instability, the ruin of children, and urban crime, the WCTU and other organizations helped to usher in Prohibition, the fourteen-year period between passage of the Eighteenth Amendment in 1919 and its subsequent repeal by the Twenty-first Amendment in 1933. The Eighteenth Amendment, enforced by the Volstead Act (the National Prohibition Act), banned the manufacture, sale, transportation, importation, and exportation of intoxicating liquors.[1]

Prohibition cut an indelible swath across American wine history, returning a thriving wine industry to its infancy. A handful of wineries survived, ones that availed themselves of Prohibition's three legislative loopholes for wine production or consumption: use for medicinal purposes, with a physician's prescription; sacramental or ritual use; or noncommercial home use in limited quantities. In a twist of history, Prohibition leveled not only the American wine industry but also, at least in part, its playing field, creating opportunities for women to participate in rebuilding the industry and, ironically, revalidating the WCTU slogan, "Never underestimate the power of a woman."[2]

Though it is produced in all fifty states, wine is nonetheless synonymous with California, the largest agricultural state, where wine is the "most valuable finished agricultural product." Home to approximately 50 percent of America's bonded wineries, California accounts for more than 90 percent of American wine production and commands a 5 percent share of the world export market. If it were a country, California "would be the fourth leading wine producer worldwide."[3]

With its temperate climate, an environment suitable for growing *Vitis vinifera,* a wine-producing heritage dating from the Spanish missionaries,[4] and an influx of energetic, entrepreneurial Europeans seeking to produce high-quality wines that had eluded them elsewhere in the country, California had risen to prominence in the American wine industry by 1900. During the first half of the twentieth century, however, California saw its wine industry devastated by Prohibition, the Great Depression, and two world wars. Not until the mid-1960s did it regain the prestige it had lost because of the decline in its winery population and the scarcity of winemaking talent.[5]

Postwar prosperity, consumer affluence, changing lifestyles, the association of fine wine with prestige and status, increased advertising, technological advances that improved wine quality, better-educated winemakers, and tax concessions that encouraged investment in wineries and vineyards—all these factors helped California to reestablish its reputation for winemaking excellence and to lead America's wine industry out of its post-Prohibition doldrums.[6] But one watershed event put the industry over the top. On May 24, 1976, at a Paris blind tasting, nine influential and experienced French judges selected California wines as superior to their French counterparts, guaranteeing worldwide prominence for the state and a boom in demand for its wines.[7]

The subsequent growth of the California wine market created demand not only for more wine but also for more people capable of producing it. Just as World War II's demand for factory workers opened new avenues for women ("Rosie the Riveter"), the expanded demand for American wine, particularly from California, changed the wine industry's criteria for entry—ability, not gender, became the prerequisite. The stage was set for women to capitalize on the growth of the state's wine industry. In the years that followed, California demonstrated both the positive effects of entrepreneurship, education, mentoring, and networking in strengthening women's position in the industry and the negative impact of industry consolidation—particularly the decline of family businesses and the increased dominance of publicly held corporations —on women's advancement within management.

GO WEST, YOUNG WOMAN

In stark contrast to the Old World, where women still acquired estate ownership primarily through inheritance, California was the land of the entrepreneur. Following in the footsteps of Josephine Tychson, the first woman to build a winery in California,[8] gutsy, pioneering women representing a wide cross-section of cultures, experience, and wealth took advantage of the California wine industry's growth spurt to found wineries in numbers unmatched elsewhere in the New World.

Sandra MacIver, hippie college dropout, wife, mother of two, and heiress to part of the Sears Roebuck fortune, could have remained among the idle rich. But, inspired by her father's love of fine wine and her grandmother's admonition to make something of herself and not let wealth paralyze her, she founded Matanzas Creek Winery in 1978, thinking that it would provide her and her husband, a law school dropout, with careers. When he sought to exclude her from the business, she kept the winery but not him.

Unprepared to handle either her inheritance or a winery, Sandra quickly proved the old axiom that to make a small fortune in the wine industry, one must start with a large one. Losing her original inheritance, she extricated herself from debt after fifteen years, helped by good advisers, a new husband, and cash from the sale of some family real estate.

Recognizing that high prices would lure status-conscious customers, Sandra advocated the elitist marketing strategy used today by most cult wineries, including some founded by other women such as Ann Colgin at Colgin Cellars or Jean Phillips at Screaming Eagle. Sandra summarized her strategy in these terms: "We are wonderful; you should want our wine; and if you're lucky, we'll sell it to you." Named one of the twenty most influential people in the modern American wine industry by *Wine Spectator* in 1996, Sandra can rightfully call herself "a self-made heiress."

Cathy Corison was no heiress, self-made or otherwise. She arrived in Napa with two hundred dollars in her pocket and a desire to make great wine. After receiving an MS in food science from the University of California at Davis and gaining years of winemaking experience working for others, she staked her life savings to found Corison Winery in 1987, becoming one of the first women in California to make the transition from winemaker to proprietor. Having no financial backing, she managed risk by steering clear of debt and using cash flow to underwrite her winery's growth. Initially reticent to put her name on the label for fear of appearing egotistical, she finally realized that her wine was her personal expression and philosophic statement. She also believed that it could be marketed more successfully if she clearly associated herself with it. Cathy's precedent led the way for other women such as Pam Starr at Crocker & Starr Wines to translate their winemaking talents into winery ownership.

Entrepreneurial immigrants like Su Hua Newton and Delia Viader fulfilled their American Dream in California, where the terroir proved suitable for the growth of their strong personalities as well as their grapes. Prepared by virtue of education, wealth, focus, vision, and steely temperament to take full advantage of New World opportunities, they retained their affinity for Old World culture, remaining consummate outsiders despite sinking their roots literally and figuratively in California soil.

The youngest of six sisters born in the People's Republic of China, Su

Hua Newton, co-founder of Newton Vineyards, maintains that she is still philosophically Chinese, despite being separated from her family since the age of eleven. Her family, who had fled to Hong Kong, later sent her to England to live with a family friend because they had no money left for her education. With a single-minded commitment to attaining success and financial independence, she became a renaissance woman, speaking four languages and accumulating college degrees.[9] A perfectionist, Su Hua claims to have refused to accept a degree in fine arts from Mills College because her transcript included a B+ for a course in which her attendance, not her performance, lowered her grade from an A.

Su Hua favors strict French-style meritocracy rather than affirmative action, prefers French winemaking practices and consultants, accepts no interns from UC Davis or California State University at Fresno, and hires only French students in their fourth and final year of study after they have experienced three crushes. Given her affinity for all things French, it is not surprising that she refused to sell Newton Vineyards to another American firm. Instead, she chose to sell a 60 percent share to LVMH Moët Hennessey Louis Vuitton, the French luxury conglomerate, in 2001, while retaining daily control and winemaking responsibility.[10] A woman who pursues physical as well as intellectual perfection and has a penchant for wearing hot yellow leather miniskirts, her appointment as an independent member of the board of directors of Krispy Kreme Doughnuts in 2003[11] may mark a mellowing.

Delia Viader, daughter of an Argentine diplomat and divorced mother of three, decided in 1984 to reside in California rather than Argentina in order to be taken seriously. Versed in six languages with three advanced degrees, including two in business,[12] Delia is nonetheless quite willing, by her own admission, to use feminine charm when necessary. Underwritten by a ten-year loan from her father, who supported her throughout her years of schooling, she built a winery, Viader Vineyards, on land he had originally purchased for a house. He obviously had not communicated with her MIT negotiation professor, who, according to Delia, said, "Here comes Delia—hold on to your wallet." Choosing an unorthodox path to set her wines apart from other Napa Cabernets, she planted vertical rather than terraced vineyards on an unusually steep slope, selecting varietals to emulate Bordeaux's Cheval Blanc. She also put her name on the label with no hesitation. Delia's entrepreneurial spirit, along with her affinity for European tradition, is further reflected by her investment in acreage along the Tuscan coast in Bolgheri to expand her winemaking reach into the Old World.

EDUCATION: THE ESSENTIAL EQUALIZER

"The opportunity to study wine and follow it with practical experience has probably been the single most important trigger in encouraging women to go into the business of making wine."[13] Before the Civil Rights Act of 1964, California had fewer than five women winemakers, all self-taught and virtually unknown.[14] This changed dramatically in 1965, when MaryAnn Graf became the first woman to earn a degree in enology from the Department of Viticulture and Enology at UC Davis. Originally admitted to study food science, which, like nutrition, was a traditionally feminine academic field, MaryAnn unwittingly pioneered a new era for women by selecting winemaking and viticulture electives as part of her curriculum. Her graduation opened the floodgates, allowing women to pour into UC Davis's enology program; by the early 1990s, they accounted for 50 percent of the students.[15] Commenting on major changes in the U.S. wine industry, Leon Adams notes, "Women trained in viticultural colleges are playing an increasingly important part in the production of both grapes and vines."[16]

MaryAnn Graff also opened new avenues for women in winemaking. She was the first woman hired as head winemaker at a major California winery (Simi). When she left Simi, shortly after it was acquired by Schieffelin, MaryAnn continued to make history by partnering with another woman, Marty Bannister, to establish Vinquiry, one of the first wine analysis and consulting firms in Sonoma. Realizing that "the laboratory is not just a part of the modern winery's quality control, but also an instrument for wine makers' creativity,"[17] they each invested twelve thousand dollars and transformed a traditional, unglamorous "women's job" into a premier, state-of-the-art, enological services company, with three locations, grossing more than $3 million per year.

WINE GODDESSES

Representing 10 to 15 percent of California's winemakers, women are disproportionately linked to the upper end of the industry, making coveted wines in minute quantities that sell for enormous amounts of money via subscription lists direct from the winery. "At the top of the business, the stars are women," one wine industry consultant noted.[18] Often referred to by others as the Wine Goddesses,[19] Heidi Peterson Barrett, Merry Edwards, Mia Klein, and Helen Turley exemplify a special breed of pacesetting: they are California winemakers who work as consulting enologists or independent contractors. Serving as full-time winemakers and making all decisions at several wineries, they differ from earlier consultants who advised on site resident winemakers.[20] They also "call their own shots."[21]

Talented entrepreneurial men and women are drawn to consulting because it has low start-up costs, is not capital intensive, provides variety, and is potentially very lucrative. Women are also attracted to it for personal reasons. Heidi Peterson Barrett calls herself a "shared winemaker" rather than a consultant because she not only tells people what to do; she also does it for them.[22] A winemaker who likes to work for small, ultra-premium producers so that she can do everything,[23] Heidi finds that consulting gives her both flexibility and control over her schedule. The antithesis of a globetrotting "flying winemaker," she confines herself to working for clients who are nice people with a sense of humor, who have the potential for making great wine by virtue of their attitude and their vineyard, and who live in Napa within a thirty-minute drive from her home. Heidi is a very traditional woman who emphasizes being a mom, bans television at home, and retains her maiden name to honor her father, Dr. Richard Peterson, a leading contributor to the modern California wine industry. She seeks recognition for her talent and accomplishments, not her gender, and bristles at being called a "woman winemaker."

Merry Edwards, whose business card proclaims her *Reine de Pinot* (Queen of Pinot), was the first winemaker at Matanzas Creek and the first person to conduct a seminar on cloning at UC Davis. She consults in part to coordinate her family and professional obligations. But it is also a financial strategy. Having experienced a financial setback when her first venture, Merry Vintners, folded because of insufficient financial backing, she now aims to diversify her risk by working for more than one vineyard[24] and to gain the financial backing to support her dream of owning her own vineyard, Meredith Vineyard Estate Inc., in which she has controlling interest. Unlike her colleagues who work only with star-quality wineries, Merry is a troubleshooting superstar specializing in winery start-ups and the rehabilitation of run-down wineries.[25] When she graduated from UC Davis, Merry refused to be relegated to a laboratory rather than a cellar. She counsels young women entering winemaking to "dress for success" by donning work clothes rather than business suits for their interviews, to demonstrate that they are ready and able to work in a cellar. Named Winemaker of the Year in 2004 by the *San Francisco Chronicle*,[26] Merry serves as a role model as well as a mentor.

The other Wine Goddesses also own small wineries and have their own labels. Heidi Peterson Barrett initially resisted having her own label because she did not want clients to think that their wines took a back seat to hers. But she now believes that owning her own winery—La Sirena (the mermaid, in Italian or Spanish), a magical name related to her favorite pastime, scuba diving—gives her a better understanding of her clients' anxieties. Mia Klein named her winery Selene, Greek for moon goddess. Helen Turley owns Marcassin, a French term for a young wild boar.

An independent woman considered by some to be as difficult as she is talented,[27] Helen Turley has set her own rules throughout her life, even

6. Heidi Peterson Barrett, winemaker and owner of La Sirena in Napa and known as one of California's Wine Goddesses, is a consultant who makes many of the region's most sought-after and expensive wines.

designing her own graduate program in flavor science at Cornell so that she could receive a BS degree without taking organic chemistry. A contrarian who considers UC Davis faculty white-coated scientists and sanitary food engineers,[28] she has "particular interest, passion and skills . . . in guiding small winegrowing projects . . . that are based on superior viticultural sites."[29] Her primary clients pay one hundred thousand dollars each per year for a minimum of two years and either obey her dictatorial commands or become victim to her single-minded philosophy, "My way or the highway."[30]

A FERTILE GROUND

The exceptional number of women who have flourished in California reflects not only their individual talent, education, and entrepreneurial spirit but also a supportive cultural climate. Family-run wineries have provided opportunities for both female and male members to display their ability. Mentors of both genders have played an active role in guiding and advancing women's careers. Networking has also added to the support system that made America an especially fertile ground for women's progress.

Inheriting family wineries has been an important route for women's advancement from as far back as 1940, when Fernande Romer de Latour and her daughter, Hélène de Pins, inherited Beaulieu Vineyards after the death of its founder, Georges Latour.[31] What sets the American experience apart from its Old World counterpart is that women's ascendancy within family wineries in the United States frequently occurred despite the presence of brothers, sons-in-law, or other male relatives. According to John De Luca, longtime president of the Wine Institute, "The increasing role of the daughters of wine families and women in general is one of the signature developments in the [American] wine industry."[32]

The poor survival rate of family-owned businesses in America has been well documented: only one-third make it to the next generation, and only 15 percent survive until the third generation. In this context, women often emerged as contenders because of the family's determination to keep the business alive for another generation. The women's success, however, depended on their standing within the family, the support and empowerment they received from the head of the family, and their ability to forge a career path reflecting their own determination, long-term commitment, and desire for advancement.[33]

Tim Tesconi, writing about the role of women in Northern California family wineries, noted that "most of the vintners' daughters . . . sought fame, fortune, independence, or their own identity far away from the wine cellar but eventually were lured home" by location, lifestyle, family ties, or loyalty to the family winemaking tradition. They also were enticed to return by the flexibility and familiarity of working for a family business, by the nurturing environment such a business can provide, by a meaningful family life, and by the potential for prestige and profits.[34]

Jean Robinson Wente succeeded her husband, Karl, as chair of the board of Wente Brothers Winery in 1977 and eventually divided ownership equally among her three children, Eric, Philip, and Carolyn. After graduating from Stanford, Carolyn worked in public relations and marketing in the banking industry. Returning to the family winery in 1980, she assumed marketing responsibilities while her brothers handled the vineyards and production. Over the course of the next ten years, the importance of her role increased as decisions became less production-driven and more consumer- or market-oriented. Today, she is president of the renamed Wente Vineyards.

Carolyn Martini left her position as inventory manager for the nine campuses of Rutgers University to run the Louis M. Martini Winery when her father, Louis P. Martini, suffered a heart attack and called her home in 1975.[35] Selected by her siblings to serve as president and CEO, she bypassed her brother Michael, the winemaker, who was serving in the military at the time.[36] Carolyn remained in control until the winery was sold to Gallo in 2002.

A clear departure from the European model that favors sons over daughters is Spottswoode Vineyard and Winery, one of California's early cult wineries. After the death of Jack Novak in 1977, his widow, Mary, assumed control. In 1982, she transformed the business from grape selling to winemaking. In 1987, Mary selected her youngest daughter and middle child of five, Beth Novak Milliken, to assume management of the winery and complete its transition to an estate winery with its own crush and bottle-aging facilities. By virtue of circumstance and atmosphere, Mary and Beth—who became the first woman to serve as president of the Napa Valley Vintners Association[37]—have maintained a predominantly female staff, including winemakers Rosemary Cakebread and Mia Klein.

The most famous face of California's largest family-owned winery, Gina Gallo, granddaughter of Julio Gallo and grandniece of Ernest, is one of thirteen third-generation Gallo children—referred to as G3s—

who work for the E.&J. Gallo Winery. Gina, who took extension courses in enology from UC Davis, became the only sister in her family of eight (four girls and four boys) to work for Gallo of Sonoma as one of its five winemakers. She proved to be a natural fit and assisted with the transition from popularly priced wines to upscale wines. According to Gina, her grandfather, Julio, and her father, Robert, encouraged her as a winemaker, as did her mentor, Marcello Monticelli, vice-president of winemaking. She notes that her older brothers taught her how to persist in a male-dominated business. Her mother instilled the sense of family and community that gives her life balance, Gina says, and she credits her granduncle, Ernest, for his remarkable sense of knowing the consumer. In an industry purported to be reticent to hire women in sales, Gina's prominence reflects her public relations value, her winemaking skills, and, most of all, her family ties.

Prominent male mentors who were not relatives were particularly important in advancing the careers of several influential women and identifying them with world-class wines. No man fit this mold better than André Tchelistcheff, who is credited not only with starting the modern wine era in Napa[38] but also with training and mentoring more women winemakers, including MaryAnn Graf, than anyone else.[39] Robert Mondavi, the visionary who raised the standard of California wines on a grand scale and became their worldwide ambassador, has been equally significant in providing opportunities for women to display their talent and establish their credentials. Mike Grgich, Mondavi's head winemaker at the time, hired Zelma Long as an intern to work the harvest of 1970, but it was Mondavi himself who promoted her to head enologist after Grgich's departure, thus launching one of the most distinguished careers in California. Mondavi's willingness to give women prominent positions remains evident today: Genevieve Janssens, for example, is director of winemaking at Mondavi. Mia Klein's consulting practice as well as her winery, Selene, were inspired by Tony Soter, who brought her into his consulting business in 1990 and showed her how to make her own wines without a lot of money, her own vineyard, or her own winery structure.[40]

Despite the support of well-regarded male mentors and a generally hospitable atmosphere, women often were excluded from male social networks. Women for WineSense (WWS), founded by Michaela Rodeno and Julie Williams in 1990, sought to overcome this problem. WWS is a not-for-profit organization with membership open to men and women. Through educational programs,[41] it promotes the benefits of moderate wine consumption as part of a healthy, balanced lifestyle and defends wine against the neo-Prohibitionist movement that pressured the government to require warning labels on wine bottles. As the group states: "Women for WineSense views wine as a natural, agriculturally-based beverage which enriches American economy, culture and way of life, differentiating the appreciation of wine and its rich tradition from the abuse of alcohol, which the organization firmly opposes."[42] WWS also serves as a network that provides a job hotline and forms "strategic alliances with other wine, food and women-oriented organizations."[43]

Like Le Donne del Vino in Italy, WWS receives uneven support from prominent women, many of whom do not have time to devote to the organization, prefer professional associations, or are disenchanted with its activities and consider it no more than a kaffeeklatch. Nonetheless, in its first ten years, WWS attracted approximately fifteen hundred members in twelve chapters[44] and bolstered the support system for women working in the U.S. wine industry.

THE EXECUTIVE SUITE: ANOTHER FRENCH PARADOX

Despite widespread success as winemakers and prominence in family wineries, women continue to be underrepresented in corporate executive suites in the California wine industry, especially at the highest levels. In 1991, Cathy Corison noted that "in recent years, as the ladders to top management have gotten longer, the progress for women seems to be slowing down temporarily."[45] Well over a decade later, the situation appears more permanent than temporary. In marked similarity to the Old World, "the barrier that probably hasn't come down is the one around the higher positions such as president or chairman or CEO of a winery which is owned by a large corporation. . . . That's the place where the least amount of progress has been made," according to Katie Wetzel Murphy, a highly respected winemaker.[46]

Ironically, on the rare occasion when a woman assumes a senior position within a winery controlled by a large public company, the firm is likely to be owned by Europeans, particularly French or Spanish sparkling wine companies. This may seem odd, given Continental personnel practices, in which few women other than the sisters, wives, or daughters of the original owners are elevated. But European firms operating in California view the acceptance of women as more than another cultural difference in an alien business environment; it is also a strategic decision.[47] Capable and ambitious women such as Eileen Crane and Michaela Rodeno are initially hired and promoted by European firms operating within the United States because they garner more publicity, are seen as less threatening than men, are considered more pliable, are willing to accept lower salaries, are considered more aesthetically in tune with wine (particularly "feminine" sparkling wine), and are viewed as trustworthy, sincere, and genuine.[48]

Originally a nutritionist who came to California to work in a pastry kitchen, Eileen Crane ignored the advice of a male faculty member at UC Davis who told her that there was no future for a woman winemaker. Heeding instead the suggestion of Dr. Ann Noble, Eileen learned on the job, working her way up from assistant winemaker at Domaine Chandon, a French-owned sparkling wine firm, to become president and winemaker at Domaine Carneros, co-owned by Champagne Taittinger and Kobrand. Along the way, she designed and guided the construction of wineries for Gloria Ferrer, a Spanish-owned sparkling wine firm, and for Domaine Carneros while also making their wines and managing the wineries.

Readily admitting that her success is unique, she says that women do not have the same opportunities as men in the California wine industry, in part because they do not play golf or belong to the "old boys' club." A vocal advocate for women's advancement,[49] Eileen counsels career-oriented women to pay attention to the number of women in management before accepting a job at a given firm. She attributes her personal success to her ability to do many jobs; to her willingness to hire and train good employees, regardless of gender, and provide a support system to meet their needs; and to her conscious decision not to have children.

With an MBA from UC Berkeley and an MA in French literature from UC Davis, Michaela Rodeno is a rarity, a married woman with children who advanced within the corporate wine world without being a winemaker. She began as the first woman tour guide at Beaulieu Vineyards but eventually worked her way up to executive vice-president and CEO of French-owned St. Supéry Vineyards in 1988. In the interim, she spent fifteen years at Domaine Chandon as assistant to the president and then as vice-president for marketing. Instilled with self-confidence by her family, Michaela, an early and innovative proponent of synthetic "corks" in colors to match the labels on bottles, attributes her success to her fluency in French, her marketing creativity, her ability to avoid the winery-related discrimination suffered by her winemaking contemporaries, and her childhood spent with three brothers—being "one of the boys" but with special privileges.

The career of Zelma Long, the first woman to leap from winemaking to senior management at a major California winery, epitomizes the highs and lows experienced by women corporate executives in California's wine industry as well as the strategies women have used for remaining at the top. Her odyssey to the executive suite began with an undergraduate degree in general science, with a minor in nutrition, and master's courses at UC Davis. Thanks to her winemaking talent, she rose from intern to chief enologist at Robert Mondavi Winery during the booming 1970s. When MaryAnn Graf left Simi, the board of directors was reluctant to replace her with another woman,[50] so in 1979 they hired Zelma in a different position, as vice-president for winemaking. Supremely self-confident, she accepted with the understanding that Simi would fund her efforts to obtain an MBA that would prepare her for the top job. In 1980, after completing the executive program at Stanford, she became Simi's president and CEO. With a $5.5 million budget, she renovated Simi, introduced new winemaking techniques, and developed estate vineyards.[51]

Well-spoken, energetic, outgoing, knowledgeable, attractive, and proactive, Zelma became more than an industry leader; she became an icon commanding near-adulation.[52] Among women in the wine industry, Zelma's mentoring efforts are legendary. Dawnine Sample Dyer, formerly vice-president of winemaking at Domaine Chandon, says, "Zelma solidified my feelings that mentoring is vital for any minority pioneering a new field."[53] Aware of her good fortune and wanting to give something back, Zelma states, "If I can do anything that either encourages or furthers the careers of younger women, I'm glad and proud of it."[54] By providing internships, jobs, promotions, and encouragement to qualified women as well as men, she has opened new avenues for women in California's wine industry. Highlighting Zelma's importance as a mentor, Cathy Corison comments that among her female contemporaries, she may be the only winemaker *not* mentored by Zelma Long.

Known as a cerebral winemaker who continued to conduct research and write professionally to enhance her enological credentials, Zelma developed a holistic concept of winegrowing, melding winemaking and vine growing. She redefined the concept of grape ripeness and founded the American Vineyard Foundation to help finance research in enology and viticulture. She is also a founder of the American Viticulture and Enology Research Network (AVERN).[55] When LVMH purchased Simi in 1981, Zelma became executive vice-president for business development of Chandon Estates (Simi and Domaine Chandon).

Zelma is an optimist, noting that "women today have incredible opportunities that they didn't have 20 and 30 years ago. Every young woman should have a sense of possibility, a sense that she can do whatever it is she wants to do in this business."[56] But she is also a realist who retired from the corporate world after twenty years, believing that French business and cultural traditions work against women. Fully ac-

7 Zelma Long, co-owner of Zelphi Wines, which operates in both Napa and South Africa, is also a flying winemaker. She was the first woman to serve as CEO of a major California winery (Simi) and is considered one of the pioneers responsible for the growth of the modern California wine industry.

cepted within the industry, she remained an outsider within the corporation. Privately, she concedes that women have the same technical possibilities for advancement but not the same business opportunities; men have a lock on executive positions in public corporations, she believes.

Today, Zelma and her husband, Phillip Freese, own Zelphi Wines, operating in California (Long Vineyards) and South Africa (Vilafonté). She has joined the ranks of the Wine Goddesses and the flying winemakers, consulting in California, the Pacific Northwest, and Israel, and has found that being her own boss is the most comfortable fit at the top.

. . .

Until the early 1960s, California replicated the Old World in excluding women from its wine industry: "Wine was a man's business . . . and remained one into the new age. While male bastions elsewhere collapsed thunderously, in the wine business they were subsiding with the speed of ivy-covered ruins."[57] Today, however, California has become the leader of a New World for women as well as wine. So numerous and well established are women in California's wine industry that the average observer assumes that they are fully accepted, integrated, and equal. For many at the top of the business, this is true.

The one dark spot is the dearth of women in senior management positions in public corporations, a fact that does not bode well for the future. As the wine industry becomes ever more consolidated and dominated by a few publicly held megacompanies, most of which are based in the "old boy" liquor and beer tradition, women in California and elsewhere are unlikely to advance to the executive suite. While women will continue to be great winemakers and gain appropriate recognition for their talent and their wines, management opportunities are likely to diminish, as is already apparent in the heavily corporate climate of Australia. Additionally, as the entrepreneurs who made their mark on the early California wine industry retire or are enticed to sell to larger enterprises, they will not be readily replaced, and the number of women in managerial positions will decline.

Nonetheless, small, privately held wineries run by women—such as Matanzas Creek, which was purchased by Artisans and Estates in 2000; Newton, in which LVMH purchased a controlling interest in 2001; and Louis M. Martini, purchased by E.&J. Gallo Winery in 2002—are the forerunners of a trend that will accelerate along with the intensification of global competition. If the current experience in corporate America serves as an example, women will play a significant role in the future as entrepreneurs, winemakers, and consultants rather than as senior executives of the public corporations that are coming to dominate the industry.[58]

CHAPTER SEVEN

The New World:
The Southern Hemisphere

The New World countries of the Southern Hemisphere—Australia, New Zealand, Argentina, Chile, and South Africa—have centuries of winemaking experience. During the past twenty-five years, they have emerged as challengers to the Old World's hegemony by producing dependable, competitively priced, and, in some cases, superior wines that gained international popularity. Following different paths consistent with each country's unique social, economic, and political environment, the wine industries of these nations agree "that quality is their salvation" and that they "are committed to producing top notch wines at affordable prices,"[1] a determination that has proven to be the salvation of women in their wine industries, too.

AUSTRALIA

Since 1788, when vines as well as convicts arrived with Captain Arthur Phillips and the British First Fleet,[2] Australia has evolved into a self-confident and spirited leader of the international wine trade, commanding a 7 percent global market share.[3] With a reputation for quality and value surpassing that of many Old World countries, Australia's wine industry is known for its pioneering and nontraditional spirit. Its willingness to experiment, invent, and blend to achieve superior results while retaining competitive prices has brought great success.[4]

Located throughout the country but concentrated in the states of New South Wales, Victoria, South Australia, and Western Australia, Australia's wine business is dominated by four multinational alcoholic beverage conglomerates—Southcorp, Constellation Brands, Pernod Ricard, and Fosters—which process and market 89 percent of the nation's grapes.[5] Despite consolidation, however, the total number of wineries has steadily increased, from 62 in 1965 to 1,899 in 2004–2005, because the creation of new boutique wineries has outpaced the demise of traditional family-owned establishments.[6]

The initial expansion of the wine industry was sparked after World War II by an influx of European immigrants from well-established wine cultures. But this expansion did little to increase the involvement of women.[7] In Australia, women had to wait for educational equity and increased international demand for their country's wine to catalyze new opportunities for them.

Roseworthy Agricultural College, a division of the University of Adelaide, is the Australian counterpart of the University of California at Davis. Founded in 1883 as an all-male institution, Roseworthy, under pressure from the Ministry of Education, reluctantly admitted Pam Dunsford in 1972 to complete her fourth year of study. To earn her degree in enology, she endured fear for her personal safety, the "silent treatment" from her classmates, and residence in an infectious disease ward so that she would not have to share the men's toilet and bathroom.[8]

Today, women make up approximately 40 percent of enology graduates.[9] "Young, energetic, and aggressive,"[10] words that describe Australia's wine industry, are equally appropriate for the women who benefited from Dunsford's pioneering experiences. One of these women was Louisa Rose, a senior winemaker at Yalumba. After graduating from an all-girls high school, where she was told she could be anything she wanted to be, and Melbourne University, where she was an honors graduate in physics, Louisa Rose earned her enology degree at Roseworthy.

She then began work at Yalumba, the country's oldest family-owned winery, where she has spent her entire career. Ever conscious of preparing herself for advancement, she chose Yalumba rather than a publicly held alcoholic beverage corporation because it was large enough to offer opportunities but relatively loosely structured and small enough to allow her accomplishments to be recognized.

Louisa has been a senior winemaker since she was twenty-five years old. Today, she is responsible for cellar and quality-control management at Yalumba and "almost [its] entire portfolio of white wines as well as a selection of single vineyard reds."[11] In 1999, the Barons of the Barossa,[12] a previously all-male wine group that had opened its doors to women (but called them Barons, not Baronesses), selected Louisa as Barossa Winemaker of the Year for her success in expanding the region's varietals to include viognier. Her résumé gained further luster in 2004 when she received the Women in Wine Award at the International Wine and Spirits Competition.[13]

Louisa is extremely poised and self-confident and takes gender-related issues in stride. She is unfazed by her status as the first woman winemaker at Yalumba or by rare instances of discrimination, such as having to taste wines in the basement of a men's club in Brisbane that barred women from its main halls. Knowing that she will have to make career choices in the future, she has been preparing herself for all options, both as a winemaker and as a manager. She has moved up in the ranks as a wine judge, has attended several leadership workshops, and was among sixteen persons (including two other women) selected by Yalumba for its inaugural Signature School management certificate, designed for the winery by the Graduate School of Management of the University of Adelaide.[14] Intensely focused on her career, Louisa makes time for a closed, informal network of women in the Barossa who are her age, who also graduated from Roseworthy, and who have equivalent winemaking experience, such as Wendy Stuckey at Beringer Blass and Fiona Donald at Penfolds.

Unlike Louisa Rose, Sarah Marquis never considered working for anyone but herself. Today, she is a partner with her husband, Sparky (Njal), in GRAPES Consulting (Great Reds and People Equal Success), serving as consulting winemakers for private clients. The two met at Roseworthy, where they participated in extracurricular entrepreneurial programs sponsored by Amway. Sarah and her husband make all decisions together, although she is responsible for the final blending of wines at GRAPES. Additionally, they make wine under their own label, Marquis Philips, an Australian/American partnership that markets its wines only in the United States. The Marquis Philips logo is a "roogle," an imaginary animal with the body of a kangaroo and the head of a bald eagle, combining the national symbols of both countries.

Despite claiming that she is not a feminist, Sarah personifies the demand for equality that is at the core of the women's movement. A competitive soccer player who refers to herself as an "old lady all-star," she points out that one of their wines, Sarah's Blend, is not named after her but exists because of her. She also bristles when her husband receives all the publicity and she is assumed to be less than an equal partner. As an example, she notes that *Winestate Magazine* selected the couple as Winemakers of the Year in 2000, publishing a picture of both of them, but then cropped her out of the same picture when they were renominated in 2001. Slights notwithstanding, however, her car's license plate HAVNFUN reflects that she has made the right personal and professional decisions.

Given the consolidation occurring in the Australian wine industry, it is hardly surprising that a substantial number of winemakers work for publicly held corporations. For women seeking to balance family and careers, such as Wendy Stuckey at Beringer Blass and Eloise (Ely) Jarvis at Cape Mentelle, corporate life has been a mixed blessing. After taking parental leaves guaranteed by national legislation,[15] both women were permitted to return on a part-time basis, an employment arrangement that has yet to receive national acceptance.[16] Their male mentors supported the unconventional work schedules because they did not want to lose the women's talent, experience, or knowledge. There was, however, a quid pro quo: Wendy and Ely were forced to relinquish their titles and

8. Sarah Marquis, director and winemaker at GRAPES Consulting, is a co-owner of Marquis Philips, which markets some of Australia's finest wines exclusively in the United States.

accept demotions. Wendy, who had been the group white winemaker for all of Beringer Blass–Australia, is now a senior winemaker; and Ely moved from production manager/winemaker to winemaker.

Although both women believe that they have sidetracked their careers only temporarily and can regain their professional footing in the future, they also acknowledge that they may be permanently on a "mommy track," defined as "a career path determined by work arrangements offering mothers certain benefits, such as flexible hours, but usually providing them with fewer opportunities for advancement."[17] Wendy notes the limited opportunities within corporations and realizes that her future advancement may depend on the timing and availability of openings. When she eventually returns to full-time status, she adds, her progress within the corporate structure will be limited because she does not want to travel extensively, a requirement in an industry heavily engaged in international trade. Gender also will make it extremely difficult to move up a corporate ladder that is dominated by men who have experience in the liquor, beer, or finance industries.

Although Wendy and Ely consider themselves to be in command of their own destinies because they have not been bound by other people's expectations and have been true to themselves, corporate life has created career choices that they might not have faced if they had been working for themselves. Sarah Marquis graduated from Roseworthy in the same class as Wendy, but she was able to work out of her home when her children were very young. Having never relinquished her position or title, she has one of the two corner offices at GRAPES. Women who work in family enterprises—such as Prue Henschke at C. A. Henschke & Company, Diana (Di) and Vanya Cullen at Cullen Wines, and Tricia Horgan at Leeuwin Estate—also are not required to choose between their careers and their personal lives.

With a degree in zoology and botany, Prue Henschke began her viticulture career by accompanying her husband, Stephen, the fifth generation in his family's winemaking tradition, to Germany's Geisenheim State Research Institute, where she worked without pay in the vineyards while he studied. After returning to Australia, she took courses at Roseworthy and Riverina College (now part of Charles Sturt University). A conservationist who does not subscribe to any one agricultural philosophy, Prue manages the vineyards for all Henschke wines, including the iconic Hill of Grace.[18] Chosen with Stephen as Joint International Red Winemaker of the Year at the International Wine and Spirits Competition in 1994–1995 and selected as Viticulturist of the Year by the Barons of the Barossa in 1997, Prue still has to defend herself against those who believe that her achievements are more related to her marriage than to her professional skills, an issue that enrages and frustrates her husband.

9. Prue Henschke, co-owner and viticulturist at C. A. Henschke & Company, is responsible for growing the grapes used in Hill of Grace, one of Australia's iconic wines.

Working in the warm environment of a family winery where she can be both creative and respected, however, more than compensates for any doubts she encounters because of her family name. Prue has no interest in working for a public corporation, noting that a corporation would rather hire a man who has headed a failed winery than elevate a woman from within to the top job.

Western Australia, "a minnow in the sea of Australian wines,"[19] is home to the Margaret River region, which "accounts for less than 1 percent of total Australian output . . . [but] bottles 20 percent of the country's premium-priced wines."[20] This area was not even considered suitable for growing wine grapes until 1965, when Dr. John Gladstone published a report entitled "The Climate and Soil of South Western Australia in Relation to Vine Growing." This region, which has yet to experience the full impact of the giant corporations, hosts approximately seventy wineries, many of which are independent family operations with women in prominent positions, including Cullen, Leeuwin, and Vasse Felix.[21]

Having received a degree in religious anthropology as a continuing education student after her four children were grown, Tricia Horgan did not anticipate becoming managing director of Leeuwin Estate, her family's elegant winery. She self-deprecatingly says that her husband, Dennis, gave her the title so that "he could say he slept with the boss." Nonetheless, she is the detail-oriented CEO responsible for the daily operation of a multifaceted business dedicated to the "art of fine wine." In addition to the winery, the Leeuwin Estate includes an art collection (original Australian paintings chosen or commissioned to adorn the labels of the Art Series wines), a first-class restaurant and catering service, a concert series that since 1985 has featured the London Philharmonic Orchestra and an array of internationally acclaimed performers, and a charter air service to help clients visit the winery.

Remarkably, she manages to keep all these balls in the air simultaneously. Tricia is known as a team builder whose attention to staff minimizes turnover. She is also ably assisted by most of her family. Her older son controls finances; her older daughter handles public relations; her younger daughter plans and markets special events, including the concerts; and her gregarious husband, whose name appears on the information label on the wine bottles, handles external relations. Like several other women profiled here, Tricia's views on feminism are inconsistent. Upholding the core principle of equality but distancing herself from a feminist label, she asserts that she prefers to be thought of as a person rather than a woman. She is unwilling to accept an appointment as a token woman, although she enjoys being the only woman in a room full of men. Tricia also notes that family businesses are more female-friendly than corporations and can handle assertive women at the top, clearly a feminist view of the business world.

Founded in 1971 by Dr. Kevin Cullen and his wife, Diana (Di), Cullen Wines is testament to the passion and talent of two women, Di and Vanya, the youngest of the Cullens' six children. A suffragist, a vociferous environmentalist, and the first woman to wear pants in Margaret River,[22] Di Cullen was a pioneer and role model. She blended not only wine but a multifaceted career that included practicing physiotherapy, managing the family's sheep and cattle farm, and managing the winery, while raising a large family and commuting long distances so that her husband could retain his medical practice and conduct research. A self-taught winemaker who read and traveled widely, Di gave up physiotherapy in 1981 to become Cullen's full time winemaker, at a time when the winery was struggling and having trouble hiring for the position. (The winery did not break even financially until 1994.) Committed to organic viticulture and quality wine, she was responsible for "creating all of the wine styles for which Cullen is still famous today."[23] Under Di's direction in 1977, Cullen was the first Margaret River winery to receive the trophy for best wine at the Canberra Wine Show. In 1984, she became the first woman to win a trophy at the Perth Royal wine show. She became a Member of the Order of Australia in 1991, for services to viticulture and wine.[24]

Vanya, a Roseworthy graduate, assumed the winemaking responsibilities in 1989 and the role of managing director in 1999.[25] Following in her mother's footsteps, she claims only to have fine-tuned the wine styles Di had developed. Nonetheless, Vanya, whose Cabernet Merlot blend has been described by Huon Hooke as "potentially a flagship wine for the country" and by Steven Spurrier as "the finest Bordeaux blend I have ever tasted from Australia," is a pioneer and role model in her own right.[26] She was named Qantas/*The Wine Magazine* Winemaker of the Year in 2000. One of the judges who awarded the prize said, "It is frustrating to see her introduced as 'one of Australia's greatest female

10. Vanya Cullen, managing director and winemaker at Cullen Wines, was named Australian Winemaker of the Year in 2000 by Qantas and *The Wine Magazine*. The wine she named after her mother, Diana Madeline, is considered one of Australia's iconic wines.

winemakers'—Vanya is without question one of the best winemakers this country has seen."[27]

Trained in viticulture as well as winemaking and inclined to lead by example, Vanya developed a three-year plan for transforming some of the vineyards from organic to biodynamic by 2004. She also followed Pam Dunsford as the second woman to qualify as a wine judge. Vanya encourages other women to become wine judges and looks forward to the day when the Royal Agricultural Society names a woman to chair an entire wine show. A woman who goes against the norm, takes on the establishment, and finds a way to accomplish whatever she wants, Vanya is credited with bringing her family's boutique winery to world-class status. She freely acknowledges the debt she believes she owes her mother, honoring her by naming the 2001 Cabernet Merlot Diana Madeline. One of Australia's iconic wines, it was released in 2003, the year of Di's death.

NEW ZEALAND

Home to the Southern Hemisphere's youngest wine industry, New Zealand's ten wine-growing regions prove that excellence rather than size or age is key to penetrating the international wine trade. New Zealand produces approximately 0.2 percent of the world's wine, but the country's focus on high-quality, high-end wines gave it the highest average wholesale price per bottle ($4.95) in the world in 2002, twice the price of the average French wine.[28] The ability to command high prices, coupled with relatively inexpensive vineyard acreage, attracted substantial overseas investment, increasing the number of wineries in the country by approximately 25 percent from 1998 to 2002 and the value of its exports by 250 percent.[29]

Beginning in 1819, when missionaries first planted grapes, a story often repeated in the New World, New Zealand's wine history is divided into three pivotal periods: the immigrations of the nineteenth century; the threat of prohibition, which did not end until about 1960 (after the absentee votes of overseas servicemen turned the tide against it); and the modern period.[30]

The industry's success remained elusive, however, until the right varietals were selected in the 1970s to accommodate the cooler climate. The savior was sauvignon blanc, a varietal previously associated with the Loire Valley in France. It was first planted in 1973 in the Marlborough region of the South Island, the site of 53 percent of New Zealand's wine production. Today, Sauvignon Blanc made from these grapes accounts for one-third of New Zealand's production and two-thirds of its exports.[31] It is particularly popular in the United Kingdom, to which 48 percent of New Zealand's exports were destined in 2002.[32] In no small part, the overwhelming acceptance of Sauvignon Blanc is the triumph of (Meredith) Jane Hunter, OBE, managing director and viticulturist of Hunter's Wines.

Jane is an Australian by birth. Precluded from enrolling in enology because Roseworthy College did not admit women to the program until her senior year, she studied agricultural science at the University of Adelaide, graduating the same day as her mother, a political science major. After teaching continuing education courses in viticulture, horticulture, and business management, she moved to New Zealand, where she became a restaurateur. She was eventually named national (chief) viticulturist for Montana, the nation's second largest winery, and married Ernie Hunter, one of the first proponents of sauvignon blanc in Marlborough and an international ambassador for New Zealand wines. When Ernie died in an auto accident in 1987, Jane decided to retain and manage Hunter's winery to keep his legacy alive, even though she had no winemaking or winery management experience. She was given little chance for success because she had always been in the background and was quiet, young (thirty-three), and female.[33]

Through tenacity and determination, Jane prevailed as the first woman in New Zealand to head a winery. Her management style was marked by financing all capital investments out of cash flow and relying on expert consultants rather than a large staff.[34] In addition to these useful practices, she would further attribute her success, tongue in cheek, to being bone-lazy and a delegater, which forced her staff to learn responsibility and independence. Believing that her business would benefit from a greater acceptance of New Zealand wines, she also assumed her late husband's ambassadorial mantle and traveled extensively, speaking on behalf of New Zealand, the Marlborough region, and Hunter's Wines.

In recognition of her extraordinary efforts, she was awarded the Order of the British Empire (OBE) in 1993 and an honorary doctorate of science degree from Massey University in 1997. The most recent acknowledgment of her achievements was her unanimous selection as the first recipient of the Women in Wine Award presented by Le Donne del Vino at the International Wine and Spirits Competition.[35] In conferring the award, Le Donne del Vino noted, "Jane Hunter OBE has spent 20 years at the forefront of the New Zealand Wine Industry where she has not only built her own Hunter's Wines into a successful company, but also worked tirelessly to promote the profile and reputation of the Marlborough region. She has shown total commitment to the New Zealand cause over a long career."[36] Her selection for this award is also a reflection of the changing balance between the New World and the Old World of wine.

Many of the women who help run family wineries in conjunction with their husbands, such as Melba Brajkovich of Kumeu River Wines, operate behind the scenes in a traditional manner reminiscent of the Old World, receiving little if any credit for their work. For more than forty-five years, Melba's life has been defined entirely by her family and Kumeu River Wines. Although she has held an official title, that of managing director, only since the death of her husband, Maté, in 1992, it is obvious when touring the winery with her that she has handled the finances; she can relate from memory the exact acquisition date and cost of every capital improvement and piece of equipment. In keeping with the team approach that she developed with her husband, Melba shares management responsibilities and lunches daily with her three sons, one of whom, Michael, is the first New Zealander to become a Master of Wine. Like her husband, Melba is the product of an émigré family from the Dalmatian Coast who came to New Zealand to work in the Kauri gumfields. Despite this Old World Croatian upbringing, she has proven herself a woman of the New World by deciding, in conjunction with her husband, to leave a 25 percent interest in the winery to their daughter, who chose a career outside the family business.

New Zealand, the first nation in the world to grant women suffrage in 1893, had only two women winemakers in 1983.[37] Today, however, young women are sprinkled throughout the wine industry, thanks to

11. Jane Hunter, OBE, managing director and viticulturist at Hunter's Wines, is credited with expanding the recognition and sales of New Zealand's wines, particularly Sauvignon Blanc from Marlborough. She was selected as the first recipient of the Women in Wine Award presented by Le Donne del Vino.

Australia's Roseworthy Agricultural College, which "has been instrumental in educating young New Zealanders."[38] Although most of these women have yet to attain positions of prominence and have received little publicity, several members of the wave of the future have gained recognition. Eveline Fraser is the senior winemaker at Cloudy Bay; and Michelle Richardson, who was chief winemaker at Villa Maria before becoming the winemaker at Peregrine Wines, was *Winestate Magazine*'s New Zealand Winemaker of the Year in 1998, 1999, and 2000.[39]

While Eveline, who changed her occupation from beer brewing to winemaking, waxes eloquent on women's ability to advance in New Zealand's wine industry, Michelle is more restrained, noting that her accomplishments have occurred without a mentor. She also wonders whether there haven't been some "totally missed opportunities" because she doesn't "go out for beers on a Friday" with men in the business. She complains that male-only wine groups have sometimes excluded her "from the wines and colleagues." There is "also an issue with mixing socially with men when you're a woman. [There's an] issue with their spouses. Ridiculous but true." Michelle has tackled part of this problem head-on by helping to found Women in Wine, a networking group for discussing industry issues and developments as well as providing wine tasting opportunities. In the future, it may also serve as a support group and a way to promote wine to women purchasers and consumers.[40]

The future for women in today's New Zealand wine industry is likely to improve because of the rising number of women entering the industry and the California-style entrepreneurial spirit of women like Kathy Lynskey, managing director of Kathy Lynskey Wines, the first winery in New Zealand founded by a woman. As in Australia, however, a few corporations dominate New Zealand's wine industry, with 80 percent of the wine production originating in wineries owned by Corban's and Montana.[41] If New Zealand follows the pattern of other New World countries, women will hold major positions as winemakers, but not as managers, in these companies. Here, too, women are likely to hold managerial positions primarily in family-owned and individually owned wineries.

ARGENTINA

Viticulture in Argentina officially dates from 1556, when the Spanish priest Juan Cidrón (or Cedrón), known as El Soñador, the dreamer, arrived from Chile with his legendary cotton and grain seeds in one hand and wine saplings in the other.[42] Today's Argentinean wine industry is more firmly rooted in the wave of European immigration, mostly from

Italy and Spain, at the end of the nineteenth century. Bringing with them both winemaking knowledge and a traditional thirst for the beverage, the immigrants profoundly altered the domestic wine market, transforming it from one in which the urban elite consumed only French wines into a mass market in which large quantities of inexpensive table wines were sold throughout the country.[43]

The fifth largest wine-producing nation in the world, Argentina was a sleeping giant, "shunted to the sidelines of the world market by protectionist economic policies, dictatorship, triple-digit inflation, and an insatiable domestic demand for wine."[44] The unstable currency, as well as violations of human rights by the dictatorship, made some countries reluctant to trade with Argentina. In the 1990s, this picture changed. During the period of convertibility, the Argentine peso was pegged to the U.S. dollar, causing the country to sink into an economic quagmire. But its wine industry began to flourish, attracting foreign investors with hard currency who were seeking new sources of grapes to make wines at bargain prices.

This capital infusion underwrote the industry's modernization, its improving wine quality, and its entry into the export market, trends that accelerated in late 2001 when the peso was devalued and permitted to float freely.[45] The wine industry derived a dual benefit from the devalued peso. Low domestic production costs allowed producers to price their wines very competitively on the international market. Simultaneously, profits from foreign sales and additional foreign investment pouring into the country provided hard currency with which to expand and improve vineyards, wineries, and wines. No winegrowing area benefited more than Mendoza, where virtually all the great Argentine vineyards are located.[46] Fortunately for women, no winery was better prepared to thrive in this new environment than Bodega Catena Zapata.

As a rule, Argentina does not provide a nurturing environment for women in or out of the wine industry. (Recall that Delia Viader felt that she had to flee to California in order to be taken seriously.) But Bodega Catena Zapata is a distinct exception. Its owner, Nicolás Catena, is a third-generation descendant of Italian immigrants to Mendoza,[47] who left an economics professorship at the University of California at Berkeley to transform his family's winery. Once Argentina's largest producer of jug wine, the firm today is a world-class vintner, utilizing international consultants, computer controls, and stainless steel tanks.[48] And, one might add, a professional staff of winemakers and marketers heavily dependent on women. Because of "a bias for women"—he believes that they work harder and are more creative, trustworthy, and loyal[49]— Nicolás Catena has employed and mentored several of the most distinguished women in the Argentine wine industry. The current winemaker, Estela Perinetti, is responsible for Caro, a classic New World/Old World joint venture between Bodega Catena Zapata and Domaines Barons de Rothschild (Lafite Rothschild).[50] Marina Gayan is the first Argentinean of either gender to become a Master of Wine.[51] Susana Balbo and Laura Catena own their own highly regarded wineries.

The first woman winemaker to practice her craft in Argentina,[52] Susana Balbo graduated at the top of her class with honors in enology from Mendoza Maza University. She was immediately offered an opportunity to continue her studies at the University of Bordeaux, but her parents refused to allow it because of her gender and her age. Instead, they asked her to work for their winery, reporting to her older brother, a dropout from the program in which she had excelled.

Despite having no resources of her own and needing to support her two children and her husband, who was unable to work, she refused her parents' offer and left her family's winery to become the winemaker and administrative manager at Mission Torino from 1981 to 1990. This winery was located in a very traditional area that was inhospitable to women, and she was excluded from all local wine events, including those where her wines were being tasted. But any discomfort or insecurity quickly evaporated when her wines received mixed reviews from local men who held themselves up as expert tasters. Unbeknownst to them, however, she had put exactly the same wine into differently marked bottles. After this experiment, Susana determined that their palates and opinions were irrelevant, and she never again worried about inclusion or doubted her own ability.

Throughout the dynamic years of the 1990s, Susana worked at Bodega Catena Zapata as the export director. Knowing that she eventually wanted to own her own winery, she also rented facilities and made her own wines. She spent her vacations and her funds traveling to other wine regions of the world to expand her knowledge. In 1999, she left Bodega Catena Zapata and established her own, eponymous winery, Susana Balbo. She also became the winemaker for Ben Marco, a winery owned by her second husband, Pedro Marchevsky, who had formerly been a viticulturist at Bodega Catena Zapata.

A woman who loves making wine and being a mother, Susana instinctively touches her wine bottles as if they were children, to check on the life inside. She also expresses her maternal sentiments on her labels. Designed by her stepdaughter, the Susana Balbo labels include a multitude of feminist and reproductive images, including a Huarpe Indian fertility symbol representing women's reproductive role in bringing together the past (vineyard), the present (winemaking), and the future (wine); two women back to back supporting each other; storks bringing children; fallopian tubes connecting everything; and a small hand within a larger one, depicting a child cared for by a mother. Those competitors who overlooked her because of her gender provided her with freedom to pursue her passions; they also underestimated her.

The primary beneficiary of Nicolás Catena's pro-female bias is undoubtedly his older daughter, Laura, an emergency room physician with degrees from Harvard and Stanford who lives in San Francisco with her husband and three children. Dividing her professional activities between her medical practice and her duties as vice-president and head of exports of Bodega Catena Zapata, she juggles her disparate roles with the help of e-mail, four or five trips per year to Argentina, and an annual two-month leave without pay from the hospital so that she can be present for the crush at the winery.

Laura is a woman of seemingly boundless energy and enthusiasm for

12. Susana Balbo, winemaker and proprietor of the eponymous winery Susana Balbo, is the first woman enology graduate to practice the craft of winemaking in Argentina.

wine who likes the challenges, human interaction, variety, and emotional stimulation afforded by her different roles. She claims to have known next to nothing about wine when her father offered her the position in 1998. A quick study, she tutored herself initially by reading *Wine for Dummies* and went on to become an integral part of the international expansion of Bodega Catena Zapata. Despite the mutual admiration evident between her and her father, Laura wanted more than a position calling for her to consult on decisions. The result was Luca, the winery she founded and named after her older son.[53] Now her father is more than her mentor; he is her grape supplier.

CHILE

Across the Andes from Argentina, Chile parallels the Pacific Ocean as it stretches over twenty-five hundred miles from the Atacama Desert in the north to Tierra del Fuego near Antarctica in the south. The first wine-producing country in the Americas, Chile has a wine heritage dating from 1541, when Spanish conquistadores and missionaries led by Pedro de Valdivia descended from Peru to plant the first vines and make wine for sacramental purposes and daily consumption.[54]

Chile's wine history is as closely linked to its political climate as to its terroir. Until 1818, the country was under Spanish rule. During those years, the wine industry flourished until its exports became globally competitive with Spanish wines. Intent on reversing this course, the Spanish government retarded the Chilean industry's development by restricting its vineyard planting and wine production, limiting its exports, banning trade except with Spanish merchants, and imposing punitive taxes.[55]

In the post-independence period of the nineteenth century, the wine industry recovered by developing an informal affiliation with France, a pattern later to be replicated at the end of the twentieth century, referred to as the "French connection." In 1830, French scientist Claudio Gay convinced the Chilean government to set up an official plant nursery, Quinta Normal, for conducting botanical research. One of the research projects involved evaluating the suitability of French grape varietals for Chilean planting. Overall, however, the French influence is primarily attributable to wealthy Chilean land and mine owners who became enamored of French culture and wine after traveling abroad. Silvestre Ochagavía paved the way in 1851 by importing classic *Vitis vinifera* for his estate, and others followed suit, buying wineries and transplanting French vines. From that point forth, the Chilean wine industry was truly rooted in Bordeaux.[56] The timing was impeccable: by 1855, the great European outbreak of phylloxera was devastating vineyards throughout the Continent. Geographically isolated, the imported vines thrived in a phylloxera-free environment, and Chile became the only major wine-growing nation in the world to have pure, ungrafted European vines.[57]

In the twentieth century, governmental intervention again adversely affected the industry. Salvador Allende's Marxist agrarian reforms between 1970 and 1973 targeted the ten families who controlled the wine industry, dividing or expropriating their large estates as part of a nationalization program. Although the military dictatorship of Augusto Pinochet Ugarto, which overthrew Allende's government in 1973, returned the wineries to their historical owners, its repressive practices created new economic uncertainties. The international community, repelled by Pinochet's atrocities, refused to import Chilean wines or to invest in the nation, thereby delaying modernization and improvements in the industry.[58]

Participation in the global wine trade and an infusion of foreign investment commenced with the return of democracy in 1990.[59] Initially, large international wine firms flocked to the country seeking a new source of economically priced varietal wines to augment their own production, in order to fill supermarket shelves. Some foreign investors, often French, partnered with domestic producers to create fine wines capable of competing globally.[60] Today, Chile is the only wine-producing nation in the world to export more wine than it sells domestically.[61]

Because of the consolidated state of Chile's wine industry—ten large wineries bottle 80 percent of the wine—"the most reliable indicator of quality [in Chile] is still the producer."[62] Although one commentator observes that "women are rare in Chile's wine world,"[63] they are well represented among the top producers making the finest wines. In the early 1990s, Gaetone Carron, a flying winemaker who now owns her own property in Italy, was the senior winemaker at Concho y Toro, Chile's largest winery, and was responsible for its premier wine, Don Melchior. María del Pilar González Tamargo joined Viña Santa Carolina in 1976 and became chief enologist in 1990. When she became the head winemaker at Viña Carmen in 2001, Consuelo Marín Gamé, her assistant, replaced her at Santa Carolina. Since 1980, Viña Santa Rita, another of the giants, has employed Cecilia Torres, winner of numerous wine prizes, as its chief enologist.[64]

But it was the reincarnation of the "French connection," spearheaded by two women from illustrious wine backgrounds, that altered the course of the Chilean wine industry at the end of the twentieth century and made it internationally competitive. One of these women was Baroness Philippine de Rothschild. Building on the precedent set by her father, Baron Philippe, in 1979, when he entered into an equal joint venture with Robert Mondavi to produce Opus One in California, Baroness Philippine developed a joint venture with Concha y Toro in 1997 to produce Almaviva, a Bordeaux-styled wine.

The second woman, and the major French force in the new Chile, is Alexandra de Bournet, who uses her family surname, Marnier-Lapostolle, professionally. With the assistance of the French flying wine-maker Michel Rolland, Alexandra has guided Casa Lapostolle, a joint venture between the Marnier-Lapostolle family (51 percent) and Chilean José Rabat (49 percent), since 1994.[65] An accountant by profession and the great-granddaughter of the founder of Grand Marnier liqueur, she was unable to continue working at the headquarters of her family's firm in Paris when she married and moved to Geneva. Wanting a project to call her own but aware that it required her to look outside France, she convinced her family to expand their wine interests from the Loire to Chile because of the latter's historical ties to France, the availability of relatively inexpensive land suitable for an excellent winery, and its openness to women.

In keeping with her family's interest in the environment,[66] Alexandra implemented organic farming and is attracted to biodynamics, which has yet to gain many adherents in Chile or elsewhere in the New World, with the exception of Vanya Cullen's work. Seeking balance in her life as well as in her wines, Alexandra is not an absentee landlord. She divides her time between Geneva and Chile so that she is available for the major stages in the winemaking process. And she further divides her passion as well as her time between her family and business interests, which leaves no time for herself. Descended from a family that has been mak-

13. Alexandra Marnier-Lapostolle (de Bournet), a member of the French family that owns Grand Marnier, established her own reputation by founding and operating Casa Lapostolle, one of Chile's finest wineries.

ing distilled drinks for six generations,[67] Alexandra has a firm knowledge of the alcoholic beverages industry. This, along with her hands-on approach to management, personal marketing of her wines, willingness to accept risk, and belief in the natural affinity of fine wine, fine art, and fine music, has made Casa Lapostolle a premier Chilean producer and global force in the wine world.

SOUTH AFRICA

Because of its history, which stretches over 350 years, the South African wine industry can identify with the Old World. But, in reality, it is a 15-year-old member of the New World. In 1652, Jan van Riebeeck, the first governor, told the Dutch East India Company that the Cape was suitable for growing grapes and could be a useful feeding station for ships on their passage to the East. The governor then made the first wine in 1659.[68] Nevertheless, February 2, 1990, is the date that defines the beginning of the modern South African wine industry. On that date, precisely 331 years to the day after van Riebeeck made his first wine, President F. W. de Klerk announced that Nelson Mandela would be released from prison.[69] Mandela's freedom and the abandonment of apartheid in 1994 lifted the stigma shrouding South Africa and altered the course of the nation's wine industry, permitting it to enter the global wine trade.

Unfortunately, the nation was ill prepared to capitalize on its new opportunity. South Africa had experienced centuries of political and economic setbacks. Its self-serving Dutch governors had been more intent on accumulating personal wealth than fostering community development. Under British colonialism, the wine industry became a pawn in British-French conflicts, with South African exports to Britain dependent on the relative availability of French products. The Boer Wars (1902–1918) marked the start of the twentieth century, followed by the rise of Afrikaner nationalism and apartheid.

The wine industry's structure and focus also inhibited its ability to compete internationally. Founded in 1918, the Cooperative Winegrowers Association of South Africa, the KWV (Kooperatiewe Wijnbouers Vereniging van Zuid Afrika Beperkt), favored high-volume, low-quality production, a poor mix for gaining global attention. Set up by the ruling National Party as the wine industry's regulatory body, the KWV sought to reduce the economic risks faced by grape growers by purchasing their entire production at a preset minimum price. The net result was a tightly controlled, anticompetitive, non-market-driven industry.[70]

Exposure to international competition altered not only South Africa's approach to producing and marketing wine but also its attitude toward women in the industry. Reminiscent of the situation in other New World nations, notably Australia, New Zealand, and the United States, women's advancement in South Africa's wine industry is integrally intertwined with the industry's emergence as a global competitor and supplier of finer

wines. As recently as 2001, Susan Low noted in *Wines & Vines,* "It used
to be that Norma Ratcliffe from Warwick Estate was the only female
winemaker that anyone ever heard about in South Africa."[71] The Cana-
dian-born Ratcliffe, a self-taught winemaker who calls herself a "style
guidance counselor," began making wine at Warwick Estate, her family's winery, in the mid-1980s. She gained her initial fame in 1992 with
her debut at the Nederburg Auction, going on to chair the Cape Winemakers Guild in 1993.[72] Today, she is no longer alone.

South Africa's reentry into the international wine community has allowed young women to gain experience in other wine regions: Storm
Kreusch-Dau, for example, worked with Paolo di Marchi at Isole é Olena
in Tuscany before founding her own winery, WhaleHaven Wines, in
1995.[73] Foreign investment in South Africa brought new ideas along with
new owners, some of whom were women with well-established roots in
the wine world, such as Zelma Long and May-Eliane de Lencquesaing.
In a pattern reminiscent of Alexandra Marnier-Lapostolle in Chile, Anne
Cointreau-Huchon, granddaughter of the founder of Remy Martin Cognac and great-granddaughter of the founder of Cointreau, bought
Morgenhof Estate and hired Rianie Strydom.[74] Born in 1970, Rianie traveled throughout France and other parts of Europe after receiving her
BS in agriculture, with a major in viticulture and enology, from the University of Stellenbosch. In 1993, before graduating, she worked as the
assistant winemaker at Morgenhof, and by 1999 she was the head winemaker. During her tenure, Morgenhof became known as a winery with
a substantial majority of female staff members.[75] In 2005, Rianie became
the winemaker at Bilton Wines.[76]

One observer describes "a growing band of women winemakers."
They include Melanie van der Merwe at JC le Roux; Lizelle Gerber of
Avontuur; Anna-Marée Mostert, the new winemaker at Warwick Estate;[77] and Ronell Wiid, winemaker at Hazendal Estate, who won the
coveted Diners Club Winemaker of the Year Award in 1999.[78] The list
will no doubt increase over time. As Vision 2020, the agenda for devel-

opment of the wine industry, is implemented,[79] it will require an influx of new talent to make internationally competitive wines, a trend that has aided women throughout the New World.

Women also are benefiting from empowerment wine projects that seek to advance wine education for black South Africans and members of other disadvantaged groups, hone their management skills, and help them to purchase their own wineries. By 1999, these programs had underwritten fourteen viticulture students, eight of whom were women,[80] and the first black investment in a winery, Papkuilsfontein Vineyards. Papkuilsfontein hired Carmen Stevens, the nation's first black female winemaker, to produce its first wine, Tukulu (a Zulu word meaning red soil). These empowerment projects also resulted in the first female-owned winery, Old Vines Cellars, which employs a predominantly female staff.[81]

Women in South Africa, like the wine industry itself, have yet to achieve their full potential. Nonetheless, the nation's support for privatization and small property ownership, its dismantling of cooperatives, and the absence of major international alcoholic beverage companies at least temporarily create conditions that have proven beneficial to women throughout the rest of the New World and allow for optimism regarding the future of South African women in the wine industry.

·   ·   ·

Despite their geographic separation and disparate histories, the New World's major wine-producing nations display startling similarities in the opportunities afforded women in their wine industries. The growing influence of women is related to the increased worldwide demand for improved wines, the introduction of educational equity, the continuation of family-owned wineries, the assistance of mentors, and the strength of entrepreneurship.

Women also confront similar challenges in the wine industries throughout the New World. Social traditions that excluded women from the wine world persist. Networking among women, if it exists at all, is informal and sporadic. Domination of the wine industry by a few alcoholic beverage corporations—already a fact of life in Australia and New Zealand—threatens to limit women's opportunity to combine careers and winemaking, as it has already limited their access to senior management positions. Women who aim to influence the wine industries in the Southern Hemisphere will need to safeguard their independence and strengthen their presence in small or family wineries that emphasize high-quality wines.

CHAPTER EIGHT

Knowledge Is Power

The increasing numbers of influential women proprietors and wine-makers who have come forward in recent years are not alone. Simultaneously, two other groups of women have influenced the wine industry by imparting valuable information. Of key importance, viticulture and enology professors and scientists have added to the operative body of knowledge in the wine world, inspiring innovations in grape growing and winemaking. In addition, writers with specialized knowledge have published books, articles, and reviews demystifying wine's complexities and influencing the buying habits of consumers, who have widely varying familiarity with wine.

EDUCATORS

No center of higher learning related to wine has been more important for women than the Department of Viticulture and Enology at the University of California at Davis, "the New World's Vatican of viticulture, the oracle of grape growing, the arbiter of winery practice."[1] UC Davis, however, did not emulate the College of Cardinals in the composition of its faculty or its student body. Ten years after the passage of the Civil Rights Act of 1964, the department hired its first woman professor. Since then, it has had continuous representation of women on its research faculty, contributing to the department's stature as the nation's premier educational institution in viticulture and enology. Ahead of its time, this UC department made it respectable for similar institutions elsewhere in the world to follow its example, such as the Geisenheim State Research Institute in Germany, which hired Prof. Dr. Monika Christmann as head of the Enology Department in 1993. At the time, she observed, "there were no women in leading positions in the German wine world," and she acknowledged that "taking the only position available in Germany in this field at a very young age was either risky or naïve."

Dr. Ann Noble, the first woman appointed to the UC Davis enology faculty, arrived as an assistant professor to fill a vacancy left by retiring department chair Maynard Amerine. A sensory scientist and flavor chemist recognized today as preeminent in the "world of analytical sensory evaluation of wine,"[2] Ann was confronted initially by skepticism and condescension. An article in *Wines & Vines* commented on her appointment by noting that she was not a "Woman's Libber" and added, "Being pretty and single makes a difference, too."[3]

Ann is most famous for the Aroma Wheel, a codification of 132 descriptive words and phrases related to wine tastes and smells. The Aroma Wheel is a graphical representation of tasting terms for aroma, the portion of the bouquet attributed to grape flavor. "The aroma, combined with odors resulting from the winemaking process . . . results in a complex array of smells collectively referred to as bouquet [or the 'nose' of the wine]." The Aroma Wheel employs a three-tier system of primary, secondary, and tertiary clusters of flavor definitions arranged in three circles, one inside the other.[4] The center or innermost circle contains general impressions of aromas (for instance, fruity or earthy) as well as specific characteristics that are too dominant to ignore, such as oxidation. The middle circle subdivides these into narrower groups (for instance, the type of fruitiness, such as citrus or berry). The largest or outer circle adds greater specificity and subtlety (for instance, the type of berry) to the groups in the middle circle.[5]

The Aroma Wheel has been translated into several languages, and tasters throughout the world use it as a common vocabulary for communicating their evaluation of a wine. Starting at the inner circle and working their way outward, they are able to describe, identify, and classify the olfactory aspects of wine,[6] "the single most important element in wine judging. It involves the most sensitive human organ, the nose, and is generally the primary factor in deciding on wine quality."[7] Through the Aroma Wheel, Ann provided the wine industry with a set of nonsubjective terms, understood by everyone, for judging flavor and aroma. Sensory evaluation rather than chemical analysis became a corollary to grape variety, growing season temperature, vineyard geographic location, and sugar/acid ratio in distinguishing between premium and standard table wine.[8]

When she retired from UC Davis in November 2002, Ann was the most senior faculty member in the Department of Viticulture and Enology by virtue of years of service. A feisty and assertive woman who educated and mentored a substantial number of California's winemakers, it was fitting tribute that she was replaced by one of her former students, Dr. Hildegarde Heymann. Co-author of *Sensory Evaluation of Foods: Principles and Practices,* currently the most prescribed sensory textbook in the world, Dr. Heymann teaches VEN125 Sensory Evaluation of Wines, the course developed by Ann Noble.[9]

Dr. Carole Meredith, a geneticist, joined the faculty of her alma mater at Davis in 1980, despite the concerns of the older men in the department's agricultural area, who, according to her, wanted to know, "How will she pee in the vineyard?" Carole initially avoided grape research because grapes represented a risky, difficult, and recalcitrant subject that would reduce the number of articles she could produce. Until she earned tenure, she strategically selected her research interests: tomatoes when she was a graduate student, and tobacco, corn, and cotton while she was an untenured faculty member.

Carole is best known for the DNA fingerprinting of cultivars (cultivated vines)—linkage mapping with molecular genetic markers to trace the ancestry of grape varietals. "With a new method of unraveling the grapevines' tangled family tree, she has shown that several of the world's best known wine grapes are not pure strains but hybrids between other varieties. . . . Her findings . . . undermine the theoretical basis for the French quality control system, the Appellation d'Origine Contrôlée, which denies its label to wines made from hybrid varieties on the assumption that such grapes are inferior to their parents."[10] Her research showed that cabernet sauvignon and chardonnay are both hybrids and that cabernet sauvignon is a cross between cabernet franc and sauvignon blanc. She also found that chardonnay descended from pinot and gouais blanc, "a grape deemed so coarse that it is no longer grown in France."[11] In a particularly intriguing finding, she determined that zinfandel in the United States and primitivo in Italy are the same variety and originated in Croatia.[12]

Carole's DNA forensic fingerprinting method for tracing grape relationships overshadowed earlier methods used by historians and ampelographers, who studied leaves. Her genetic techniques, involving microsatellite analysis, use patterns of repetitive DNA segments as markers for determining linkages between grape varietals.[13] To encourage international dialogue and information sharing among scientists with similar interests, she formed the Vitis Microsatellite Consortium, with twenty-one members in ten countries; they have developed three hundred DNA markers.

Carole's findings have also contributed to understanding why the same grape variety thrives in one environment and not in another.[14] "Her work allows growers to be certain of the varieties in their vineyards and gives geneticists help in preserving old grape varieties and developing new ones."[15] Using DNA analysis, she helped grape breeders develop new varieties, gave people a window into wine history, and connected science with history, especially in Europe. In 2000, she was awarded the Ordre du Mérite Agricole by the French government for her contribution to viticulture. She retired from UC Davis in January 2003 and now makes wine with her husband, Steven Lagier, at Lagier Meredith Vine-

14. Carole Meredith, PhD, professor emerita of the Department of Viticulture and Enology at the University of California at Davis, is known for her work on grape DNA fingerprinting and her contributions to viticulture. She now co-owns Lagier Meredith Vineyards, a highly regarded Napa winery.

yards. Today, she finds time for her favorite pastimes, rock and roll and photography. Some of her photographs appear on the labels of her wine bottles.

After receiving her PhD in microbiology from UC Berkeley and doing postdoctoral work at Harvard Medical School, Dr. Linda Bisson considered it a risk to come to UC Davis in 1986 rather than remaining with mainstream hard sciences, where her career path would have been more predictable. Her subsequent prominence as a faculty member, administrator, and industry consultant, however, proved the wisdom of her decision.

Linda's philosophical position is that gender issues are usually people issues rather than discrimination. Her strong "people skills," combined with the leadership skills she attributes to her years at an all-girls parochial high school, led to her selection as chair of the Department of Viticulture and Enology in 1991. She declined reappointment in 1996 in order to devote herself to research on yeast metabolism and fermentation, teaching and publishing works such as *Principles and Practices of Winemaking*, for which she and her co-authors received the 1998 book prize from the Office International de la Vigne et du Vin.

Through her research and during her administrative years, Linda gained the respect of California's state legislators and the state's wine industry. In particular, she became a wine industry heroine by proving scientifically that ethyl carbonate, a carcinogen, was a natural component of wine rather than a manufactured one. The wine industry was being pressured to remove ethyl carbonate from wine in order to comply with U.S. Department of Agriculture export guidelines, but since the guidelines applied only to additives, her findings rescued wine producers. In recognition of her accomplishments and the high regard in which she is held by the wine industry, the department awarded her the Maynard A. Amerine Endowed Chair, after conducting a full international search. Linda, along with Hildegarde Heymann and Dr. Susan Ebeler, an associate professor conducting research on the ability of red wine's components to deter cancer,[16] exemplifies women's continuing influence on the faculty of UC Davis's Department of Viticulture and Enology.

Not all wine educators prepare students to be viticulturists or winemakers. Many conduct classes for people seeking greater knowledge and appreciation of wine, either for personal or professional reasons. Some educators teach in formal academic settings, such as Dr. Marian Baldy, in the College of Agriculture at California State University, Chico. Others teach in specialized wine education programs, including Mary Ewing-

Mulligan, president of the International Wine Center (IWC) in New York; and Karen MacNeil, who heads the Rudd Center for Professional Wine Studies at the Culinary Institute of America (CIA), Greystone, in Napa Valley, California. In addition to the direct impact these women have had on their students, they also have written books that reach large, worldwide audiences.

Dr. Marian Baldy, a geneticist, received her undergraduate degree summa cum laude at UC Davis, was elected to Phi Beta Kappa, and also earned her doctorate at Davis. Two years of postdoctoral work at the University of Oregon Medical School convinced her that she did not like laboratory work. In 1972, when her husband accepted a position at Cal State Chico, she decided to make teaching her career. The only woman on the agriculture faculty for twenty years, she refers to herself as a "tall poppy," a person who was out of place for much of her career. Marian has taught more than six thousand students in her Introduction to Wine class, which she still teaches despite taking early retirement in 2000.[17]

In 1993, Marian's influence expanded far beyond Cal State Chico when she authored *The University Wine Course: A Wine Appreciation Text and Self-Tutorial,* the first comprehensive book of its kind. Published by the Wine Appreciation Guild in San Francisco, it has sold more than twenty-five thousand copies. In 1996, it was named one of the twenty-five books on the Basic Shelf of Wine Books by the Society of Medical Friends of Wine. Marian served on the board of directors of the Society of Wine Educators, an international organization that made her an honorary life member in 1997. In 2002, she also received the Award of Merit of the American Wine Society for her advancement of the field of wine appreciation.

Karen MacNeil did not start her career focused on wine; she focused on survival. She began supporting herself at the age of fourteen. Karen describes her career as a bike trip: pedaling her bike fast, never stopping, always being ready to ride, and taking whatever road seemed most advantageous. Initially, she wrote about food in order to obtain food samples as well as money to end her dependency on food stamps; her first published article, which appeared in the *Village Voice,* was about butter. Only in the mid-1980s did she write her first wine article. She has since contributed to the *New York Times, Food & Wine, Wine Spectator, USA Today,* and the *Los Angeles Times.* For several years, she served as the wine correspondent for NBC's *Today Show,* and she hosted the public broadcasting program *Wine, Food, and Friends.*

A self-made woman, Karen has no time for networking; avoids adopting female role models, so that she can forge her own path; and does not take no for an answer. Seeing obstacles as catalysts for creativity, she circumvents them rather than allowing them to become permanent roadblocks. These attributes, along with her willingness to dive into the deep end of the pool and then figure out how to swim, helped her bypass everyone to become chairman (the title is not a problem for her) of the wine studies program at the CIA's Rudd Center. By her own admission demanding, difficult to work with and for, and not one of the boys, Karen believes that the quality of one's work, not gender, determines success.

In 2001, Karen published her major book, *The Wine Bible,* whose sales exceed three hundred thousand copies. At the CIA, Greystone, the continuing education campus of the premier American culinary school, she directs the professional wine certification programs. An authority on service and professional restaurant management, she also conducts corporate seminars and private wine tutorials for individuals, restaurants, and corporations such as Oracle. In addition, she finds time for Fife Vineyards in Napa, which she owns with her husband.[18]

MASTERS OF WINE

Requiring an encyclopedic knowledge of wine plus great taste buds,[19] the designation MW, Master of Wine, is "the most coveted and difficult to attain credential in the world of wine. . . . To be admitted into the program, candidates are expected to have at least five years of in-depth professional experience buying, selling or writing about wine and, with a few exceptions, to have taken preparatory courses. They must submit a 1,000-word essay on wine theory and a detailed practical tasting analysis of three wines assigned by the [Institute of Masters of Wine]."[20]

In the absence of a set curriculum, candidates for this credential follow an independent study course with a suggested reading list that covers viticulture and vinification, fermentation procedures, and all aspects of the commercial trade. The four-day exam consists of two sections, a theory section with twelve essays, plus a tasting exam. The half-day tasting sessions are held on three days. During each of the unlabeled (blind) tastings, candidates must identify information such as grape type, climate, fermentation techniques, wine style, region, and vineyard for twelve wines. They spend an average of eleven minutes and fifteen seconds per wine.[21] The key to success is the reasoning used to defend the identification.[22] With a minimum passing grade of B-minus, the exam pass rate is about 10 percent. Candidates must wait three years to retake the exam if they fail it three times.

The first MW exam was held in 1953 "under the auspices of the 'Worshipful Company of Vintners' and the 'Wine and Spirits Association.'" There were six successful candidates.[23] The Institute of Masters of Wine (IMW), which administers the exam today, was established in 1955. Originally open only to British citizens in the wine trade (importers, merchants, and retailers), the exam was made available in 1983 to "people who made their living through wine" and in 1988 to those who were not British subjects.[24] Today, the exam is open to "anyone anywhere in the world who can write a satisfactory dissertation on one of that year's three chosen subjects." Exams are now administered in June in Sydney, San Francisco, and London and can be taken in languages other than English, with the cost of translation assumed by the individual.[25] As of 2005, the membership represented eighteen nationalities and included persons residing in nineteen countries.[26]

In a development that paralleled the emerging educational equity in the United States and Australia, Sarah Morphew of England became the first woman to receive the MW, in 1970. By the mid-1980s, women made up approximately one-tenth of the nearly 100 MWs, but by 2005, women's representation had doubled to 22.98 percent, or 57 out of 248.[27]

In addition to administering the MW exam, the IMW publishes the *Journal of Wine Research* "to enhance and encourage scholarly and scientific interdisciplinary research" in the fields of viticulture, enology, and the wine trade. In October 2003, the organization also signed a strategic partnership with the Geisenheim State Research Institute whereby the IMW will teach new master courses developed at Geisenheim, students from Geisenheim will visit the United Kingdom to learn more about global markets for international wines, and MWs and MW candidates will visit Geisenheim to study viticulture and winemaking firsthand with Geisenheim professors such as Monika Christmann.[28]

Mary Ewing-Mulligan, MW, became the first American woman to earn the designation Master of Wine in 1993. Applying the lessons she had learned as a marathon runner (small steps can lead to long distances, never give up before reaching the goal), she passed the written exam on the second try and the tasting exams on the fifth.

Mary made several strategic decisions in building her career. She decided not to become a journalist and not to work for one brand or one company because it would diminish her freedom to express her opinion. While employed at the Italian Trade Commission, she chose not to pursue fashion and instead focused on wine. And she was willing to accept salary cuts if the positions she sought offered possibilities for advancement.

After graduating from the University of Pennsylvania as an English literature major, Mary went to work for the Italian Trade Commission, eventually becoming director of the Italian Wine Promotion Center (later called the Italian Wine Center). After a brief period as a wine broker, during which she discovered that wine sales did not interest her, she became public relations director for Pepsico Wines and Spirits. In 1984, she joined the International Wine Center in New York as director of educational services. In 1988, she bought fifty percent of the IWC from its founder, Albert Hotchin, and became sole proprietor in 1997.

In 2004, Mary was named executive director of the U.S. branch of the

15. Mary Ewing-Mulligan, MW, director of the International Wine Center in New York, was the first American woman to earn the designation Master of Wine. She gained international fame as the co-author of *Wine for Dummies.*

London-based Wine and Spirits Educational Trust (WSET), the only organization authorized to provide courses for people studying for the MW. In her new capacity, she will conduct WSET courses at the IWC in New York as well as at thirteen additional U.S. locations including Copia in Napa, California; and Phillywine.com in Philadelphia. She may add more U.S. sites in the future.[29]

Mary also is a wine columnist for the *New York Daily News,* a contributing writer for several publications in the United States and England, a wine judge and, formerly, a wine correspondent for the public radio program *The Splendid Table*. Her greatest source of fame and influence, however, is the book she co-authored with her husband, Ed Mc-Carthy, *Wine for Dummies.* Along with its many offspring, such as *Red Wine for Dummies* and *Italian Wine for Dummies,* it has become an industry unto itself, selling more than 750,000 copies since 1995. The fastest-selling wine book ever published in the United States, it has also been translated into seventeen languages.[30]

Although she has little time for networking or organizations other than the Society of Wine Educators, Mary goes out of her way to help women. Among the people with whom she has worked, Sheryl Sauter is the second and only other American woman to earn the MW. Sheryl is a member of the IWC faculty.

Describing the wine business as unwelcoming to newcomers and hard to break into, but hospitable to those in it, Mary advises women to seek advancement in technical areas with defined curricula. If you earn credentials in those areas, making your qualifications clear and unequivocal, recognition and jobs follow. She admits that wine is more than a career; it is also a time-consuming hobby and a lifestyle that requires irregular hours, considerable socializing, and a supportive spouse (if a woman wants to marry). Mary remains convinced that women do not have the same possibilities as men in the industry because it is harder for them to get in the door and more difficult for them to be taken seriously once inside.

WRITERS AND PUBLISHERS

Wine writers capable of swaying consumers' choices have exceptional influence. "The fact that a highly regarded writer can sell wine is something with which the industry, however unhappily, must contend. Few other businesses support a coterie of journalists in such an intimate fashion."[31] Although men outnumber women among the wine writers, "the few women who do sell or write about wine exert an influence far exceeding their numbers," one observer claims.[32]

British women journalists, in particular, are a substantial segment of the world's most prominent wine writers. They include Joanna Simon, former editor of *Wine & Spirits* and a correspondent for the *Sunday Times* (London); and Jane MacQuitty, wine editor for *Good Housekeeping* and wine correspondent for *The Times* (London). Several of the British writers have earned the MW designation, including Rosemary George, whose books include *The Wines of New Zealand* and *Chablis;* Serena Sutcliffe, head of the International Wine Department at Sotheby's, whose numerous works include *Champagne: The History and the Character of the World's Most Celebrated Wine* and *The Simon and Schuster Guide to the Wines of Burgundy;* and Jancis Robinson, editor of *The Oxford Companion to Wine.*

The first British woman to write seriously about wine was Pamela Vandyke Price, who asserted that wine was the "predominant and passionate interest of my life."[33] During her career, she edited *House & Garden* and *Wine & Food.* She was the wine correspondent for the London *Sunday Times* and the wine writer for *The Times* and *The Observer.* She also authored or edited more than twenty-five wine books, including *The Wine Lover's Handbook; The Taste of Wine; The Penguin Wine Book; Wine: Lore, Legends, and Traditions;* and the fourth volume of *Christie's Wine Companion.*[34]

Despite her pioneering contributions, Pamela Vandyke Price provided a mixed legacy for women who sought to use her as a role model. A self-described independent personality who hated "team spirit" and "never thought of myself as a woman," she preferred the company of men because women "weaken and trivialize what they propound." In her autobiography, *Woman of Taste,* she writes, "Prejudice against women has been rare in my life: either I simply haven't noticed it or, if it has been made obvious, I have dismissed it as of no importance—because it *has* no importance within the wine trade as I've known it." Other comments in her book belie this statement, however. She points out that "learning about wine in the late 1950's was not always easy, unless one were already able to enter the wine trade in some junior capacity . . . for a woman it would have been as a telephonist, secretary or some type of bookkeeper." She felt it necessary to go out of her way to get along with older male wine writers, being careful not to offend them, but was offended herself when many people assumed erroneously that she had been accepted by the wine trade because of her involvement with some man or because a man had written her articles for her. In the late 1950s, she was still ignored when attending wine education lectures, where "none of the young men wanted to sit by me."[35]

One of Pamela's colleagues was Jancis Robinson, MW, OBE, considered by some to be one of the twentieth century's two great wine writers (the other is Hugh Johnson), who changed the wine world through writings "documented with great accuracy, intricacy and intelligence."[36] Gaining an appreciation for fine wine at Oxford University while reading in mathematics and philosophy, she began her wine writing career in 1975 as an assistant editor of *Wine & Spirits.* Since then, she has written for the *Sunday Times,* the London *Evening Standard,* the *Financial Times,* and *Wine Spectator,* which did not have another woman writing regularly about wine for ten years after her departure in 1995 and still has no MWs on its editorial staff.[37]

Jancis has authored numerous books, many of which have appeared in multiple editions and translations, including *Masterglass; The Oxford Companion to Wine,* which she edited; *The Great Wine Book; The Wine Book; The World Atlas of Wine,* with Hugh Johnson; and *Vines, Grapes, and Wine,* a groundbreaking work that introduced readers to the concept of identifying wines by grape varietals rather than by their place of origin or the name for blends of lower-quality wines.[38] A multimedia communicator, Jancis wrote and presented the first TV series on wine, *The Wine Programme,* and has been a frequent writer, presenter, or narrator for a host of other TV shows aired worldwide, including *Jancis Robinson's Wine Course,* a ten-part series on U.S. public television.

Married, with three grown children, Jancis has now given up writing books, other than updating *The Oxford Companion to Wine,* in order to devote herself to her wine ratings and informational Web site, www .jancisrobinson.com. The site, which is completely independent, with no ads or sponsorship, provides her with a vehicle for self-promotion and

16. Jancis Robinson, MW, OBE, legendary wine critic and author of many books, including *The Oxford Companion to Wine,* was the first journalist to earn the designation Master of Wine and the first wine journalist to be accorded the Order of the British Empire. She sponsors an informational Web site, www.jancisrobinson.com.

pays its way through subscriptions received from sixty countries. She believes that it has gained popularity because of its "less aggressive 'feminine' tone." In addition to all her other activities, she also manages to serve as a consultant for clients such as British Airways.

Risking her career in 1984 by pursuing the MW, because failure could have tarnished her image, Jancis secured her reputation by obtaining the credential. She was the first journalist or person outside the wine trade to become an MW and one of the few people to pass both parts of the exam on the first try.[39] She notes in her autobiography, *Tasting Pleasure,* that she studied for the MW exam with a group composed solely of women[40] and, according to her, without any dominant, know-it-all men.

Jancis is most proud of "being a woman in what is seen as a masculine world, without being consciously feminist about it."[41] Nonetheless, she is well aware that being a woman brought some advantages, such as publicity and special courtesy; it also made her easily distinguishable for members of the wine trade.[42] Although she believes that women generally have to do more to prove themselves, she says that this was not true in journalism, where women were given a fair shake and were protected against the gender discrimination prevalent in the wine trade itself. Despite the continued existence of male-only clubs, she feels totally accepted as part of the larger "club."

Jancis's accomplishments have garnered her numerous awards, including an honorary doctorate from The Open University in 1997, the Wine Literary Award from the Wine Appreciation Guild "for an exceptional contribution to the literature of wine in the English language,"[43] and *Decanter* magazine's Woman of the Year award in 1999. In 2003, she received the Order of the British Empire (OBE), the first wine writer accorded this honor.[44]

Among the many people who have given British women wine writers fair treatment is Sarah Kemp, publisher of *Decanter* magazine, Britain's leading wine magazine (now owned by Time-Warner). A wine enthusiast rather than a connoisseur, Sarah rose in the publishing world because of her advertising and publishing acumen. Founder of *Decanter*'s Fine Wine Encounter, a two-day extravaganza of wine tastings, wine seminars, and food, she is proud of putting together a bright, young, talented team that includes several women. Believing that the wine trade still has gender barriers, Sarah states that the same is not true in publishing, except possibly at the top, where there is a fear of women. Although she makes few distinctions between male and female publishers, she admits that as a woman publisher she might pursue different topics than a man would, such as encouraging women to buy finer wines.

In addition to the British women, female wine writers in other coun-

17. Sarah Kemp is the publisher of Great Britain's leading wine publication, *Decanter,* and the founder of *Decanter*'s Fine Wine Encounter events.

tries have also provided valuable contributions, including Chantale Lecouty, who wrote for and co-owned the *Revue de Vin de France;* and Phyllis Hands, who co-authored *The Complete Book of South African Wines* (despite her belief that "women do not belong in the South African wine industry").[45]

. . .

Globalization, increased competition, and consumers' desire for consistent and better-quality wines have created opportunities for well-educated women and men to carve out professional niches from which they can significantly influence the wine industry. They have helped to improve the quality of wine, to train viticulturists and winemakers, to educate wine enthusiasts, and to influence what wines people buy and how much they are prepared to pay for them. Women professors, authors, and journalists specializing in wine have paved the way for other entrepreneurial, self-confident, and well-educated women. They have demonstrated that obtaining solid credentials and building a useful niche are key.

CHAPTER NINE

Uncorking Sales

Women with perseverance, expertise, and marketing flair occupy niche positions throughout the multitiered global wine trade. Successfully selling wine, from the great auction houses of the world to the local supermarkets, they have beaten not only their competition but also the odds in the segment of the wine industry least hospitable to women.

AUCTIONEERS

The advent of corks in the seventeenth century transformed wine from a short-term commodity to one that could be bottle aged for many decades. Auctions of young wines in barrels were eventually transformed into events where rare vintages and fine wines at all stages of maturity were sold.[1] Whereas other commodities are often offered at auction simply because of the three "Ds" (death, divorce, and debt), costly wines have become "liquid gold," investments purchased by connoisseurs, collectors, and status seekers for the express purpose of capitalizing on financial, as well as aesthetic, appreciation. "The most important salesrooms for high-priced wines—whether classics or cult wines—are auction houses. Roughly 90 percent of the trading in long-lived top wines is accomplished in the wine auction houses of Christie's and Sotheby's in London and their branches in America, Asia and Australia."[2]

Serena Sutcliffe, MW, senior director and head of the International Wine Department of Sotheby's, gained sway over the world of wine auctions by transforming Sotheby's from a poor, unprofitable cousin of its arch competitor, Christie's, into the world's top wine auction house. Earning a profit for Sotheby's every year since joining the firm in 1991, she increased annual turnover from under 2 million British pounds to 33 million British pounds by 1999. She accomplished this through bold steps such as holding the first international wine auction in New York in 1994, acquiring the American auction house Davis & Company in 1998, and raising 8.8 million British pounds in the Millennium sale in 1999. Her reward was an appointment to Sotheby's European board of directors.[3]

Born in 1945 ("an incredible vintage, so I never hide my age," she says),[4] Serena chose to travel rather than attend Cambridge, where she had been admitted. Her early career was spent as a French translator and interpreter for NATO and UNESCO, capitalizing on her natural talent for languages, which had been honed through her travels. Propelled into the wine trade in 1971 by her love of wine, she refused to accept a "woman's" position in public relations or administration. Relying on sheer persistence, exceptional preparation, and a willingness to work harder than others, she became an importer. After passing the MW exam on the first attempt in 1976 and becoming only the second woman MW, she married David Peppercorn, another MW, and the two were in business together until she joined Sotheby's.[5] Awarded the Chevalier dans l'Ordre des Artes et des Lettres by the French government in 1988 as one of the world's leading wine authorities, Serena also chaired the Institute of Masters of Wine in 1994–1995.[6]

The author of several books (*The Simon and Schuster Guide to the Wines of Burgundy; Champagne: The History and the Character of the World's Most Celebrated Wine*), Serena considers writing a sideline. She describes her occupation as "the buying, selling, consulting end of the fine wine business, leading eventually to the fascinating world of wine auctions. It gave me the opportunity to do what I love best, which is tasting, evaluating, analyzing and comparing great wines—although one also has to do mundane things like add up, negotiate, plan and market in order to hold down a job."[7]

Serena's lofty position did not come without a struggle. She notes that being a woman was a massive hindrance at the outset of her career—and still remains a serious disadvantage because some "blinkered" men will never fully accept her. Although she now considers male-only private clubs largely irrelevant and antediluvian, she concedes that these remnants of a discriminatory bygone era can adversely affect women's ability to conduct business by limiting their interaction with clientele and networks. She therefore refuses to address any group that excludes women as members and staunchly supports serious women who are seeking to become involved in the wine industry. "Of course, in the 21st Century, we should no longer be talking of Women in Wine—just People. But, the fact remains that women are something of a rare commodity around the grape although, be warned, we are on the increase!"[8]

The United States has become the modern proponent of wine auctions as charitable fund-raising events, emulating the wine auctions of the Hospices de Beaune.[9] Raising phenomenal amounts of money for a variety of causes, charity wine auctions also enhance the aura of wines, winemakers, and wineries that command top dollar. A classic example of the impact of a wine auction on the reputation of a winery and its winemaker occurred at the 2000 Napa Valley Wine Auction, when a six-liter bottle of Screaming Eagle, made by Heidi Peterson Barrett for the winery owned by Jean Phillips, commanded half a million dollars, the highest price ever paid for a single bottle of wine.[10]

U.S. charity wine auctions are "a magnificent game in which there are no losers but the taxman. Donors of wine can write off whatever they estimate is the lot's fair market value, in total, against tax. Successful bidders can write off the entire difference between that fair market value

18. Serena Sutcliffe, MW, senior director and head of the International Wine Department of Sotheby's, helped to transform Sotheby's into the world's top wine auction house. She is the author of several books about the wines of Burgundy and Champagne. The second woman to earn the designation Master of Wine, she is the only woman to head the Institute of Masters of Wine.

and whatever crazy price they paid for the lot."[11] The largest of these events is the annual Napa Valley Wine Auction, "five days of hedonism sanctioned by the fact that it has so far [from 1981 through 2003] raised more than 30 million dollars for local causes." The superstar of American charity wine auctions and the first woman auctioneer in Napa Valley is Ursula Hermacinscki, the "Goddess of the Gavel."[12]

Ursula hardly fits the image of an auctioneer—described by one commentator as a "British male, wearing a bow tie and half moon glasses."[13] As far back as her senior year in high school, she knew that she wanted to work in the auction world. With her mother's help, she developed a plan to build a career at Christie's. After graduating from Marquette University with a major in Spanish literature, she pursued her dream and her interest in art and antiques by enrolling in Christie's fine art course in London. She was hired by Ann Colgin at Christie's in New York[14] in 1985, as a secretary assigned to catalog furniture and decorative arts in the rug department. Ursula took advantage of the auctioneering opportunity offered to all Christie's employees, becoming their youngest female auctioneer.

In 1989, Ursula transferred to Christie's Los Angeles office to catalog Liberace's estate.[15] Hooked on auctioneering, however, she enrolled in a year-long wine course at the University of California at Los Angeles. In 1992, she became the only woman auctioning wines in Los Angeles.[16] After a brief transfer back to New York to set up Zachys-Christie's wine auction department, she returned to Los Angeles to set up a similar department in 1998.

Ursula's success rested on recognizing that charity wine auctioneering is part showmanship, part sales, and part fun.[17] It also rested on mentoring from Michael Broadbent, head of Christie's international wine auctions. Initially treating her as a novelty, he taught her to combine her personal and professional life into one, making her clients her friends.

After fourteen years at Christie's and a car wreck that broke her back, hospitalized her for six months, and gave her time to wonder, "How dare they have wine auctions on the Internet without me?" Ursula became executive vice-president of Winebid.com. As was the case with many other Internet-related ventures, Ursula's position at Winebid.com was short lived. She has returned to live auctions as senior adviser and auctioneer for Zachys Wine Auctions in New York and is writing a guide to wine auctions.

With a clientele that is well over 90 percent male, Ursula claims to have experienced no discrimination as a woman, although she admits that one of the attractions of the Internet was that it was faceless, making gender a nonissue. Thinking of herself more as an auctioneer than as a woman, Ursula loves being top dog on the podium but is more comfortable as a strong number two person in an organization rather than number one. Conceding that "this is a guy's world" and not wanting the responsibility that accompanies authority, she does not demand the top position, a stance rarely adopted by influential women.

TRADE REPRESENTATIVES

One of the most significant phenomena of recent years has been the rise of Australia as a competitive force in the international wine industry. A relative latecomer to the global wine trade, Australia made up for lost time in large part because of the vision, creativity, and dedication of Hazel Murphy, chief executive for Europe of the Australia Wine Export Council–United Kingdom. In 1986, when she founded the Australian Wine Bureau, the predecessor of the Australia Wine Export Council, in the United Kingdom,[18] Australia exported only eighty-five thousand cases of wine to that country, accounting for 1 to 2 percent of U.K. wine imports. When she retired in February 2003, Australia was flooding the British market with 20 million cases of wine, 25 percent of U.K. wine imports, bypassing the French as the United Kingdom's greatest source of wine on the basis of value.[19]

A marketing professional experienced in textiles, Hazel joined the Australian Trade Commission (Austrade) in 1979, with responsibility for all Australian retail exports. In 1984–1985, Hazel's forecast that, within the range of export products she handled, Australian wine had the greatest potential in the U.K. market[20] encouraged nine Australian wine companies to ask her to promote their wines. They guaranteed her salary for three years and gave her a telephone but no staff. Hazel single-handedly assumed the task of increasing Australian wines sales in the United Kingdom and, eventually, throughout Europe. It was a daunting challenge for at least three reasons: Australian wines had no unique image; wine drinking in Great Britain was a mark of privilege that excluded the average citizen; and, for centuries, whatever wines were consumed in the United Kingdom were primarily from Bordeaux.[21]

Emphasizing Australian wines' price-to-quality ratio[22] in a marketing campaign called "putting glasses into hands," Hazel targeted the untapped portion of the British wine market, the average consumer. Her innovative strategies included joint tastings by several different wineries; "wine flights," which were educational trips to Australia for British wine journalists, sommeliers, and buyers;[23] wine tours for MWs; Australian wine courses; a Web site for consumers; Australian wine newsletters for the United Kingdom and Europe; and a focus on supermarkets (especially Safeway, which agreed to put its own label on Australian wines at a low price point). She organized promotions at large wine retailers such as Odd Bins and set up tastings at golf tournaments to capitalize on Australia's sports image and a captive audience. She also made it a point to introduce the wines of the larger Australian producers to help pave the way for others.

Referring to herself self-deprecatingly as "a legend in her own lunchtime," Hazel notes that she was born in 1948, the Year of the Rat on the Chinese calendar. In 1996, the Rat horoscope predicted that she would achieve success far beyond expectations that year—and she did. The Australian government, which had never given her any funding, recognized her importance by awarding her the Order of Australia; she was also named Honorary Australian of the Year in 2004. In 1996, the Australian wine industry recognized its indebtedness to her by giving her its highest honor, the Maurice O'Shea Award, "presented to an individual or group who has made a significant contribution to the Australian wine industry."[24]

By 2003, the volume of Australian wine exports to Europe had become too great for her to handle with only a small, primarily part-time staff in London and limited auxiliary offices in Ireland and Germany. Hazel restructured her operations into two sections, a London office to handle only the United Kingdom and Ireland, and an office in The Hague responsible for continental Europe. She also restructured herself out of a job. Realizing that if she remained in London, she would again become responsible for all of Europe, she resigned and was replaced by two men. Today, Hazel runs her own market consulting firm with an Australian wine and olive oil clientele.

Every nation has a unique array of specialists serving as commercial intermediaries between wineries and their final customers. In France, there are brokers (*courtiers*) and négociants (discussed in chapter 4). Brokers neither handle nor stock wine. Serving as intermediaries between producers and négociants, their tasks are to ensure that the quality of the wine delivered by producers to négociants is identical or equivalent to the original samples, to mediate any disputes between the parties, and to make certain that payments are duly made. For their services, brokers earn commissions from producers and négociants.[25]

Since the first half of the eighteenth century in France, however, it has been négociants who have flourished. In Burgundy, with its famous vineyards divided among many owners, "the traditional role of the négociant was to buy a multitude of different lots of wine, blend them, bring them up (*élevage*) and bottle them" under the négociant's own label.[26] In Bordeaux, however, with its large estates, négociants are wine merchants who inventory and sell the wines rather than producing them.

Inheritance has been key for women who gained ownership of French négociant houses, just as it was to women who became proprietors of wine estates. Few women négociants gained the personal prominence of Jeanne Descaves, the "doyenne of the Bordeaux wine trade."[27] Born in 1902, Jeanne Descaves married and joined her husband's négociant house, Maison Jean Descaves, in 1921. From the time of his death in 1968 until her own at the age of ninety-seven, she continued to run the firm with thirty-seven thousand cases of Grands Vins de Bordeaux Authentiques in her cellar.[28] During her seventy-nine years as a leading Bordeaux négociant, she converted her husband's business from one that sold cheap bulk wines to one that specialized in top château-bottled wines.[29] Determined to retain sole ownership and run the business, she refused to accept a partner and took calculated risks, always adamant that she would not borrow even one French franc from the bank. She was aided by her self-confidence, her outstanding energy, her memory, and her belief that she had nothing to prove. She considered herself hampered because she had not been born in Bordeaux and because she had never been well integrated into the social part of the wine business—with two children to care for, she did not party. In 1996, at the age of ninety-four, when she was forced to hire a managing director to help her because her children were not interested in the business, she hired a woman.[30]

Inheritance has been of little value in helping French women secure other types of intermediary positions, however. The few women who have become brokers, such as Becky Wasserman-Hone, were forced to start their own business. Becky, an American who now holds dual citizenship, emigrated to France in 1968 with her husband and two children. In 1976, needing financial independence but with no assets other than a partially completed music degree from Bryn Mawr and her bilingualism, she eschewed being a bilingual receptionist and chose the riskier path of helping French coopers sell their barrels in the growing markets of California and Oregon. With the steady income from the cooperage trade, she qualified for her first bank loan in 1979, using the money to found her export company, SARL Le Serbet. Specializing in wines produced from low-yielding vineyards with a high percentage of old vines, Becky represents sixty to seventy small Burgundian and southern French winemakers whose wine she liked and who were having difficulty entering the U.S. market.

Becky is a matchmaker who brings together buyers and sellers. Considered a broker because she owns no vineyards, winery, or stock, Becky considers herself a principal, or dealer, rather than a broker because she takes legal title to the wines she handles and exports. Stubbornness, which she calls her greatest personal strength, helped her stay in business despite handling a volatile product and despite facing American bankruptcies, trade requirements, fluctuating currencies, and other financial hurdles that kept her from profitability until 1996. Unlike

Jeanne Descaves, who refused to ever take out a loan, Becky has been heavily dependent on bank loans from Crédit Agricole, shareholders who were willing to invest with a woman, two recapitalizations, and three mortgages. Along the way, she never lost control of her firm, even though she owns only 26 percent of it. Like Jeanne Descaves, Becky never accepted a partner because women do not get fifty-fifty deals. Because of a 75 percent voting requirement, she had retained veto rights over all decisions.

Becky believes that women are at the high end of the wine industry because they are uncomfortable making money on mediocrity. Despite this common affinity for fine wines, she notes that women producers do not gravitate to women sellers and that there is no "old girls' network."

THE AMERICAN MARKET

Among American women and men, there is consensus that the last great barrier to women in the wine trade is the three-tiered system of importing, distributing, and retailing. Even Becky Wasserman-Hone claims that she had more trouble selling wine in the United States than she did in convincing producers to sell their wines to her in France.

The top wine marketing tier in the United States, and the only one governed by federal law, is importing. All wine importers must obtain a national license entitling them to bring wines into the country but not to distribute them after arrival. Distribution (wholesaling) is regulated on a state-by-state basis, a remnant of Prohibition. Importers, then, must depend on distributors to transfer their wines to the third tier, the final customers—retail outlets and restaurants. Within this structure, influential women are found infrequently at the importing or distribution levels and somewhat more often in the retail and restaurant worlds.

Among the few prominent women who import and market wine in the United States is Mireille Guiliano, president and CEO of Clicquot Inc. and author of the best-seller *French Women Don't Get Fat*. She increased her product's market share from 1 percent in 1984 to 15 percent in 2001 by focusing on brand identification in a manner similar to that employed by her wine's namesake, the original Veuve Clicquot (described in chapter 3). True to her brand's history and tradition, Mireille emphasized Champagne's elegance, not just as a special event wine but also as a wine that could accompany a meal. Known for her frequent and lavish entertaining—a Halloween bash that rotates among six cities, an annual Bastille Day gala in New York, and a Fourth of July event at her home—Mireille's parties are a soft selling technique that associates Veuve Clicquot Champagne with refinement and fun.[31]

She also enhanced Veuve Clicquot's aura of exclusivity by convincing the finest restaurants to feature her Champagne and shunning discounts in order to position her brand as the most prestigious and most expensive nonvintage brut.[32] She is determined to meet three new customers for Veuve Clicquot every day. A hands-on executive, she appeared in radio ads to help Americans pronounce Veuve Clicquot and further stimulate brand awareness. When Veuve Clicquot was acquired by LVMH, Mireille expanded her portfolio to include other ultra-premium wines and Champagnes consistent with her marketing niche.[33]

Having studied French and English literature at the Sorbonne and languages at the Institut Supérieur d'Interprétariat et de Traduction,[34] it was natural for Mireille to use her multilingual talents as a United Nations translator when she accompanied her future husband to New York in 1973. Becoming bored with translating technical material, she changed careers in 1979, transferring to the Champagne News and Information Bureau, a public relations firm, where she was assigned to the Veuve Clicquot account. In 1984, at the behest of Veuve Clicquot's chair, she established the U.S marketing subsidiary Clicquot Inc. She was promoted to president and CEO in 1991, a position she doubts would have been available to her in France.

A tough, no-nonsense executive who serves on the Committee of 200, a professional organization of prominent women entrepreneurs and corporate leaders,[35] Mireille's success is based on several rules. The first is that "you must be happy" and must have passion in work as well as in love. No fan of job-hopping, she expects total loyalty from her employees and will not rehire someone who leaves.[36] She promotes from within, using the motto "the best grow, the rest go."

Mireille says that she "learned about life's inequalities early on when I saw my little brother get beaten up after school because we were Protestant in Catholic France." She also believes in the survival of the fittest, the need to outthink the competition and to take chances to deal with inequality. Always optimistic and never scared, she attributes her ability to take risks to her mother, who asked, "What's the worst that can happen?" when assessing life's turning points.[37]

Mireille is persistent and finds ways to get where she has to go without letting gender become a hindrance. She claims that most distributors give her no trouble because her brand is so successful and because she had the advantage of knowing a lot of people from the Champagne Bureau before coming to Clicquot Inc. Mireille works in a relaxed office atmosphere with open doors, no secretaries, and employees who multitask in order to encourage openness and integration. Wanting everyone to know everything and handling all sales, marketing, and communications in-house,[38] she holds meetings only as needed rather than at preset times. She wants her staff to respect, not necessarily love, her. Having set her own rules in the United States, she says that she cannot imagine returning to work in France with its bureaucracy and unions that create endless meetings and force her to retain lazy or incompetent people.

Believing that people must avoid trying to do too much and must have equilibrium in their lives (she is an advocate of yoga), Mireille chose not to have children, arguing that one cannot give equal weight to career advancement, a husband, children, and free time.[39] She says that she traded the pleasures of having children for the pleasures of not having them, because you cannot give 100 percent to everything with children and a career. Married to Edward Guiliano, president of the New York Institute of Technology, Mireille's only complaint about her two-CEO marriage is that she does double duty and really needs a wife.

19. Mireille Guiliano, president and CEO of Cliquot Inc., expanded the U.S. market for Veuve Clicquot Champagne and authored the bestseller *French Women Don't Get Fat.*

Cristina Mariani-May, vice-president of marketing of Banfi, is a graduate of Georgetown University. She earned an MBA in international management from Columbia University Business School and is the first woman to hold an executive position in her family's company, the largest wine importer in the United States. Because her sister has chosen not to be part of the business, Cristina also is heir apparent to her father's 50 percent of Banfi's voting stock.

Despite his success in convincing Cristina to join the business rather than become an art curator, her father, who is Banfi's chair and her role model and mentor, has yet to convince her to replace him as chair in the future. Although Cristina sees herself more as her father's "son" than his daughter and considers herself a competitive person, she is reluctant to assume this leadership role, believing that owning half of the voting shares will provide her with sufficient control. A nonconfrontational person, she may allow a male cousin who will control only 12.5 percent of the voting shares to have the CEO title he covets.[40] The recent birth of her first child and the frequently offensive comments she must endure from distributors, especially the older cigar and cognac guys, weigh against her taking the top position. If disagreeing with her father remains painful, however, she cannot be counted out.

"The distributor is the middle tier of the deservedly maligned American three-tier system of wine distribution. Distributors are the funnel through which all wines must pass before reaching retailers and restaurants who then sell to consumers. The distributor tier has a stranglehold on what is or is not sold in their individual markets."[41] Cristina Mariani-May refers to distribution as a male club, a view some, such as Robert Parker, would call charitable. Parker refers to liquor and spirits distributors now handling wine as "Neanderthals." According to Michaela Rodeno, women working within distribution channels rather than working for one winery are severely disadvantaged and beleaguered, because as spirits and liquor companies gain dominance of wine distribution, the opportunities for women to advance in sales evaporate.[42] From Sandra MacIver, who used a special business card listing her as president when she met with distributors so that they would not turn their backs on her and talk only to her husband, to Delia Viader, who exploits her femininity and good looks in dealing with distributors by being coy and disarming to camouflage a first-rate mind, women in the American wine industry concede that distribution remains a problem for them.

Among the very few women who own a wine distribution company in the United States is Debra Crestoni, proprietor of Connoisseur Wines, which imports, markets, and distributes ultra-premium wines from throughout the world in the Midwest, primarily Illinois, Michigan, Minnesota, and Wisconsin.[43] Educated at the Chicago Academy of Fine Arts and the Art Institute of Chicago, from which she received a master's degree, Debra's career in wine began in the mid-1970s at the original Connoisseur Wines, owned by her mentor, Pete Stern, who introduced her to fine wine, especially small boutique wines from overseas. She honored Pete by adopting his firm's name.

Debra sold wine in retail stores and was a sommelier at fine restaurants for a decade. In 1989, she opened her first distribution firm, Vintage Wine Selections, to represent five wineries that were among the crème de la crème of California's cutting-edge cult wineries. Because of her experience and extraordinary ties in California, she was able to sell her firm to Chicago Brands in 1992 and become a partner, the position she held until 1999 when she established Connoisseur Wines.

Debra credits her survival to the extraordinary loyalty she has earned from her clients (all of whom have remained with her), to her ability to think outside the box, and to her ethical conduct—eschewing multiple layers of pricing, under-the-table incentives, and discounts for product positioning.[44] She realized early on that large distributors needed to represent larger wineries in order to gain economies of scale from their warehouses, trucking fleets, and frequent inventory turnover and economies of scope associated with multiple clients and a wide variety of products. But by subcontracting with a larger distributor to handle her warehousing and trucking requirements, she has been able to fill her portfolio with small to medium-sized high-quality wineries,[45] turn her inventory twice a year, and avoid major capital expenditures. Although she worked for two years from her apartment in order to get Connoisseur Wines off the ground, she now has an office, a substantial facility, and six employees. She is able to consider expanding her portfolio, increasing her inventory turnover to three times per year, and branching out into a wine school to provide professional training for retailers and sommeliers.

Like Jeanne Descaves, Debra is insular, not socializing with competitors and consciously keeping herself apart in order to avoid unwelcome gender issues, a problem for women in wine sales. Her major professional activities include the Chicago Society of Sommeliers, the Women's Advisory Board of the Lyric Opera of Chicago's Wine Auction, and Les Dames d'Escoffier, an international organization of well-regarded and experienced professional women in the food and wine industries.

SOMMELIERS

The last marketing tier directly serving consumers consists of retail stores and restaurants. Although the former are the sites at which most sales occur, getting an upscale brand into top restaurants is essential "because demand for a wine often trickles down from sommeliers."[46]

The stereotypical sommelier, "a supercilious male in a tuxedo with a silver tastevin around his neck," has become history as "the stubbornness of European-born restaurateurs, who favored all-male staffs,"[47] has succumbed to legal pressures. Patrons also have come to rely on talent and knowledge rather than gender as they select wines.

An elite group of sommeliers has earned the designation Master Sommelier, MS, the highest professional distinction in fine wine and beverage service. This credential is conferred by the Court of Master Sommeliers, headquartered in London. Unlike the more academic MW exam, the MS exam contains three, increasingly difficult stages—Basic Certificate, Advanced Sommelier Certificate, and Master Sommelier Diploma. Conducted orally because wine service is regarded as a performance craft, the exams include a comprehensive theory section, a tasting examination, and a practicum "where candidates walk through a mock dining-room situation and are graded on their responses to questions and situations covering every aspect of beverage service."[48] As of June 2005, 138 individuals had earned the MS designation. Of these, 15, or 10.87 percent, were women.[49]

Madeline Triffon, MS, director of wine and beverages for the Unique Restaurant Corporation in suburban Detroit, was the first American woman awarded the Master Sommelier designation, in 1987. She is a permanent member of the board of directors of the American chapter of the Court of Master Sommeliers.[50] It has been said that in Detroit the sommelier hierarchy is "Madeline Triffon, and then there's everybody else."[51] *Wine Spectator* has given her wine lists its Grand Award of the World's 100 Best Wine Lists, and *Restaurant Business Magazine* has called her the "Grand Dame of America's Sommeliers."

Born in Connecticut, Madeline grew up in Greece and has spent her entire professional career in the Detroit area. Her sommelier career began at a French restaurant ("thanks in no small part to a good French accent") before she completed her theater studies at the University of Michigan or knew anything about wine. Her training consisted of being told to read a copy of Hugh Johnson's *Atlas of World Wines.*

Madeline speaks to women's groups but does not join them because she subscribes to the unfortunate misrepresentation of feminism as male bashing. She also does not view her "accomplishments as advancing gender equality in the wine trade so much as . . . affirmation of . . . [her] own dedication and determination to succeed."[52] Although she admits that she is still seen as an oddity, she does not consider gender a problem. She thanks her former boss, Max Pincus of London Chop House, for paying her fee to take the MS exam. She muses that a female sommelier may help in soothing egos and bolstering customer self-confidence in ordering wine. Madeline would rather ignore discrimination, fearing that she might develop a poisoned attitude or a chip on her shoulder that might adversely affect her work in the service/hospitality industry.

Nonetheless, in retrospect, she admits that she had to prove herself because being at least as good as a man was not good enough. Saddened rather than angered by discrimination, she acknowledges that the distribution network discriminates against women; that there is a "buddy network" among her MS colleagues, who do not call to include her in trips or to seek out her opinion; and that predominantly male collector groups do not invite her or ask her to join.

Unlike other women who also disavow a feminist label, Madeline seems to eschew recognition for her accomplishments by saying that she "hides right out in the open" and avoids the limelight. Nonetheless, she,

20. Madeline Triffon, MS, director of wine and beverages for Detroit's Unique Restaurant Corporation, was the first American woman to earn the title Master Sommelier.

too, contradicts her antifeminism by aggressively pursuing her salary demands, another form of recognition. Consulting for Marriott and United Airlines, she concentrates on advancing herself rather than helping other women, although she is happy to see them get ahead and is considered a mentor by many other women sommeliers.

Andrea Immer, MS, became a superstar soon after earning her Master Sommelier credentials in 1996. (She now uses Andrea Robinson as her professional name.) The very next year, she became the first woman to be named Best Sommelier in America by the Sommelier Society of America. In June 1998, she was the U.S. representative in the Concours

Mondial, or "Wine Olympics," in Vienna, the triennial Sommelier World Championship. She enhanced her fame through television appearances as the host of *Quench* on the Food Network[53] and through her numerous books, including *Great Tastes Made Simple* and *Andrea Immer's Wine Buying Guide for Everyone.*

With economics and finance degrees from Southern Methodist University, Andrea originally came to New York as a financial analyst for Morgan Stanley. But her command of languages, her theater background, and her love of wine spurred her interest in being a sommelier who could present fine wine to the public. Consciously planning her career, Andrea took courses with Mary Ewing-Mulligan, who taught her how to blind taste and how to balance her love of wine with the study of wine. Mentored by Kevin Zraly, she took his advice to go to Europe to learn more about wine. With the help of a Eurail pass and a student identification card, she spent six months working the harvest. She also methodically noted wines she liked, people she met, tastings she attended, and everything else that could help her career. Zraly then put her career on the fast track when he hired her as beverage director at Windows on the World in New York's World Trade Center in 1996.

In 1999, Andrea became the first corporate director of beverage programs for Starwood Hotels and Resorts. She later attended and graduated from New York's French Culinary Institute, where she is now the first dean of wine studies. Andrea maintains an active nonacademic schedule as a speaker and as a consultant for several clients including Hilton, Marriott International, Olive Garden, and Target and as a wine columnist for *Esquire* and *F&B Executive.* She also maintains her own Web site, www.andreaimmer.com.[54]

Andrea attributes her success to knowledge and hard work, the prerequisites for a woman to get in the door and gain power and credibility, and to her employers. Confident that she would do a good job, they gave her flexible schedules that allowed her to balance family and her career. Being a woman also was helpful because she was not threatening to customers and attracted publicity.

Heeding the advice of Kevin Zraly, who emphasized the importance of safeguarding her integrity, Andrea is emphatic that there is a double standard for women and men around alcohol. Harking back to arguments used in ancient cultures, she says that women must have pristine judgment in their conduct around alcohol because their reputation and honor are paramount. She does not drink "with the boys," in order to protect her personal and professional reputation.

Andrea has faced rejection more often from women than from men. Nonetheless, she says, the worldwide "old boys' distribution network" creates disadvantages for women sommeliers by not making all wines available to them. She also sees poor prospects for women in wine and liquor conglomerates.

Alpana Singh, MS, director of wine and spirits for Lettuce Entertain You Enterprises and former sommelier at Everest in Chicago, is the youngest person to earn a Master Sommelier credential. A member of a nondrinking Hindu family of Indian origin who emigrated from Fiji, Alpana acquired an introduction to wine in order to land a waitress job at a local bistro to earn money for college. Eventually, she quit school and used her income to pay the expenses associated with earning her MS. Although she is now passionate about wine, she originally considered it her ticket to a new life. Even today, she says that the MS is hers because she paid for it; no one has a hold on her, and she incurred no obligations. Simply put, she is a young woman who does not want anyone to tell her what to do and who is determined to set her own course.

Having grown up, in her words, as a mini-adult, trying to please her elders and lacking her own interests or activities, Alpana is now trying to build a life apart from wine. Overcoming her inclination to be a loner and avoid publicity, she is attempting to capitalize on the attention she receives because of her gender, age, and minority status, hoping to relate to people her own age and to overcome her workaholic tendencies. Her regular appearance on the television show *Check, Please!* is part of this effort.

Alpana is never casual. Ever conscious of her appearance and reputation, she is not at ease among wine people and does not relax with them as she would with friends outside the wine business. Grateful to the chef Jean Joho for hiring her at Everest when she had completed only the second level of the MS exam and for protecting her from unpleasant customers and distributors, Alpana is influential because of her credentials, experience, and determination.

. . .

The remarkable accomplishments of the women who market wine throughout the world are less a sign of a level playing field and more a testament to their tenacity, their ability to develop a market niche, and their talent. Not immune from the effects of bias, each one has found a strategy with which she is comfortable. Some have chosen to ignore bias. Others have chosen to accede to it by not seeking the top job, by trying to appear less competitive or threatening. Several limit social interactions in their professional lives in order to protect their reputations. Prejudice against women in wine has not disappeared, nor is it more prevalent in the Old World than in the New, especially with the increased importance of liquor and wine conglomerates in the wine trade. Nonetheless, for determined and capable women who can withstand the sexism that still permeates wine distribution networks worldwide, opportunities for career advancement do exist.

CHAPTER TEN

Past, Present, Future

Where are the women? Everywhere. They own great wineries, make fine wine, contribute to advances in viticulture and enology, educate wine consumers, guide wine connoisseurs, and market wine throughout the world. As John Stimpfig noted in *Decanter*, "Wine, like many things, used to be a man's world. Not any more. You only have to look at the growing number of women in every area of the wine trade to see that there's an awful lot of girl power in its upper echelons."[1] Although such a statement might seem obvious today, the growing presence of women in the wine industry is a relatively recent phenomenon, shaped by globalization and societal advances in the late twentieth century. For most of recorded history, traditions, social mores, cultural practices, religious customs, superstition, and widespread gender prejudice—often disguised as protectionism—prevented women from owning wineries, making wine, drinking it, appreciating it, or selling it. This is no longer true. Throughout the wine landscape, women have created a mosaic of acceptance, accomplishment, and influence.

On closer observation, however, the picture is more complex. One purpose of this study has been to give this picture texture, definition, and detail and to call attention to the contradictions that remain. Each woman's story is unique. Degrees of acceptance and success differ by profession, region, and country. Traditional barriers that had seemingly faded into the background reappear, sometimes with diminished significance, but at other times transformed into new, equally onerous challenges. Women's presence in the wine world is permanent. The extent of their influence in the future is less certain.

No longer excluded from the Old World's wine industry, women such as Chiara Lungarotti, Corinne Mentzelopoulos, and Annegret Reh-Gartner own and manage some of the largest and most prestigious wineries in the world. Others, such as Albiera Antinori, are poised to assume positions of immense responsibility running vast wine empires. Young women such as Anne Gros, Elisabetta Foradori, and Heidi Schröck make some of the most honored wines in the world and are not reluctant to display their names prominently on the labels.

The beneficiaries of family circumstance and the vagaries of fate, female proprietors in the Old World inherited family-owned wineries that withstood the international tidal wave of consolidation. Their inheritance made possible by the absence of competitive male heirs in their generation, these women are talented, industrious, and tough—but also lucky. Historically, capable widows chose to retain their husbands' legacies: Lily Bollinger, Veuve Clicquot, Jeanne Descaves, Colette Faller, and Madame Pommery inherited, controlled, and enhanced the reputations of their wineries or wine-related businesses. The late-twentieth-century women proprietors, however, are less likely to be widows than daughters, who inherit wineries with no male siblings or cousins able or willing to run the family business. It is the coming of age of these daughters in numbers previously unknown throughout the Old World that has strengthened women's prominence and influence in the European wine world. In the nineteenth century, Dona Antónia Adelaide Ferreira was an anomaly; today, she would be one of a crowd.

Is this change permanent or transitory? It is too soon to tell. Sons, regardless of birth order, are still traditionally given the right of first refusal before a daughter such as Sylvie Spielmann can inherit her family's winery. Male cousins or brothers sometimes must fail before competent women such as Anne-Claude Leflaive and May-Eliane de Lenc-quesaing grasp the reins of the family firm. Generally, it is only in the absence of male heirs that parents, particularly fathers such as Piero Antinori, Giancarlo Gloder, Giorgio Lungarotti, and Baron Philippe de Rothschild, mentor their daughters in order to keep the winery in the family. Even then, daughters must prove their mettle and work harder to retain their inheritance; they cannot assume, as male heirs might, that it will remain in their hands.

If the traditional preference for male heirs remains intact in the Old World, there is no guarantee that women will retain their current level of prominence. Traditional inheritance patterns must be altered permanently rather than occasionally if women's place within the Old World wine industry is to be secure. Until women are judged on their ability rather than their gender, their position in the family firm will remain uncertain, and their influence will vary from generation to generation. Sensitivity to this issue differs among women. Only a few such as May-Eliane de Lencquesaing are prepared to break with tradition and give equal consideration to female successors. Like Veuve Cliquot, many women view themselves as the exception while they continue to support the rule.

Apart from historical and geographic differences, New World women proprietors display collective characteristics that distinguish them from their Old World counterparts. One still finds widows who inherited distinguished wineries and added to their luster, including Melba Brajkovich, Naoko Dalla Valle, Jane Hunter, and Mary Novak. By and large, however, the New World no longer requires wives to become widows in order to be recognized for their achievements. Barbara Banke, Prue Henschke, Tricia Horgan, Sarah Marquis, Su Hua Newton, and Norma Ratcliffe are not silent partners. They share the limelight as well as the work with their husbands. By eschewing the inheritance template, the New World has encouraged greater advancement of daughters. Carolyn Martini and Carolyn Wente rose to prominence in their families' wineries despite the presence of interested and capable male relatives. Cristina Mariani-May is poised to follow suit; the choice is hers.

Entrepreneurship is the defining trait of many New World women proprietors who were not the beneficiaries of inheritance. Susana Balbo, Ann Colgin, Cathy Corison, Debra Crestoni, Di Cullen, Merry Edwards, MaryAnn Graf, Kathy Lynskey, Sandra MacIver, and Jean Phillips mapped their own courses, accepted the associated risks, and eventually won fame within the wine world. Some New World women, such as Delia Viader and Becky Wasserman-Hone, transplanted their entrepreneurial spirit overseas. And, in a kind of reverse migration, some Old World daughters such as Anne Cointreau-Huchon and Alexandra Marnier-Lapostolle found the New World more fertile for their own personal growth.[2]

Despite its professed egalitarianism, the New World also poses questions regarding the sustainability of women's influence. Not all women have daughters like Vanya Cullen or Beth Novak Milliken who are prepared to inherit their mothers' mantle. The entrepreneurial spirit may live on, but the chances of establishing a successful, new, high-end winery—the heart of women's current success—is being curtailed. The increased scarcity of good land, skyrocketing real estate costs, and the enormous investments required for technology, automation, and advertising create almost prohibitive barriers to entering the industry.[3] Corporate beverage giants have entered the upper end of the business, intensifying competition in that market segment as well as in the supermarkets. Financing, a traditional problem for women without family wealth, remains difficult to obtain. The patience and determination required to save money, buy land, and build a new winery—as Susana Balbo, Cathy Corison, Merry Edwards, and Kathy Lynskey did—will be more difficult in the future. More women will need the good fortune of a Pam Starr, who partnered with a wealthy absentee landowner, in order to continue the entrepreneurial tradition.

The growth of educational equity was a common denominator fueling women's wine-related careers in both the Old World and the New World. It provided essential, recognizable credentials attesting to women's knowledge and competence, key factors in their professional success. "In order to take advantage of equal opportunity women must believe they are, and in fact must be, as competent as their male counterparts. In-depth competence in their chosen field has traditionally been one of women's outstanding strengths."[4] Coincident with the expanded de-mand for California wine in the late 1960s, American women wine-makers gained a platform from which to launch their careers by obtain-ing degrees in enology.[5] Their example was soon emulated throughout the New World and eventually the Old World as well. Thanks to the pioneering efforts of women such as Susana Balbo, Pam Dunsford, Mary Ann Graf, Mechthild Hammel, and Teresa Severini, women armed with degrees in enology and viticulture have established beachheads of global influence. It is increasingly rare for a woman winemaker like Lalou Bize-Leroy to hold a position of importance based on an entirely experiential education.

Although educational advances have been international, women winemakers have not attained comparable levels of influence in all coun-tries. In the New World, the paths to success and influence are diverse and well traveled. Women such as Dawnine Dyer, Michelle Richardson, and Wendy Stuckey have made wines for large international firms; others, such as Heidi Peterson Barrett, Mia Klein, and Sarah Marquis, consult for small, prestigious wineries while also producing wines un-der their own labels. In the Old World, however, the path is generally narrower. Despite exceptions such as Nadine Gublin, the Old World's women enologists who work outside a family setting are still more likely to be relegated to the anonymity of a laboratory. A few women such as Laurence Faller and Teresa Severini have attained recognition by mak-ing wine in their families' wineries. Internationally, the common thread of success for women winemakers remains their association with pre-mium wines. They, like their wines, must simply be better. Women still have no "wiggle room."

Looking beyond winemaking itself to the broad spectrum of wine-related occupations in academia, journalism, and business, obtaining cre-dentials through formal degrees or professional certifications has been key. Reflecting the increased presence of women on faculties through-out American higher education, women professors such as Marian Baldy, Linda Bisson, Susan Ebeler, Hildegarde Heymann, Carole Mere-dith, and Ann Noble are or have been prominent faculty members at enological and viticultural teaching and research centers.[6] Outside the United States, however, women's representation on university enology faculties lags in all regions, despite an occasional exception such as Monika Christmann at Geisenheim.

In wine-related journalism, Great Britain has led the way for women as wine columnists and critics. Thanks to the pioneering efforts of Sarah Morphew, Serena Sutcliffe, and Jancis Robinson, women writing about or marketing wine throughout the world have gained recognition, stature and influence by earning the coveted Master of Wine designation—including Mary Ewing-Mulligan, Marina Gayan, Rosemary George, Fiona Morrison, and Toni Paterson. Women sommeliers such as Madeline Triffon, Andrea (Immer) Robinson, and Alpana Singh have won professional advancement by becoming Master Sommeliers. As more women successfully complete the MW or MS examination, wine-related professions that prize these credentials hold great potential.

Business skills and credentials such as an MBA are similarly important for women aspiring to senior management positions throughout the wine world. Globalization and the increased scope and complexity of the industry require a firm command of financial statements, myriad legal requirements, and global marketing savvy. These skills are as crucial in family-owned businesses as in large public corporations. It is increasingly common to find a woman attorney, such as Barbara Banke or Laura Bianchi, or one who has earned an MBA, such as Lorenza Sebasti, at the helm of a family firm.

When asked to explain their success, however, women frequently attribute it to passion for wine rather than to education or credentials. For them, their chosen profession is their calling, their essence, and their identity. They claim that passion gave them the single-minded determination, unwavering focus, and self-confidence to achieve their goals despite the setbacks, loneliness, and even abuse that may have plagued their careers. They testify, "If you have the soul and you have the passion for the industry, you will succeed, male or female."[7] Some women even draw attention to their gender, hoping to capitalize on it for publicity, special attention, or preferential treatment. Winemakers and proprietors such as Susana Balbo, Cathy Corison, Elisabetta Foradori, Lalou Bize-Leroy, Kathy Lynskey, Heidi Schröck, Sylvie Spielmann, and Delia Viader proudly display their names on their labels as a sign of assertiveness and self-identification. Others, including Mia Klein, with her Selene (moon goddess) label, and Heidi Peterson Barrett, with La Sirena (the mermaid), use female symbolism to identify their labels with their gender.

Passion and pride may have been essential elements for women's successes in the past, and may remain so, but in the future they will no longer be sufficient without solid credentials, particularly in positions outside a family winery. Consolidation of the wine industry is clearly the wave of the future, even though its pace might be uneven from country to country.[8] By absorbing the small family-owned wineries in which women have achieved their greatest successes, the move toward consolidation, particularly given the accelerated domination of the alcoholic beverage giants, generates some uncertainty about women's future influence. Few women are found in senior management within these companies, and there is no reason to believe that this will change measurably in the foreseeable future. Even in California, where women have attained their most commanding positions in the international wine community, fewer women are found in the upper echelons of large corporate wineries today than a decade ago. The few who have managed to retain their positions, such as Eileen Crane and Michaela Rodeno, work for subsidiaries of Old World corporations, most often in the area of sparkling wines. A recent study revealed that women managers in these large alcoholic beverage companies are confronted with the traditional barriers to advancement: exclusion from informal networks, a paucity of role models, and gender-based stereotypes, particularly those related to balancing a career and a family. These are remarkably similar to the barriers faced by women in another male-dominated industry, high technology.[9]

Even with improved access and impressive credentials, women will need to do more if they wish to pursue successful managerial careers in the increasingly consolidated wine world. Mutual support through networking and mentoring will need to be taken more seriously. With rare exceptions, such as Zelma Long, the experience of women in all wine-related professions has tended to be insular. It can, of course, be argued that these women had little alternative, given the climate in which they were struggling. Working within an almost exclusively male enclave, older women were most likely to have had male mentors—either relatives, friends, or colleagues. Unfortunately, this has not changed; younger women rarely refer to another woman as a mentor.

Networking has received unenthusiastic or at best sporadic support from women, a majority of whom either do not affiliate with organizations such as Women for Winesense or Le Donne del Vino or fail to actively participate when they do. Many of these women see little potential for collective assistance from what they deem to be fringe groups or gripe sessions. Some appear to fear that identification with other women will be an admission of defeat or, worse, a sign of disaffection that will translate into further isolation from the male mainstream. Younger women, such as Louisa Rose and Albiera Antinori, dismiss or ignore issues of gender discrimination as not worth their time or energy, arguing that only individual effort will help them attain their goals. Certainly networking is no substitute for personal achievement, but as the successful women members of the Committee of 200 can attest, collective action can be a dynamic force for achieving mutual goals, and role models are an important source of encouragement.

Despite examples to the contrary, the historical double standard of the symposia, consortia, and male social clubs continues to play a prominent role in the industry. The structures may be largely extinct, but the pall they cast over socializing between men and women in the wine industry remains. In some instances, women such as Debra Crestoni and

Andrea (Immer) Robinson restrict their socializing with men to professional settings for fear of tarnishing their reputation. In the vast majority of situations, however, women such as Michelle Richardson or Madeline Triffon—who would like to participate in informal gatherings, tastings, or winery trips with male colleagues—claim that they are systematically excluded or overlooked. Joining women's networks may not solve this problem, but at least it does not exacerbate it. Opening women's networks to supportive male members might help to break through the remaining gender tensions. In addition, women in powerful positions speaking more openly for equity could have an important impact on establishing more comfortable interactions with male colleagues, fostering greater concern for mentoring and networking, and eradicating ongoing discrimination. But this will not be possible unless more of these women acknowledge themselves as beneficiaries of modern feminism's strides toward economic, political, and social equality and admit that theirs remains an uphill battle.

Despite the progress they have made, women are not about to overtake men's commanding presence in the world of wine. Individually, however, many women have attained indelible influence as proprietors throughout the world's great wine regions, as winemakers of many of the world's most prestigious wines, and as academicians, journalists, and marketers helping to shape the global wine industry. In the future, it seems safe to say, individual women will continue to wield an influence comparable to or greater than that of many men. Who these women will be, where they will reside, and what positions they will use to leverage themselves may change over time. But rest assured, they will be there, and they will be there in large measure because of the ground broken by the women discussed in this book, women who have already altered the wine industry forever.

NOTES

1. WOMEN NEED NOT APPLY

1. Genesis 9:20–21.

2. Rod Phillips, *A Short History of Wine* (New York: Ecco, 2002), p. xiv.

3. Ibid., p. 46.

4. Phillips, *Short History of Wine*, p. 23. An in depth study of the role of wine in ancient Egypt can be found in Mu-Chou Poo, *Wine and Wine Offerings in the Religion of Ancient Egypt* (London: Kegan Paul, 1995).

5. Phillips, *Short History of Wine*, p. 44; Jancis Robinson, ed., *The Oxford Companion to Wine* (New York: Oxford University Press, 1994), p. 465.

6. Phillips, *Short History of Wine*, pp. 42–45.

7. Ibid., pp. 45–47, 57.

8. Ibid., pp. 204, 205.

9. Robert C. Fuller, *Religion and Wine: A Cultural History of Wine Drinking in the United States* (Knoxville: University of Tennessee Press, 1996), pp. 16, 22.

10. T. A. Layton, *Wines and People of Alsace* (London: Cassell and Cassell, 1970), p. 102.

11. Alan Spencer, "Saint-Emilion Women Enfranchised after 800 Years," *Decanter*, April 12, 2001, www.decanter.com/news/46862.html.

12. The Qur'an does not forbid alcohol consumption. "A careful and critical analysis of all references [to wine] reveals that the Qur'an treats wine with a great ambivalence; the potent liquid that constitutes an abomination in one verse becomes a source of 'good food' in another . . . the Qur'an condemns wine

only when consumption takes place in contexts deemed unsuitable or inappropriate; the prohibition is hardly unconditional or absolute" (Kathryn Kueny, *The Rhetoric of Sobriety: Wine in Early Islam* [Albany: State University of New York Press, 2001], p. 1). Some argue that Muhammad created the prohibition on alcohol consumption in order to eliminate the excessive drunkenness that had become prevalent among Muslims (Fuller, *Religion and Wine,* p. 6). "The *prohibition* of wine was not a Qur'anic invention, but rather a strict legal proposition developed through analytic and narrative discourses that sought to 'clarify' the revelation's ambivalent treatment of wine's ambiguities as a social and conceptual substance. This legal proposition implies a uniformly negative view of wine in the Hadith [accounts of Muhammad's sayings or behavior]" (Kueny, *Rhetoric of Sobriety,* p. 89).

13. Phillips, *Short History of Wine,* p. 60.

14. Fuller, *Religion and Wine,* p. 50. According to the Talmud, women were more likely to enjoy a new garment than to enjoy wine. Nonetheless, allotments of wine were provided for two groups of women: nursing mothers, to improve lactation, and affluent women who had grown up surrounded by wine (Michal Dayagi-Mendels, *Drink and Be Merry: Wine and Beer in Ancient Times* [Jerusalem: The Israel Museum, 1999], p. 60).

15. "Kosher Wine . . . A Little History," www.abarbanel.com/history.shtml; Fuller, *Religion and Wine,* p. 40.

16. For a wine to be deemed kosher, it must conform to specific agricultural rules (e.g., *shmeetah,* which specifies that Jewish fields from which the grapes are gathered must lie fallow every seventh year; and *orla,* which forbids picking grapes from vines that are less than four years old), historically symbolic rules (e.g., *ma'aser,* the requirement that 1 percent of the winery production be poured away as symbolic tithing to the high priests of the ancient temples), and Mevushal (pasteurization) rules that prevent its adulteration by non-Jews who might use it for non-Jewish religious purposes, especially idolatrous practices ("Kashrut," www.abarbanel.com/kashrut.shtml).

17. Rabbi Moshe Feinstein, *Igros Moshe Yoreh Deah II* (Brooklyn: Moriah Offset, 1973), sec. 45, p. 63, col. 2: A woman who is trustworthy and known to be G-d fearing may serve as a Mashgicha (feminine of Mashgiach), a supervisor of Kosher food production. This applies only in certain circumstances such as a widow needing to sustain herself and her children.

18. Tillich quoted in Fuller, *Religion and Wine,* p. viii.

19. John 2:7–10; Matthew 26:27–28.

20. Richard P. Vine et al., *Winemaking: From Grape Growing to Marketplace* (New York: Chapman and Hall, 1997), p. xix.

21. Daphne Boutwood of the *Sunday Times* (London), quoted in Layton, *Wines and People of Alsace,* p. 102.

22. Jeni Port, *Crushed by Women: Women and Wine* (Melbourne: Arcadia, 2000), p. 13.

23. Leo A. Loubère, *The Red and the White* (Albany: State University of New York Press, 1978), pp. xix, 86; e-mail message to the author dated June 13, 2000, from Elvira Henni Angela Ackermann, Cantine Lungarotti.

24. Fiona Beeston, *The Wine Men* (London: Sinclair-Stevenson, 1991), p. 141.

25. The 1908 U.S. Supreme Court case *Muller v. Oregon* (208 US 412) set the American precedent for gender distinctions in labor law. Incorporating attorney Louis Brandeis's nonlegal, social arguments, the "Brandeis Brief," the case upheld an employer's decision to specify different working conditions (maximum hours) for women in order to preserve their health and their ability to meet familial obligations. What began as progressive protections eventually became gender-based restrictions, however, and women as a class came to be viewed as physically frail and less able than men to perform many jobs, particularly those requiring stamina or strength.

26. Beeston, *Wine Men,* p. 89; Port, *Crushed by Women,* p. 28.

27. Richard L. Doty et al., "Sex Differences in Odor Identification Ability: A Cross-Cultural Analysis," *Neuropsychologia* 23, no. 5 (1985): 667, 669; Kate Fox, "The Smell Report: Sex Differences," Social Issues Research Centre, www.sirc.org/publik/smell_diffs.html.

28. *Scientific American Frontiers,* "Ask the Scientists: Linda Bartoshuk," www.pbs.org/safarchive/3_ask/archive/bio/94_bartoshuk_bio.html; "Linda Bartoshuk," http://info.med.yale.edu/bbs/faculty/bar_li.html.

29. Port, *Crushed by Women,* pp. 23, 26.

30. One study argued that men have a higher-risk life strategy and, by virtue of evolution, are more likely to seek status, to be competitive, and to accept risks, while women are nurturing and display "affiliative" behavior; see Kingsley R. Browne, "Sex and Temperament in Modern Society: A Darwinian View of the Glass Ceiling and the Gender Gap," *Arizona Law Review* 37 (Winter 1995): 1103, 1104, 1106.

31. James Lawther, "Women in a Man's World," *Decanter,* September 1999, p. 44.

32. Thomas Matthews, "Where Are the Women?" *Wine Spectator,* November

30, 1999, www.winespectator.com/Wine/Archives/Show_Article/10,1275,2431.00
.html.

33. Information received from Jim Gordon, former managing editor of *Wine Spectator.*

2. THE CHANGING FACE OF THE WINE BUSINESS

1. Hugh Johnson, "Foreword," in Pierre Spahni, *The International Wine Trade,* 2nd ed. (Cambridge: Woodhead, 2000), p. vii.

2. For statistics on the labor force, see Richard P. Vine et al., *Winemaking: From Grape Growing to Marketplace* (New York: Chapman and Hall, 1997), p. xx. Acreage figures can be found at Wine Institute, "Key Facts: World Vineyard Acreage by Country," www.wineinstitute.org/communications/statistics/keyfacts_worldacreage4.htm. The total worldwide vineyard acreage in 2000 was 19,409,000. For information on total wine production, see Wine Institute, "Key Facts: World Wine Production by Country," www.wineinstitute.org/communications/statistics/keyfacts_worldwineproduction02.htm. Worldwide wine production in 2000 totaled 7,288,514,856 gallons.

3. Tim Unwin, *Wine and the Vine: An Historical Geography of Viticulture and the Wine Trade* (London: Routledge, 1991), p. 342.

4. Gideon Rachman, "The Globe in a Glass," *The Economist* 323, December 18–30, 1999, p. 92.

5. Ibid., p. 91.

6. Wine Institute, "Key Facts: Wine Consumption in the U.S., 1934 to 2002," www.wineinstitute.org/communications/statistics/consumption1934_99.html.

7. Unwin, *Wine and the Vine,* p. 352.

8. Robert M. Parker Jr., "25 Years in Wine: The Critic Robert M. Parker, Jr.," *Food & Wine,* September 2003, p. 132.

9. Dr. Philip Norrie, "The Wine Doctor: Wine and Health," *Winestate Magazine,* May/June 2000, www.winestate.com.au/magazine/article.asp?articleno=131.

10. The discovery of the French paradox is attributed to Dr. S. Renaud and Dr. M de Lorgeril, who considered the "high intake of saturated fats but low mortality from [coronary heart disease]" among the French to be paradoxical (S. Renaud and M. de Lorgeril, "Wine, Alcohol, Platelets, and the French Paradox for Coronary Heart Disease," *The Lancet* 339 [June 20, 1992]: 1523). Spahni

attributes the general use of the term and the public's awareness of the medical benefits of red wine to a CBS *60 Minutes* television broadcast in November 1991 that contained a segment titled "The French Paradox" (Spahni, *International Wine Trade,* pp. 79, 90).

11. Wine is believed to aid in the treatment of several ailments, including cancer, Alzheimer's disease, kidney stones, stomach problems, blood clots, osteoporosis, and macular degeneration. See Norrie, "Wine Doctor"; and Ágata Székely, "Red Wine: The Healthiest Drink," *Vuelo,* February 2003, p. 42.

12. Norrie, "Wine Doctor."

13. Rachman, "Globe in a Glass," pp. 99, 103.

14. Mouton Rothschild is a first growth Bordeaux château that also produces Mouton Cadet, a popularly priced wine that is the single largest export from Bordeaux. Mondavi is the California wine company credited with revolutionizing the quality of California's wines. Its moderately priced wines, sold under the Woodbridge label, have detracted from the firm's stature.

15. Rachman, "Globe in a Glass," p. 99.

16. A recent academic study conducted by two economics professors from the University of Montpellier, France, observed: "About 20 leading companies are transforming their strategic configurations in 'multinational firms of the wine industry.' . . . Furthermore, the industry is becoming an 'oligopoly with fringes.'" The conglomerates, they note, "co-exist [with] a large number of small wineries" (Alfredo Manual Coelho and Jean-Louis Rastoin, "Globalization of the Wine Industry and the Restructuring of Multinational Enterprises" [paper presented at Oenometrie XI, Université de Bourgogne, Dijon, France, May 21–22, 2004]).

17. Rachman, "Globe in a Glass," pp. 98, 99.

18. Unwin, *Wine and the Vine,* pp. 341, 349; Spahni, *International Wine Trade,* p. xii.

19. Rachman, "Globe in a Glass," p. 101.

20. Unwin, *Wine and the Vine,* p. 344; Jeni Port, *Crushed by Women: Women and Wine* (Melbourne: Arcadia, 2000), p. 21.

21. Rachman, "Globe in a Glass," p. 95.

22. A highly rated wine is one that receives a score of 90 points or better on a 100-point scale from Robert M. Parker Jr. in his quarterly publication *The Wine Advocate,* from Steve Tanzer in his bimonthly publication *International Wine Cellar,* or from *Wine Spectator,* a major U.S. wine publication. Although there are other influential critics who rate wine, these three publications have a dis-

proportionate influence on premium wine buyers. Parker's and Tanzer's scores are particularly powerful because they accept no advertising in their publications and have well-respected palates.

23. Spencer E. Ante, "Heavyweights behind the Great Wines," *Business Week,* March 19, 2001, p. 102.

24. Unwin, *Wine and the Vine,* p. 353.

25. Parker, "25 Years in Wine," pp. 135, 164.

26. Mary Ewing-Mulligan, MW, confirmed the information regarding the examination's essay question in an e-mail to the author dated May 2, 2005. The Master of Wine (MW) designation and its qualifying examination are discussed in chapter 8. Appendix 2 lists the women who have earned the MW.

27. A combination of circumstances made Australians the original "flying winemakers." Positioned to take advantage of two harvests, one in the Northern Hemisphere in the fall and one in the Southern Hemisphere in the spring, they were not bound by tradition, understood the needs of a consumer-led market for wines, were quality conscious, and were at the forefront of technological advances in winemaking. The ranks of these consultants now include individuals from many producing nations, including modern European winemakers. See Andrew Williams, *Flying Winemakers: The New World of Wine* (Adelaide: Winetitles, 1995), pp. 2, 6, 27.

3. A TOAST TO THE PAST

1. Melanie Parry, ed., *Larousse Dictionary of Women* (New York: Larousse Kingfisher Chambers, 1996), p. 732.

2. Anthony Rhodes, *Princes of the Grape* (London: Weidenfeld and Nicolson, 1975), p. 8.

3. Ibid.

4. Serena Sutcliffe, *Champagne: The History and the Character of the World's Most Celebrated Wine* (New York: Simon and Schuster, 1988), p. 167.

5. Tom Stevenson, *The New Sotheby's Wine Encyclopedia: A Comprehensive Reference Guide to the Wines of the World* (New York: DK Publishing, 1997), p. 167; Andrew Jones, *Wine Talk: A Vintage Collection of Facts and Legends for Wine Lovers* (London: Judy Piatkus, 1997), p. 12.

6. Princess Jean de Caraman Chimay, *Madame Veuve Clicquot Ponsardin: Her Life and Time* (Reims: 1961), p. 19.

7. Kolleen M. Guy, "Drowning Her Sorrows: Widowhood and Entrepre-

neurship in the Champagne Industry," *Business and Economic History* 26, no. 2 (Winter 1997): 508.

8. Karen MacNeil, "Veuve Clicquot in Russia," *Quarterly Review of Wines,* August 1992, p. 30.

9. Chimay, *Madame Veuve Clicquot Ponsardin,* p. 14.

10. Marion Winik, "The Women of Champagne," *American Way,* March 1, 1997, p. 113.

11. Rhodes, *Princes of the Grape,* p. 13; Frédérique Crestin-Billet, *Veuve Clicquot: La Grand Dame de la Champagne,* trans. Carole Fahy (Grenoble: Glenát, 1992), pp. 132, 136.

12. Patrick Forbes, *Champagne: The Wine, the Land, and the People* (New York: Reynal, 1967), p. 439.

13. Kolleen M. Guy, "Wine, Work, and Wealth: Class Relations and Modernization in the Champagne Wine Industry, 1870–1914" (PhD diss., Indiana University, 1996), pp. 37, 441–443.

14. Guy, "Drowning Her Sorrows," p. 507.

15. *Champagne Pommery* (Reims: Champagne Pommery, n.d.).

16. Guy, "Drowning Her Sorrows," p. 507; Sutcliffe, *Champagne,* p. 152; *Champagne Pommery.*

17. Rhodes, *Princes of the Grape,* pp. 20, 21.

18. *Champagne Pommery.* In 1888, Madame Pommery used art to protect her reputation against rumors claiming that she was experiencing financial difficulties. She squelched the rumors by purchasing Millet's *Les Glaneuses (Women Gleaning)* for three hundred thousand gold francs in order to prevent its sale in the United States. She then contributed it to the Louvre. Today it is part of the collection of the Musée d'Orsay (*Pommery* [Reims: Champagne Pommery, n.d.], p. 6; Forbes, *Champagne,* p. 462).

19. *Champagne Pommery.*

20. Guy, "Drowning Her Sorrows," p. 505.

21. Forbes, *Champagne,* p. 460.

22. Andre L. Simon, *The History of Champagne* (London: Octopus Books, 1971), p. 74; Guy, "Drowning Her Sorrows," p. 510.

23. *Pommery,* pp. 1, 3.

24. Guy, "Drowning Her Sorrows," p. 512.

25. Ibid., p. 507.

26. A. H. de Oliveira Marques, *History of Portugal,* vol. 2, *From Empire to Corporate State,* 2nd ed. (New York: Columbia University Press, 1976), p. 123.

27. Ibid., pp. 134, 135.

28. Eric Solsten, ed., *Portugal: A Country Study,* 2nd ed. (Washington, D.C.: Federal Research Division, Library of Congress, 1994), pp. 82, 83.

29. James Suckling, *Vintage Port* (San Francisco: Wine Spectator Press, 1990), p. 97.

30. "Ferreirinha 'A. Ferreira,'" *ABC,* May 1988, p. 18.

31. Jane MacQuitty, "Woman Who Built a Portuguese Empire," *The Times* (London), January 11, 1986.

32. Sarah Bradford, *The Story of Port: The Englishman's Wine,* rev. ed. (London: Christie's Wine Publications, 1978), p. 51.

33. Dwindling production necessitated the consolidation of small parcels of land and the blending of wines from several quintas into "shippers' declared vintages." See Alex Liddell, *Port Wine Quintas of the Douro* (London: Sotheby's, 1992), pp. 20, 21; Jan Read, *The Wines of Portugal* (London: Faber and Faber, 1982), p. 124; Suckling, *Vintage Port,* p. 97.

34. Liddell, *Port Wine Quintas,* p. 79; MacQuitty, "Woman Who Built a Portuguese Empire"; Wyndham Fletcher, *Port: An Introduction to Its History and Delights* (San Francisco: Wine Appreciation Guild, 1981), p. 72.

35. Liddell, *Port Wine Quintas,* p. 79; Richard Mayson, "Port's Home Side," *Decanter,* May 1998, p. 56; Suckling, *Vintage Port,* p. 97.

36. "Arrival in Australia," www.nicks.com.au/index.aspx?link_id=67.701.

37. Jeni Port, *Crushed by Women: Women and Wine* (Melbourne: Arcadia, 2000), p. 7.

38. Andre L. Simon, *The Wines, Vineyards, and Vignerons of Australia* (Melbourne: Lansdown Press, 1967), pp. 66, 67.

39. Port, *Crushed by Women*, p. 8; "Arrival in Australia."

40. "Expansion and Reputation," www.nicks.com.au/index.aspx?link_id=67.702; John Beeston, *A Concise History of Australian Wine* (St. Leonards, New South Wales: Allen and Unwin, 1994), p. 130.

4. *VITICULTRICES ET PROPRIÉTAIRES*

1. Ed McCarthy and Mary Ewing-Mulligan, *Wine for Dummies* (Foster City: IDG Books, 1997), pp. 143–145. The second growth classification (cru classés) originally contained fourteen châteaux; the third also had fourteen; the fourth had ten; and the fifth had eighteen. Most châteaux, however, remained unclassified. A complete list of the classified châteaux can be found in Jancis Robin-

son, ed., *The Oxford Companion to Wine* (New York: Oxford University Press, 1994), p. 246.

2. American-born Joan Dillon is the granddaughter of Clarence Dillon, who bought Château Haut-Brion. As president of Domaine Clarence Dillon S.A., she also oversees three additional Bordeaux estates owned by her family: La Mission Haut-Brion, La Tour Haut-Brion, and Laville Haut-Brion ("Château Haut-Brion: Joan Dillon, Duchesse de Mouchy," www.haut-brion.com/chb/history/jdem.htm).

3. James Seely, *Great Bordeaux Wines* (Boston: Little, Brown, 1986), p. 343.

4. James Lawther, "Women in a Man's World," *Decanter,* September 1999, p. 41.

5. Serena Sutcliffe, *The Simon and Schuster Guide to the Wines of Burgundy* (New York: Simon and Schuster, 1992), pp. 12, 13.

6. McCarthy and Ewing-Mulligan, *Wine for Dummies,* p. 149.

7. Alex Liddell, *Port Wine Quintas of the Douro* (London: Sothcby's, 1992), p. 16.

8. Sutcliffe, *Simon and Schuster Guide,* pp. 7, 13.

9. Ibid., p. 11.

10. McCarthy and Ewing-Mulligan, *Wine for Dummies,* pp. 152, 153.

11. The international wine critic Robert Parker has stated that Lalou "stands alone at the top of the Burgundy hierarchy" (T. J. Foderaro, "Women around the World Are Making Excellent Wines," *Star-Ledger* [New Brunswick, N.J.], May 27, 1998, www.stageleft.com/sl/press/article.asp?ID=21).

12. Per-Henrik Mansson, "Americans in Burgundy," *Wine Spectator Online,* November 15, 1998, www.winespectator.com/wine/Archives/Show_Article/0,1275,1966,00.html.

13. Serena Sutcliffe, "Bollinger Today," in *Bollinger: Tradition of a Champagne Family,* by Cyril Ray (London: Heinemann, 1994), pp. 6, 73, 74, 150, 154. Other widows notable for running their wineries during major crises or for substantial periods of time include Mathilde-Emilie Laurent-Perrier, Madame Joseph Krug, Camille Orly-Roederer, and Odette Pol-Roger, who recruited her wine's most famous devotee, Winston Churchill (Anthony Rhodes, *Princes of the Grape* [London: Weidenfeld and Nicolson, 1975], pp. 24, 25). Since 1991, the tradition of *grand marque* Champagne widows has been maintained by Carol Duval-Leroy, chair and CEO of Duval-Leroy (Gerald D. Boyd, "Duval-Leroy Returns to the U.S.," *Decanter,* March 2004, p. 94).

14. "LVMH Announces Appointment of Cécile Bonnefond as President and

CEO of Veuve Clicquot," www.findarticles.com/p/articles/mi_m0EIN/is_2000_Dec_7/ai_67685778.

15. Jacqueline Friedrich, *A Wine and Food Guide to the Loire* (New York: Henry Holt, 1996), p. 137; Fiona Beeston, *The Wine Men* (London: Sinclair-Stevenson, 1991), p. 45. Curnonsky was the pen name of Maurice Edmund Sailland. He was a gourmet who attained the title Curnonsky, Prince of Gastronomy, by public referendum in France in 1927; see "Curnonsky (Maurice Edmund Sailland)," www.foodreference.com/html/w-curnonsky.html.

16. Jancis Robinson, "Stars of Burgundy," *Food & Wine,* October 1999, p. 138.

17. In the absence of any other bidders, André Mentzelopoulos, head of the French grocery and finance conglomerate Félix-Potin, purchased a declining Château Margaux for the bargain basement sum of 72 million French francs, or approximately $14.4 million, a sale that included $4.4 million of unsold wine, in December 1976 (Per-Henrik Mansson and Thomas Matthews, "*Wine Spectator*'s Distinguished Service Award Winners," *Wine Spectator,* November 15, 1995, p. 20).

18. Joan Littlewood, *Milady Vine: The Autobiography of Philippe de Rothschild* (London: Jonathan Cape, 1984), p. 118.

19. Lawther, "Women in a Man's World," p. 42.

20. Per-Henrik Mansson, "The Billionaires," *Wine Spectator,* November 30, 1995, p. 75.

21. Corinne became managing partner of Château Margaux in 1980, when her father died. She was only twenty-seven. Having kept a 25 percent personal stake, she sold the other 75 percent to Exor/Group, a holding company controlled by the Italian Agnelli family of Fiat fame and in which she held an undisclosed percentage. In 2003, after the death of Gianni Agnelli, the Agnelli family decided to sell its 75 percent ownership in Château Margaux in order to alleviate its financial difficulties. Corinne had right of first refusal and chose to purchase the outstanding portion for $400 million. To enable her family's holding company, Soparexo, to acquire the entire Exor portion, she separately sold all her shares in Exor (Per-Henrik Mansson and Kim Marcus, "Château Margaux Sold to Former Owner," *Wine Spectator,* May 15, 2003, www.winespectator.com/Wine/Archives/Show_Article/0,1275,4113,00.html; Adam Lechmere, "Mentzelopoulos Is Sole Owner of Margaux," *Decanter,* March 10, 2003, www.decanter.com/news/46155.html).

22. Since 1943, when Philippe Jullian was commissioned to create its label, Mouton Rothschild's labels have been distinguished by artwork from many of

the world's greatest artists, including Cocteau (1945), Braque (1947), Dali (1958), Miró (1969), Chagall (1970), Kandinsky (1971), and Picasso (1973).

23. Robinson, *Oxford Companion to Wine,* p. 563; Remington Norman, *The Great Domaines of Burgundy,* 2nd ed. (London: Kyle Cathie, 1996), p. 186.

24. Robinson, *Oxford Companion to Wine,* pp. 333, 334.

25. Per-Henrik Mansson, "Behind the Breakup," *Wine Spectator,* February 15, 1993, p. 24. Aubert de Villaine believed that Lalou Bize-Leroy was enhancing the reputation and price of her négociant wines at the expense of DRC's wines. Additionally, de Villaine was concerned that she might be adversely affecting the price of DRC's full line of wines by selling its finest and most expensive wines separately rather than making them available only in mixed cases, a practice that had helped to increase the sales and price of DRC's lesser wines. If Lalou allowed the most expensive wines to be sold separately in markets where she had exclusive rights, de Villaine also feared that a pricing disparity would develop for the same wines in different global markets, creating problems with customers in the United States and the United Kingdom. Although his fears were not unfounded, Lalou categorically denied responsibility for the difficulties and in fact disclaimed any knowledge of or participation in these market schemes. Instead, she averred that persons to whom she had sold wine were conducting gray-market operations without her authorization and after she was no longer in control of the wine. When DRC was sued by American customers and forced to pay millions of dollars to compensate them for price discrepancies created by differential marketing patterns in other regions of the world, truth became irrelevant and her protestations of innocence were of no avail.

26. Richard Olney, *Romanée-Conti: The World's Most Fabled Wine* (New York: Rizzoli, 1991), p. 60. In a most unfortunate turn of fate, Charles died soon after in an accident and was replaced by his younger brother, Henri Frédéric.

27. Per-Henrik Mansson, "Bize-Leroy Loses Suit in Bitter Burgundy Feud," *Wine Spectator,* November 15, 1992, p. 9.

28. Biodynamic farming practices are referred to as homeopathic medicine for the vineyard. Founded by Rudolf Steiner in 1924, biodynamics considers the earth a living, breathing, and balanced organism, interrelated and in tune with the spiritual forces of the cosmos. To facilitate a harmonious balance between themselves, plants, soil, and the universe as well as a renewal of natural life forces, advocates of biodynamics incorporate the calendar and the signs of the zodiac into the timing of their farming activities. Like organic farming, biodynamic practices do not allow synthetic pesticides. They also mandate se-

vere pruning of vines to reduce yields (Dave Broom, "Heads in the Stars," *Decanter,* September 1999, p. 68).

29. Pichon Longueville was the dowry given to Térèse de Pichon Longueville. Through egalitarian inheritance practices, it was eventually divided into two distinct wineries, one male (Pichon Longueville Baron) and the other female (Pichon Longueville Comtesse de Lalande). Pichon Longueville Comtesse de Lalande was named for Virginie de Pichon Longueville, who inherited and managed the firm after 1850. In the twentieth century, the Pichon Longueville and Lalande families died out, and the winery was passed from aunts to nieces (information supplied by the winery).

30. Colin Parnell, "Madame May-Eliane De Lencquesaing," *Decanter,* March 1994, p, 35.

31. Patrick Forbes, *Champagne: The Wine, the Land, and the People* (New York: Reynal, 1967), pp. 469, 470.

32. Don Kladstrup and Petie Kladstrup, *Wine and War: The French, the Nazis, and the Battle for France's Greatest Treasure* (New York: Broadway Books, 2001), p. 141.

5. *LE DONNE DEL VINO*

1. Joseph Bastianich and David Lynch, *Vino Italiano: The Regional Wines of Italy* (New York: Clarkson Potter, 2002), pp. 7, 9.

2. Information obtained from the Italian Trade Commission, 33 East Sixty-seventh Street, New York, New York, 10021.

3. Sheldon Wasserman and Pauline Wasserman, *Italy's Noble Red Wines,* 2nd ed. (New York: Macmillan, 1991), p. xxxi.

4. Bastianich and Lynch, *Vino Italiano,* pp. 10, 11.

5. Karen MacNeil, *The Wine Bible* (New York: Workman, 2001), pp. 320–323; information obtained from the Italian Trade Commission.

6. MacNeil, *Wine Bible,* p. 320.

7. Technically, the first challenge to DOC regulations was Sassicaia, a cabernet-based wine produced by Piero Antinori's cousin, Marchese Mario Incisa della Rocchetta, in the Tuscan coastal area of Bolgheri. Tignanello, nevertheless, is considered the primary regulatory challenger because it was produced within the Chianti zone but defied Chianti restrictions by adding some cabernet sauvignon to the sangiovese-based wine (ibid., p. 378).

8. Victor Hazan, *Italian Wine* (New York: Alfred A. Knopf, 1982), p. 52.

9. MacNeil, *Wine Bible,* pp. 316, 320.

10. In a book devoted to wine rather than to women in the wine industry, one would add the region of Veneto, which is famous for Amarone and Valpolicella.

11. Bastianich and Lynch, *Vino Italiano,* pp. 10, 11, 195, 198.

12. Ibid., p. 198.

13. *Italian Wines 2003* (New York: Gambero Rosso, 2003), p. 40.

14. Daniele Cernilli, Fabbio Rizzari, and Marco Sabellico, "The Lords of the Vines," *Gambero Rosso,* no. 14, 1998, p. 65.

15. Michèlle Shah, "Prima Donna," *Decanter,* May 2002, p. 33.

16. Tom Mueller, "Grape Expectations," *Hemisphere Magazine,* January 2001, p. 39.

17. Shah, "Prima Donna," p. 33.

18. Daniele Cernilli, "A Chianti Life," *Gambero Rosso,* no. 33, 2003, p. 21.

19. "Lungarotti Sisters Embody New Face of Italian Wines," press release, February 10, 2000, Public Relations Department, Paterno Imports, Tangley Oaks, Lake Bluff, Illinois.

20. Ibid.

21. Doreen Schmid, "Italy's Women of Wine," *Quarterly Review of Wines,* Autumn 1989, pp. 34, 36.

22. Official material supplied by the secretariat of Le Donne del Vino.

23. The first recipient of the Le Donne del Vino Women in Wine Award was Jane Hunter, managing director/viticulturist of Hunter's in New Zealand ("Treasured Hunter," *Harpers Supplement: Treasured Trophies,* October 2003, p. 19).

24. Official material supplied by Beate Klingenmeier, president of Vinissima.

25. Giles MacDonogh, "They're Back," *Decanter,* December 1998, p. 113; Stephen Tanzer, *International Wine Cellar,* November/December 2004, p. 53.

26. "Erste Diplom-Ingenieurin für Weinbau," *Der Deutsche Weinbau,* no. 4, February 28, 2003, p. 34.

27. Official material supplied by Beate Klingenmeier, president of Vinissima.

6. THE NEW WORLD: CALIFORNIA

1. Passed on October 28, 1919, over the veto of President Woodrow Wilson, the Volstead Act (*National Prohibition Act of 1919,* Public Law 41, 66th Cong., *U.S. Statutes at Large* [1919]: pt. 1, 305–323) prohibited "beverages which contain one-half of 1 per centum or more of alcohol by volume." It allowed three

major exemptions, for religious use, medicinal use, and domestic use, which was defined as wine made at home by "male heads of households," who could "make up to two hundred gallons of wine per year legally, provided that this wine was not intended for commercial use." See "Volstead Act," http://college.hmco.com/history/readerscomp/rcah/html/ah_089600_volsteadact.htm; "Volstead Act: 1920," www.multied.com/documents/volstead.html; Robert C. Fuller, *Religion and Wine: A Cultural History of Wine Drinking in the United States* (Knoxville: University of Tennessee Press, 1996), pp. 92–93.

Ratified by conventions in the required three-quarters of the states (rather than by state legislatures), the Twenty-first Amendment nullified the Volstead Act in 1933 (Stanley K. Schultz, "The Politics of Prohibition: The 1920s," http://us.history.wisc.edu/hist102/lectures/lecture17.html). However, the Twenty-first Amendment allowed states to continue Prohibition's restrictions within their borders and excluded alcoholic beverages, including wine, from protections regarding interstate commerce (Ralph Burton Hutchinson, "The California Wine Industry" [PhD diss., University of California at Los Angeles, 1969], p. 184). The Supreme Court ended this protection in 2005.

2. This quote is attributed to Nellie McClung (1873–1951), a Canadian journalist, suffragist, and member of the Women's Christian Temperance Union (Teresa Wippel, "President's Message," Association for Women in Communications, Seattle branch, newsletter, September 2001, www.seattleawc.org/prez_msg_sept01.html).

3. "Winery Locator by State within the USA," www.allamericanwineries.com/AAWMain/locate.htm; Wine Institute, "Key Facts: California Wine Industry Statistical Highlights," www.wineinstitute.org/communications/statistics/stathio1.htm; Wine Institute, "Economic Importance of California Wine Is $33 Billion to State," news release, January 20, 2000, www.wineinstitute.org/communications/statistics/economicimportance.htm.

4. California's commercial wine production began in the early 1830s, when the missions were secularized (Hutchinson, "California Wine Industry," p. 137).

5. Victor W. Geraci, "Grape Growing to Vintibusiness: A History of the Santa Barbara, California, Regional Wine Industry, 1965–1995" (PhD diss., University of California at Santa Barbara, 1997), pp. viii, ix. Prohibition reduced the number of wineries in California from 700 to 140 (Karen MacNeil, *The Wine Bible* [New York: Workman, 2001], p. 630; Fuller, *Religion and Wine,* p. 94).

6. Geraci, "Grape Growing," p. ix; Tim Unwin, *Wine and the Vine: An Historical Geography of Viticulture and the Wine Trade* (London: Routledge, 1991), pp. 24, 25.

7. James T. Lapsley, *Bottled Poetry: Napa Winemaking from Prohibition to the Modern Era* (Berkeley: University of California Press, 1996), pp. 203, 204. The California wines that starred in Paris were the 1973 Cabernet Sauvignon from Stag's Leap Wine Cellars and the 1973 Chardonnay from Chateau Montelena. Neither winery was even ten years old at the time of the tasting. According to William Heintz, a California wine historian, California wines first competed with French wines in the 1889 World Exposition in Paris. At that time, a medal was given to John Wineburger, even though he had died many years before and the wine had been made by his widow (Blake Green, "The Women behind Those Vineyards," *San Francisco Chronicle,* June 24, 1976).

8. Josephine Tychson founded her winery in 1886. See Dolly Prchal, "Josephine Marlin Tychson: The First Woman Winemaker in California," *Napa County Historical Society Gleanings* 4, no. 3 (December 1986): preface, 2.

9. Su Hua Newton speaks English, French, Chinese, and Japanese. She holds a bachelor's degree from Cambridge University in England, a master's degree in clinical and industrial psychology from Victoria University in New Zealand, an MD and a PhD from London University, and a degree in French literature from the Sorbonne.

10. Dana Nigro and staff, "LVMH Takes Controlling Stake in Napa and Aussie Wineries," *Wine Spectator,* March 31, 2001, www.winespectator.com/Wine/Archives/Show_Article/0,1275,3140,00.html.

11. "Krispy Kreme Restructures Board to Establish an Independent Majority; Announces Board of Directors Appointment," press release, April 27, 2003, http://phx.corporate-ir.net/phoenix.zhtml?c=120929&p=irol-newsArticle&ID=609912&highlight=.

12. Delia is now a twice-divorced mother of four who speaks the major romance languages, has a PhD in philosophy from the Sorbonne, an MBA from the University of California at Berkeley, and an MS in finance from MIT. She has also completed several courses at the University of California at Davis, although she did not receive a degree from that institution.

13. Christine Austin, "A Woman's Touch," *Hilton Guest,* no. 1, 2000, p. 64.

14. MacNeil, *Wine Bible,* p. 646.

15. Eryn Brown, "Breaking the Wineglass Ceiling," *Fortune,* August 14, 2000, pp. 222, 224.

16. Leon Adams, *The Wines of America,* 4th ed. (New York: McGraw-Hill, 1990), p. ix.

17. Pierre Spahni, *The International Wine Trade,* 2nd ed. (Cambridge: Woodhead, 2000), p. 31.

18. Jane Fuhrman, "Women Winemakers Barreling to the Top," *San Francisco Chronicle,* October 6, 2000, p. 3.

19. Zelma Long founded the original Goddesses, an informal group of women in the wine industry and related fields who celebrated life and their achievements through group activities such as rafting, hiking, camping, and riding (Zelma R. Long, "The Past Is the Beginning of the Future: Simi Winery in Its Second Century," interview by Carole Hicks, oral history transcript, 1992, Regional Oral History Office, Bancroft Library, University of California at Berkeley, p. vi; introduction by Ann Noble). As applied to the current group of women consulting winemakers, the term "Goddesses" is attributable to Jane Fuhrman ("Women Winemakers," p. 3).

20. Norm Roby, "A New Breed of Winemaker," *Wine News,* June/July 1995, p. 17. Other women such as Celia Welch Masyczek could also be added to this list.

21. Fuhrman, "Women Winemakers," p. 3.

22. Andrew Essex, "The Golden Grape Awards," *Food & Wine,* October 1998, p. 82.

23. Roby, "New Breed," p. 20.

24. Ibid., p. 18.

25. Dan Berger, "Drink, Wine, Brothers, and Song," *Los Angeles Times,* August 19, 1998, p. 9.

26. Linda Murphy, "Winemaker of the Year," December 9, 2004, www.news .ucdavis.edu/in_the_news/full_text/view_clip.lasso?id=9927.

27. Jason Pahlmeyer, an owner for whom Helen Turley once worked, said, "Helen is famous for her low tolerance and lack of diplomacy. She has burnt a lot of bridges storming out of vineyards telling growers they're stupid. I just used to follow in her trail and pick up the dead bodies" (John Stimpfig and Susan Keevil, "The Woman Who Outsold Bordeaux," *Decanter,* August 2000, p. 31).

28. Richard Paul Hinkle, "From Gunslinger to 'Winegrower Counselor,'" *Wines & Vines,* August 1994, p. 32.

29. Steve Pitcher, "Napa Valley's Most Coveted Cabs (and the People Who Make Them)," *Wine News,* June/July 1997, www.thewinenews.com/ junjul97napacabs.htm.

30. Roby, "New Breed," p. 23. Hinkle, "Gunslinger," pp. 13, 32; Jerry Shriver, "Coaxing Greatness from Grapes: Turley Fine Wines Put Taste over Technology," *USA Today,* July 8, 1997, p. D1

31. James Conaway, *Napa: The Story of an American Eden* (New York: Avon Books, 1990), pp. 111, 112.

32. Tim Tesconi, "Vintners' Daughters," *Santa Rosa Press-Democrat,* September 20, 1998, p. A1.

33. Renée Edelman, "When Little Sister Means Business," *Working Woman,* February 1990, pp. 82, 83, 88.

34. Tesconi, "Vintners' Daughters," p. A6

35. Ibid.

36. Cheryll Aimee Barron, *Dreamers of the Valley of Plenty* (New York: Scribners, 1995), pp. 220, 241; Conaway, *Napa,* p. 372; Lapsley, *Bottled Poetry,* pp. 221, 222.

37. Linda Rieff has been executive director of the Napa Valley Vintners Association since 1995. Born into a farming and winemaking family, she gained the requisite experience for this position as a congressional staff member and journalist (Kathie Fowler, "Linda Rieff and the NVVA: A Perfect Fit to Lead Vintners on Critical Issues," *Spring Valley Times,* Joseph Phelps Vineyards seasonal newsletter, Fall–Winter 2002, pp. 2, 6). Other women who have held senior positions in major California wine industry organizations include Margaret Shahenian, who in 1975 became the first woman elected to the board of directors of the Wine Institute; Dianne S. Nury, who chaired the Wine Institute in 1998–1999; and Karen Ross, who assumed the presidency of the California Association of Winegrape Growers (CAWG) ("Margaret Shahenian: A Woman of Many 'Firsts,'" *Wines & Vines,* July 1975, p. 24; Tesconi, "Vintners' Daughters," p. A1; Larry Walker, "Larry Walker Talks with Karen Ross," *Wines & Vines,* June 1998, p. 16).

38. Barron, *Dreamers,* p. 25.

39. Alan Goldfarb, "Di Vine," *Guest West,* October 1993, p. 8.

40. "Winemaker of the Year: Mia Klein," *Food & Wine,* October 2003, p. 139.

41. The educational activities of WWS included Wine Appreciation Week, celebrated in February since 1993; the Trunk Show, a traveling exhibit used in schools to teach children about viticultural history; a speakers' bureau; and local, regional, and national conferences.

42. Unpublished statement distributed by Women for WineSense in 1995.

43. See www.womenforwinesense.org.

44. Larry Walker, "Women for Winesense," *Wines & Vines,* November 2001, www.findarticles.com/cf_dls/m3488/11_82/80234987.

45. Goldfarb, "Di Vine," p. 9.

46. Jean T. Barrett, "Climbing the Vine," *Market Watch,* November 1991, p. 26.

47. Caroline E. Mayer, "Women Break Barriers at Wineries," *St. Louis Post-Dispatch,* July 2, 1994, p. D4.

48. Barrett, "Climbing the Vine," p. 26.

49. With the assistance of Champagne Taittinger and Domaine Carneros, Eileen created La Rêve (The Dream) Foundation, named after her premier sparkling wine, to provide two annual scholarships for two thousand dollars (one at the Culinary Institute of America, Greystone; and one at the UC Davis Department of Viticulture and Enology) to further women's careers as chefs and winemakers.

50. Jay Stuller and Glen Martin, *Through the Grapevine: The Real Story behind America's $8 Billion Wine Industry* (New York: HarperCollins West, 1994), p. 181.

51. Long, "The Past Is the Beginning," p. viii.

52. Stuller and Martin, *Through the Grapevine,* p. 183.

53. Paul Franson, "Wine, Women, and Strong," *San Francisco Examiner,* July 5, 1998, p. D4.

54. Randy Sheahan, "Zelma Long and the New Simi," *Quarterly Review of Wines,* Autumn 1987, p. 30.

55. *California Wine Pioneers,* 1995 ed. (San Francisco: *Wine Spectator* Scholarship Fund/M. Shanken Communications, 1994), p. 19; Long, "The Past Is the Beginning," p. 88.

56. Linda Murphy, "Ten Leading Ladies," *Decanter,* October 2001, www .decanter.com/archive/4445.html

57. Conaway, *Napa,* p. 354.

58. According to Catalyst, an organization that studies women in business, only 744 of the largest 1,000 corporations in the United States had at least one woman on their board of directors in 2001. Of these firms, only 317 had more than one female director. Catalyst projected that, at the current pace, women's representation on the boards of these corporations would reach 25 percent by 2027 (Catalyst for Women, "Catalyst Charts Growth of Women on America's Corporate Boards," December 4, 2001, www.charitywire.com/charity34/02605.html).

7. THE NEW WORLD: THE SOUTHERN HEMISPHERE

1. Hrayr Berberoglu, *New World Wine Producing Countries* (Toronto: Food and Beverage Consultants, 2001), p. vi.

2. "Centenary of Federation Wine Project," brochure, National Wine Centre of Australia/Winemakers' Federation of Australia, 2001; Berberoglu, *New World,* p. 60.

3. John Shaw, "Constellation Brands Agrees to Buy Australian Winery," *New York Times,* January 18, 2003, p. B3.

4. Berberoglu, *New World,* p. 59. While retaining high yields in order to keep prices competitively low, Australians have also adopted various technological innovations for designing good wines, including increasing grape juice concentration by removing excess water through vacuum concentration; eliminating the cost and risk associated with heavy pruning in the vineyard; removing excess alcohol with spinning cones; adding alcohol to perk up flabby wines or powdered tannins to give red wines structure; and using sawdust or woodchips to add oak flavor without the expense of purchasing barrels or aging wines (Frank J. Prial, " 'Making Sense' Still Making Sense," *New York Times,* October 8, 2003, p. D6). Another recent innovation widely adopted in Australia and New Zealand is the replacement of traditional corks by screw caps on high-end bottles in order to prevent them from becoming corked.

5. Berberoglu, *New World,* pp. 67, 88; Prial, " 'Making Sense,' " p. D6; Shaw, "Constellation Brands," p. B3.

6. For information on the number of wineries, see "Centenary of Federation Wine Project"; and Australian Wine and Brandy Corporation, "Australian Wine Industry at a Glance," www.awbc.com.au/winefacts/data/free.asp?subcatid= 93. On the growth of boutique wineries, see John Beeston, *A Concise History of Australian Wine* (St. Leonards, New South Wales: Allen and Unwin, 1994), pp. 234, 235.

7. Jeni Port, *Crushed by Women: Women and Wine* (Melbourne: Arcadia, 2000), p. 10.

8. Ibid., pp. 21, 22, 23.

9. Vintage Cellars, "Winemaker of the Year," *Cellar News,* September 2000, www.vintagecellars.com.au/shared/html/sec/cellar/archive/winemaker.htm.

10. Berberoglu, *New World,* p. 89.

11. "Yalumba: Winemakers," www.yalumba.com/content.asp?p=209.

12. Modeled after European wine fraternities, the Barons of the Barossa, whose motto is "Glory to Barossa," is an organization that promotes and protects regional traditions. Its members are selected for life (WinePros, "Barons of Barossa: The Winds of Change Dinner," March 21, 2003, www.winepros .com.au/jsp/cda/authors/article.jsp?ID=5018; membership list provided by Stephen Henschke).

13. "Yalumba: Winemakers."

14. The program consisted of an intensive two-week course followed by teamwork, several months of individual assignments, and an exam. Two other

women from Yalumba, an accountant and a director of international sales from New Zealand, were selected along with Louisa.

15. According to Jarvis, Australia's parental leave policy guarantees a twelve-month leave to the child's primary caregiver at a salary to be negotiated with the employer.

16. Cosima Marriner, "Part-Time Workplace: Labor's Bid for Women," *Sydney Morning Herald,* January 26, 2004, p. 4.

17. *The American Heritage Dictionary of the English Language,* 4th ed. (New York: Houghton Mifflin, 2000); www.bartleby.com/61/92/M0379250.html.

18. The classification of Hill of Grace as an iconic Australian wine (a most highly sought-after and prized wine) was made by Langton's Fine Wine Auctions and is not an official Australian designation, according to Prue Henschke.

19. Ray Jordan, "Best Western," *Decanter,* February 2004, p. 35.

20. R. W. Apple Jr., "From a Granite Coast, Velvet Wines," *New York Times,* January 2, 2002, p. B13.

21. Founded in 1965, Vasse Felix, the region's first winery, is now a subsidiary of Heytesbury Pty Ltd., chaired by Janet Holmes à Court ("Janet Holmes à Court," www.abc.net.au/btn/australians/acourt.htm).

22. Richard Woodham, "Di Cullen Dies," *Decanter,* March 4, 2003, www .decanter.com/news/46162.html.

23. Huon Hooke, "Pioneers of the West," *Australian Gourmet Traveller,* October/November 2003, p. 90.

24. "Di Cullen: A Life of Passion," *Scoop: The Essential Western Australian Lifestyle Magazine,* no. 24, Winter 2003.

25. Until 1998, Cullen Wines was a partnership in which the six Cullen children owned the land, while their parents, Di and Kevin, owned the business and winery contents. Starting in 1999, Cullen Wines became a company in which all family members held equal shares, with Vanya becoming the managing director.

26. Huon Hooke is quoted in the announcement of the award on the Cullen Web site; see Cullen Wines, "Qantas/*The Wine Magazine* Winemaker of the Year Award 2000," www.cullenwines.com.au/pages/qwoty.htm. For Spurrier's assessment, see Steven Spurrier, "Spurrier's Choice," *Decanter,* February 2004, p. 56. Spurrier is well known for having staged the Paris tasting of 1976 at which California wines were judged superior to French wines.

27. Peter Forrestal quoted in the Vintage Cellars announcement of the award (Vintage Cellars, "Winemaker of the Year"). This award is particularly signif-

icant because it is one of the few that considers all the nation's winemakers, regardless of winery size.

28. Otto Pohl, "New Zealand Stokes Its Wine Ambitions," *New York Times,* March 3, 2004, p. W7. In 2004, land prices for vineyard acreage in New Zealand averaged forty thousand dollars per acre, compared to seventy thousand dollars in California.

29. The number of wineries increased from 293 in 1998 to 398 in 2002. From 1998 to 2002, the value of New Zealand's wine exports jumped by 250 percent, from NZ\$97.6333 million to NZ\$246.413 million (New Zealand Wines Online, "Overview," www.nzwine.com/statistics/overview.php3). By 2004, foreign investment had gained partial ownership of 85 percent of New Zealand's wineries (Pohl, "New Zealand," p. W1).

30. Caroline Courtney, *Wine in New Zealand* (Auckland: Random House New Zealand, 2003), pp. 11, 12, 13.

31. Pohl, "New Zealand," p. W7. As Pohl reports, Pinot Noir also may be a major component of New Zealand's global appeal in the future.

32. New Zealand Wines Online, "Wine Exports," www.nzwine.com/statistics/exports1.php3.

33. Michael Cooper, "In the Wake of Ernie Hunter," *North & South,* September 1988, pp. 117, 158; Cynthia Brooks, *Marlborough Wines and Vines,* vol. 1 (Wellington: Graham and Cynthia Brooks, 1992), pp. 96, 97; Yvonne Dasler, "Jane Hunter," *MORE,* p. 139.

34. Graham Kitty, "Vin Superieur," *International Business,* October 1993, p. 22.

35. "Treasured Hunter," *Harpers Supplement: Treasured Trophies,* October 2003, p. 19.

36. "Top International Award for Jane," *Hunter's Club Newsletter,* Summer 2003.

37. Port, *Crushed by Women,* p. 119.

38. Berberoglu, *New World,* p. 96.

39. "All of a Ferment," *Massey,* November 2001, http://masseynews.massey.ac.nz/magazine/2001_Nov/stories/cover_story.html.

40. Tracey Barker, "Women-Only Wine Group Launches in New Zealand," *Decanter,* October 9, 2002, www.decanter.com/news/46278.html.

41. Berberoglu, *New World,* p. 103.

42. "Sonador Wines: History," www.sonadorwines.com/default.asp?V_DOC_ID=834.

43. Christopher Fielden, *The Wines of Argentina, Chile, and Latin America* (London: Mitchell Beazley, 2003), pp. 11, 13.

44. Fincas Patagónicas Bodega Tapiz, "Argentina: History of Winemaking," www.tapiz.com/argentina.

45. David Sax with James Molesworth, "Argentina's Wine Industry Rises above Country's Economic Crisis," *Wine Spectator,* January 30, 2004, www.wine spectator.com/Wine/Daily/News/0,1145,2330,00.html. Moët and Chandon invested in Argentina in 1959 originally to make sparkling wine but expanded into still wine in 1999 at Bodega Terrazas, where they partnered with Cheval Blanc. Following a pattern set in California, Moët and Chandon chose a woman, Margareth Henriquez, as the president of this New World operation (John Downes, "The Fab Four: Argentine Producers," *Decanter,* February 2004, p. 40, www.decanter.com/archive/article.php?id=47623).

46. Michael Schachner, "A Giant Awakens in South America," *Wine Enthusiast,* October 2001, www.winemag.com/ME2/dirmod.asp?sid=&nm=&type=Publishing&mod=Publications%3A%3AArticle&mid=8F3A7027421841978F1 8BE895F87F791&tier=4&id=D04244EC39584E319BFB99B387150415.

47. R. W. Apple, "Mile-High Vineyards Reach the Stars," *The Age,* July 16, 2002, www.theage.com.au/articles/2002/07/16/1026185175197.html.

48. Joshua Goodman, "Don't Cry for These Argentine Wines," *Business Week,* October 14, 2002, p. 162.

49. Laura Catena describes her father's views in Emma Clark, "Mixing Wine with Medicine," BBC News Online, October 3, 2002, http://news.bbc.co.uk/1/hi/business/2261885.stm.

50. James Molesworth, "Catena and Rothschild Release Their First Joint Wine," *Wine Spectator,* October 25, 2002, www.winespectator.com/Wine/Daily/News/0,1145,1868,00.html.

51. Clark, "Mixing Wine with Medicine."

52. Susana is careful to point out that three women in fact preceded her as winemakers, although all three left Argentina in order to make wine.

53. Labels on the bottles of Luca wines display her husband's McDermott family crest in the background.

54. Viña Santa Carolina, "Chilean Wine History," www.vscwine.com/aboutchile/history.htm; Viña Santa Carolina, "The Land," www.vscwine.com/aboutchile/land.htm; Hubrecht Duijker, *The Wines of Chile* (Utrecht: Uitgeverij Het Spectrum B.V./Segrave Foulkes, 1999), p. 13.

55. Duijker, *Wines of Chile,* p. 13.

56. Ibid., p. 14; Saratoga Wine Exchange, "Chilean Wine History," www

.saratogawinex.com/chilean-wine.htm#his; Viña Santa Carolina, "Chilean Wine History."

57. "Visit Chile," www.visitchile.com/detalle_noticia.asp?codigo_noticia= 8&idioma=ing.

58. Duijker, *Wines of Chile,* p. 14.

59. Berberoglu, *New World,* p. 135.

60. Saratoga Wine Exchange, "Chilean Wine History"; Jeff Morgan, "Mad Rush to Chile by California and French Vintners," *Wine Spectator,* May 31, 1996, www.winespectator.com/Wine/Archives/Show_Article/0,1275,831,00.html.

61. Berberoglu, *New World,* p. 142.

62. Viña Errazuriz, "Chilean Wine History," www.errazurizwines.com/ Chilean%20Wine%20History.htm; Thomas Matthews, "New Directions in Chile," *Wine Spectator,* June 30, 1997, www.winespectator.com/Wine/Archives/ Show_Article/0,1275,1276,00.html.

63. Thomas Matthews, "Chile's Two Worlds of Wine," *Wine Spectator,* June 15, 1995, www.winespectator.com/Wine/Archives/Show_Article/0,1275,457,00 .html.

64. For information about Gaetone Carron, see Richard L. Elia, "Concho y Toro's Bonne Femme," *Quarterly Review of Wines,* Winter 1995, pp. 26, 28. To learn about the career of María del Pilar González Tamargo, see Carmen, "Winemakers," www.carmen.com/OpenDocs/asp/pagDefault.asp?boton= Doc86&argInstanciaId=86&argCarpetaId=&argTreeNodoSel=. For a description of the work of Consuelo Marín Gamé, see Viña Santa Carolina, "Consuelo Marín Gamé, Winemaker," www.vscwine.com/about/winemaker.htm. For background on Cecilia Torres, see Viña Santa Rita, "Winemakers," www.santarita .com/tour7.asp.

65. Fielden, *Wines,* p. 140.

66. The Marnier-Lapostolle family owns the largest personal botanical garden in the world.

67. Duijker, *Wines of Chile,* p. 128.

68. Graham Knox, *Wines of South Africa* (Vlaeberg: Fernwood Press, 2002), p. 20.

69. National Library of South Africa, "Fruits of the Vine: Empowerment," www.nlsa.ac.za/vine/empowerment.html.

70. Wendy Toerien, *Wines and Vineyards of South Africa* (Cape Town: Struik, 2000), p. 6; Susan Low, "New Breed of South African Winemakers," *Wines & Vines,* November 2001, www.findarticles.com/cf_dls/m3488/11_82/80234972/ print.jhtml; Knox, *Wines of South Africa,* p. 29.

71. Low, "New Breed."

72. Since 1975, the Nederburg Auction has been the premier event of the South African wine calendar. It is intended to promote higher standards for South African wines, to develop international awareness of the country's wines, and to ensure an equitable distribution of fine rare wines (Martin Fuller, "News from the Cape Winelands," www.wineloverspage.com/martinfuller/martin032500.shtml; "Women Winemakers Make a Stand at Nederburg Auction," March 30, 2001, http://iafrica.com/highlife/herlife/news/250851.htm). "All of South Africa's estates, wineries and co-operatives are invited to submit a wide range of categories of their finest wines each year. These are carefully vetted and sampled by the tasting panel, whose strictly applied criteria ensure that only the Cape's finest wines are entered into the auction each year" (James Seely, *The Wines of South Africa* [London: Faber and Faber, 1997], p. 184).

73. "SA Pinot Producer: WhaleHaven," www.megweb.uct.ac.za/ell400w/students/projects/reviewed/pinotnoir/whalehaven1.htm.

74. Flagship Wines, "Weingut: Morgenhof Estate," www.flagshipwines.ch/d/John_Platter/JP_Morgenhof.htm.

75. Lilyane Weston, "How South Africa Has Developed into a Major Wine Maker," *Bucks Free Press,* January 3, 2002, www.bucksfreepress.co.uk/search/display.var.33205.0.how_south_africa_has_developed_into_a_major_wine_maker.php; Southern Starz, "Morgenhof," www.southernstarz.com/vineyard.cfm?preview=500.

76. "New Winemaker Heralds New Era at Bilton Wines," www.wine.co.za/directory/news.aspx?newsid=7119&producerid=4293.

77. Low, "New Breed."

78. See "Ronell Wiid," www.wine.co.za/Directory/Contact.aspx?CONTACTID=230&PRODUCERID=1102; "Wine, Women, and Song," *Sunday Times* (Cape Town), November 21, 1999, www.sundaytimes.co.za/1999/11/21/lifestyle/life03.htm.

79. Toerien, *Wines and Vineyards,* p. 6. Vision 2020 was developed in 1999 by Winetech (Wine Industry Network of Expertise and Technology) to help create strategies that would make the South African wine industry "innovation driven, market directed, globally competitive, and highly profitable, while retaining strong cultural roots, instituting ethical trade practices and meaningful social responsibility programmes, and implementing strategies for affirmative action" ("Wines of South Africa: Transformation of the Wine Industry," www.wosa.co.za/sa/industry_plan.htm).

80. National Library of South Africa, "Fruits of the Vine: Empowerment."

81. Melvyn Minnaar, "A Trio of Firsts Signals Shift in South Africa's Wine Industry," *Wine Spectator,* December 31, 1999, www.winespectator.com/Wine/ Archives/Show_Article/0,1275,2350,00.html.

8. KNOWLEDGE IS POWER

1. Nicholas Wade, "Vintage Genetics Turns Out to Be Ordinaire," *New York Times,* November 23, 1999, Science Times, p. 1.

2. Jeni Port, *Crushed by Women: Women and Wine* (Melbourne: Arcadia, 2000), p. 82.

3. "Dr. Ann C. Noble: She's a 'First,'" *Wines and Vines,* April 1974, p. 24.

4. Richard P. Vine et al., *Winemaking: From Grape Growing to Marketplace* (New York: Chapman and Hall, 1997), pp. 353, 354.

5. Hugh Johnson, *The World Atlas of Wine,* 4th ed. (New York: Simon and Schuster, 1994), p. 45.

6. Ibid.

7. Vine et al., *Winemaking,* p. 353.

8. Ralph Burton Hutchinson, "The California Wine Industry" (PhD diss., University of California at Los Angeles, 1969), p. 14.

9. "Dr. Hildegard Heymann," http://wineserver.ucdavis.edu/people/faculty .php?id=9.

10. Wade, "Vintage Genetics," p. 1.

11. Nicholas Wade, "DNA Testing Digs Up Lowly Roots of an Aristocratic Wine Grape," *International Herald Tribune,* September 4–5, 1999, pp. 1, 6.

12. Linda Murphy, "Ten Leading Ladies," *Decanter,* October 2001, www .decanter.com/archive/44445.html. Carole Meredith's work on the origins of zinfandel is described in depth in Charles L. Sullivan's *Zinfandel: A History of a Grape and Its Wine* (Berkeley: University of California Press, 2003), pp. 156–165.

13. Wade, "Vintage Genetics," pp. 1, 2; "In Vino Veritas," *The Economist,* February 24–March 2, 2001, p. 82; "What Is a Microsatellite?" www.geocities.com/ jsonnentag/iguana/microsat.htm; Genetics Home Reference, "Microsatellite: Glossary Entry," ghr.nlm.nih.gov/ghr/glossary/microsatellite.

14. Wade, "Vintage Genetics," p. 2

15. Murphy, "Ten Leading Ladies."

16. See www.ucdmc.ucdavis.edu/pulse/scripts/99_00/wine_health_research .html.

17. "Wine Expert Marian Baldy Tastes National Success," *Inside Chico State*

3, no. 8, December 12, 2002, www.csuchico.edu/pub/inside/archive/02_12_12/03_wine.html.

18. Fife Vineyards, "Karen MacNeil," www.fifevineyards.com/fife/kfbio.html.

19. Irene Sax, "Master Mind," *New York Newsday,* August 11, 1991, p. 69.

20. Sam Perkins, "Noses Seek Wine Geekdom's Biggest Prize," *New York Times,* April 7, 2004, pp. D1, D4. The High Certificate exam of the Wine and Spirit Education Trust is a two-year diploma course. Because it serves as a preliminary test to qualify for the MW exam, it is recommended for those who choose to sit for the MW (Leslie Brenner, "The Grape Communicator," *Avenue,* January 1995, p. 55). In the United States, however, there are no requirements regarding preparatory courses.

21. Perkins, "Noses," p. D4; Fred Ferretti, "A Gourmet at Large: Master of Wine—Mary Ewing-Mulligan," *Gourmet,* August 1998, p. 57.

22. Sax, "Master Mind," p. 69.

23. Institute of Masters of Wine, "About the IMW," www.masters-of-wine.org/about.aspx.

24. Jancis Robinson, *Tasting Pleasure: Confessions of a Wine Lover* (New York: Viking Penguin, 1997), p. 192. Sax ("Master Mind," p. 69) notes the 1988 change.

25. Robinson, *Tasting Pleasure,* p. 202.

26. Institute of Masters of Wine, "About the IMW." Appendix 2 provides a list of the fifty-seven women who were MWs in 2005.

27. For the mid-1980s figures, see Robinson, *Tasting Pleasure,* p. 192; for the 2005 statistics, see Institute of Masters of Wine, "IMW Members: Who Are Members?" www.masters-of-wine.org/MembersWhoAre.aspx.

28. This partnership was described at www.masters-of-wine.org/asp/IMWnewsindexBODY.asp?Action=View+NewsID=161 (accessed April 8, 2004; no longer available).

29. "Ewing-Mulligan to Head Prestigious Wine Programs in U.S.," *Wine & Spirits,* December 2003, p. 14.

30. See International Wine Center, "About International Wine Center," www.learnwine.com/aboutus2.asp.

31. Pierre Spahni, *The International Wine Trade,* 2d ed. (Cambridge: Woodhead, 2000), p. 84.

32. Paul Levy, "Wine Women," p. 11 (William F. Heintz Archives, Napa Valley Wine Library, St. Helena, Calif.; source unknown).

33. Jancis Robinson, ed., *The Oxford Companion to Wine* (New York: Oxford

University Press, 1994), p. 1012; Price quoted from her autobiography, *Woman of Taste: Memoirs from the Wine World* (London: John Murray, 1990), p. 2.

34. Price, *Woman of Taste,* pp. 25, 53, 156.

35. Ibid., pp. 18, 3, 82, 3, 91, 51, 197, 198, 96.

36. See Andrew Jefford, "Wine, Geography, and Transport," in *A Century of Wine: The Story of a Wine Revolution,* ed. Stephen Brook (San Francisco: Wine Appreciation Guild, 2000), p. 49.

37. In 2005, Dana Nigro was promoted to senior editor.

38. Robinson, *Tasting Pleasure,* p. 205.

39. Andrew Jefford, "Jancis Robinson, MW," *Decanter,* March 1999, p. 28.

40. Robinson, *Tasting Pleasure,* p. 199.

41. Jefford, "Jancis Robinson," p. 29.

42. Robinson, *Tasting Pleasure,* p. 62.

43. "Jancis Robinson," *Financial Times* (London), January 21, 2004, http://news.ft.com/cms/s/a69472e2-b72d-11d9-9f22-00000e2511c8.html.

44. "OBE for Jancis Robinson," *Asia Cuisine: Weekly Ezine* 5, no. 26, June 21, 2003, http://asiacuisine.com.sg/ezine/ezine5-26.html.

45. Peter Garrett, "Phyllis Hands and Her Influence on the South African Wine Industry," *International Journal of Wine Marketing* 5, no. 4 (1993): 31

9. UNCORKING SALES

1. Jancis Robinson, ed., *The Oxford Companion to Wine* (New York: Oxford University Press, 1994), p. 62.

2. Jens Priewe, *Wine: From Grape to Glass,* rev ed. (New York: Abbeville Press, 2001), p. 233.

3. John Stimpfig, "Still Waters Run Deep," *Decanter,* September 2000, pp. 56–58.

4. Peter D. Meltzer, "Sotheby's Serena Sutcliffe," *Wine Spectator,* May 15, 1995, www.winespectator.com/Wine/Archives/Show_Article/0,,414,00.html.

5. Stimpfig, "Still Waters," p. 58.

6. Meltzer, "Sotheby's Serena Sutcliffe."

7. Serena Sutcliffe, "Women in Wine: A Personal View," www.sothebys.com/connoisseur/expert/ei_wiw_0900.html (no longer available). Despite her professional love of wine, Serena asserts that she "could live without wine but not without music" and would rather lose her palate than her hearing.

8. Ibid. Like several women executives in the wine industry, Serena avoided

having children in order to advance in business. Unlike the others, she refuses to hire young women of childbearing age, believing that women with children are bad risks who will not produce as much work even if they stay on the job.

9. Inaugurated in 1851, the charitable wine auction of the Hospices de Beaune is held on the third Sunday of November to raise funds for the combined charitable organizations of the Hôtel Dieu (Robinson, *Oxford Companion to Wine,* p. 494).

10. "American Charity Wine Auctions: Everyone a Winner," www.jancis robinson.com/winenews/jr413.

11. Ibid. More precisely, individuals can write off against their income tax only that portion of the auction price exceeding the fair market value of the wine.

12. Ibid. The moniker "Goddess of the Gavel" was given to Ursula in 1998 by *Food & Wine* magazine along with the Golden Grape Award that designated her as one of the ten most influential members of the wine industry (Andrew Essex, "The Golden Grape Awards," *Food & Wine,* October 1998, p. 74).

13. Kay Kipling, "Wine Bid-ness," *Sarasota Magazine,* April 1998, p. 21.

14. In the early 1990s, Ann Colgin became co-owner with her husband of Colgin-Schrader, which became one of Napa Valley's premier cult wineries when Helen Turley was hired as the winemaker. After her divorce in 1997, Ann kept the winery and vineyard and returned to the auction world as head of Sotheby's Los Angeles wine department (Jeff Morgan, "Lady in Red," *Wine Spectator,* November 30, 1997, www.winespectator.com/Wine/Archives/Show_ Article/0,1275,1479.00.html).

15. Essex, "Golden Grape Awards," p. 74.

16. Kipling, "Wine Bid-ness," p. 21.

17. Ibid.

18. The Australian Wine and Brandy Corporation (AWBC), an industry organization that helps to regulate the industry for the Australian government, authorized the Australian Wine Bureau in October 1985. By the mid-1990s, as more wineries participated in its export activities, another organization, the Australian Wine Export Council, was established in the hierarchy between the bureau and the AWBC. Hazel's activities became the European arm of the new organization.

19. Hazel accurately predicted that by mid-2004 Australian wine imports would exceed French imports in the United Kingdom on the basis of volume as well.

20. James Halliday, *A History of the Australian Wine Industry: 1949–1994* (Adelaide: Winetitles, 1994), p. 96.

21. Patrick Matthews, "Grape Britain," *Food & Wine,* April 19, 2004, www .foodandwine.com/articles/invoke.cfm?label=grape-britain.

22. Tim Atkin, "Critical Juncture," *Harpers Supplement: Australia,* January 2002, p. 2.

23. After the first wine flight in 1992, which included 110 people, sales of Australian wines in the United Kingdom rose by 77 percent. Hazel organized other tours every two years for smaller groups of journalists and sommeliers.

24. McWilliam's Wine, "Maurice O'Shea Award," www.mcwilliams.com.au/ Awards/Oshea.asp.

25. Serena Sutcliffe, *The Simon and Schuster Guide to the Wines of Burgundy* (New York: Simon and Schuster, 1992), p. 37; Per V. Jenster, Lars V. Jenster, and Neville Watchurst, *The Business of Wine: An Analysis of the Global Wine Industry* (Lausanne: SMC Publishing, CIMID SA, 1993), p. 85.

26. Sutcliffe, *Simon and Schuster Guide,* p. 34.

27. Jancis Robinson, *Tasting Pleasure: Confessions of a Wine Lover* (New York: Viking Penguin, 1997), p. 291. A substantial portion of the information regarding Jeanne Descaves is contained in the answers she provided to the questionnaire sent by the author.

28. Robinson, *Tasting Pleasure,* p. 292.

29. Julia Mann and James Suckling, "Grand Dame of Bordeaux Dies," *Wine Spectator,* March 31, 2000, pp. 130, 132.

30. Ibid., pp. 132, 133.

31. Jane L. Levere, "Mireille Guiliano: The Bubbly Biz's Bon Vivant," *BIZBash,* March 5, 2001, http://bizbash.com/content/editorial/e236.asp.

32. "Veuve Clicquot in the US," *Messages: Management Review LVMH/FA,* no. 16 (January 1997): 20, 21.

33. Susannah B. Mintz, "Poised for the Future," *Quarterly Review of Wines,* Summer 1999, p. 91. Among the wines Mireille added to her portfolio are Castello di Monsanto, Cloudy Bay, Krug Champagne, Cape Mentelle, and Newton.

34. Mireille received a diploma equivalent to an MA in German and English as well as a certificate as an interpreter/translator. She is fluent in Italian and conversant in several other languages.

35. The Committee of 200 is an international network of women at the top echelons of business. Seventy percent of its members are entrepreneurs running businesses with annual revenues of at least $15 million. Thirty percent are corporate executives who are either CEOs, senior executives who lead divisions producing annual revenues of at least $250 million for companies based in the United States or $30 million for divisions based outside the United States, sen-

ior executives who can prove their indirect impact on such gross revenues, or executives reporting to the CEO with profit-and-loss responsibility and an expense budget of at least $100 million. Lifetime membership in the organization is also based on considerations such as one's sphere of influence and level of commitment, corporate profitability, and industry demographics and geographic location ("The Committee of 200: Membership Requirements," www.c200.org/external/committee/requirements.asp).

36. Mireille Guiliano, with Alice Feiring, "No Hiccups in Risk Taking," *New York Times,* November 8, 2000, p. C8.

37. Ibid.

38. Mintz, "Poised for the Future," p. 92.

39. Guiliano, with Feiring, "No Hiccups," p. C8.

40. Cristina's father and her uncle each own 50 percent of Banfi. While Cristina's father is bequeathing her his entire block of voting shares, her uncle chose to divide his shares equally among his four children, thereby entitling each of them to 12.5 percent of the firm in the future (information provided by Cristina Mariani-May).

41. Craig Camp, "Wine Camp: The Food (Wine) Chain," *The Daily Gullet,* February 13, 2004, www.vinocibo.com/winecamp/winechain.htm (no longer available).

42. Jean T. Barrett, "Climbing the Vine," *Market Watch,* November 1991, p. 22.

43. Every state determines its own distribution licensing requirements. Most states require a distributor to be a state resident, although the definition of residency is not uniform. Small distributors are limited in how large a region they can cover if they cannot be licensed in more than one state. Consolidating distributorships into larger firms not only boosts efficiency and cost-effectiveness but also allows the larger firms to hire people who are licensed in various states, thus expanding their reach. This consolidation, however, limits the number of distributors to whom wineries can turn for marketing their products, reduces competition among distributors, and eventually increases the prices paid by consumers and reduces their wine choices.

44. Erica Duecy, "Wine Connoisseur Builds Reputation on Honesty, Ethics," *Daily Herald* (Arlington Heights, Ill.), October 15, 2003, p. 6B.

45. Among the wineries Debra represents are Araujo, Dalla Valle, Colgin, Bryant Family, Harlan Estates, Qupe, Tony Soter, Selection Becky Wasserman, Isole é Olena, Foradori, and Crocker & Starr.

46. Bethany McLean, "Growing Up Gallo," *Fortune,* August 14, 2000, p. 218.

47. Brendan Koerner, "Leading Ladies," *Food & Wine,* October 2003, pp. 116, 118.

48. Court of Master Sommeliers, www.gs-design.co.uk/court/ms.html; Jenny Hedden, "These Women of the Vine Have Mastered the Wine Industry," www.thewineman.com/women.htm.

49. Court of Master Sommeliers, "Master Sommeliers 1969–2005," www .gs-design.co.uk/court/ms.html.

50. Court of Master Sommeliers, "Board of Directors," www.mastersom meliers.org/board_of_dir.html.

51. Chris Kassel, "WINE: Detroit's Best Is Madeline Triffon," *Detroit Free Press,* August 19, 2003, www.freep.com/features/food/eps19_20030919.htm.

52. Hedden, "These Women of the Vine."

53. Anne-Marie O'Neill, "Andrea Immer," *People,* May 4, 1998, pp. 87, 88.

54. See "Biography: Andrea (Immer) Robinson," www.andreaimmer.com/ biography.cfm.

10. PAST, PRESENT, FUTURE

1. John Stimpfig, "Wine, Women, Misconceptions," *Decanter,* December 1999, p. 54.

2. In the United States, entrepreneurship is a defining characteristic of women in business generally. According to a study conducted in 2003 by the Center for Women's Business Research, 10.6 million firms in the United States were at least 50 percent owned by a woman or women. A woman or women also had at least 50 percent ownership in 48 percent of the nation's privately held firms. Additionally, from 1997 to 2004, the estimated growth of women-owned firms was nearly twice that of all firms, 17 percent versus 9 percent, respectively (Center for Women's Business Research, "Top Facts about Women-Owned Businesses," www.womensbusinessresearch.org/topfacts.html).

3. Michael A. Roberto, "The Changing Structure of the Global Wine Industry," *International Business and Economic Research Journal* 2, no. 9 (September 2003): 3.

4 Margaret Hennig and Anne Jardim, *The Managerial Woman* (Garden City, N.Y.: Anchor Press, 1976), p. xiv.

5. Within a national context, the experience of American women enologists paralleled that of women entering other male-dominated scientific professions, such as medicine. For example, from the academic year 1974–1975 to 2002–2003,

the number of women graduating from American medical schools rose from 1,706 (13.4 percent) to 6,978 (44.5 percent) (American Association of Medical Colleges, "Table 1: Women Applicants, Enrollees and Graduates, Selected Years, 1949–1950 through 2002–2003," www.aamc.org/members/wim/statistics/stats03 /table1.pdf).

6. Based on a recent study conducted by the American Association of University Women (AAUW) Legal Advocacy Fund, women made up 37.5 percent of all full-time faculty in 1999–2000 (AAUW Educational Foundation and AAUW Legal Advocacy Fund, *Tenure Denied: Cases of Sex Discrimination in Academia* [Washington, D.C.: AAUW, 2004], "Table 2: Percentage of Full-Time Faculty by Academic Rank and Gender, Academic Years 1981–1982 to 1999– 2000," p. 85).

7. Iain Riggs, winemaker at Brokenwood in the Hunter Valley of Australia, quoted in Jeni Port, *Crushed by Women: Women and Wine* (Melbourne: Arcadia, 2004), p. 147.

8. Domination of the wine industry by a few firms is the established norm in the New World. In Australia, four firms control 75 percent of the indigenous wine industry, and the twenty largest firms control 75 percent of the American wine industry. By contrast, the Old World's consolidation has been slower, leaving the region more fragmented and dependent on smaller producers. France, for example, has 232,900 wine producers, and its top ten brands control only 4 percent of the market (Roberto, "Changing Structure," pp. 1, 2, 3).

9. Catalyst, "Bit by Bit: Catalyst's Guide to Advancing Women in High Tech Companies," www.catalystwomen.org/knowledge/titles/title.php?page=lead_ bitbybit_03.

LIST OF INTERVIEWS

INTERVIEWEE	POSITION(S)
Albiera Antinori	Director of marketing Cantine Marchesi Antinori Florence, Italy
Susana Balbo	Winemaker/consultant/proprietor Susana Balbo Mendoza, Argentina
Marian Baldy, PhD	Professor emerita College of Agriculture California State University at Chico Chico, California Author: *The University Wine Course*
Heidi Peterson Barrett	Winemaker/consultant/owner La Sirena St. Helena, California
Laura Bianchi	Managing director Castello di Monsanto Barberino d'Elsa (Tuscany), Italy

* Individuals who were interviewed by phone rather than in person.
** Individuals who granted the author permission to use their responses to the question-
naire in lieu of being interviewed.

Linda Bisson, PhD   Maynard A. Amerine Professor of Enology
                    University of California at Davis
                    Davis, California

                    Former chair, Department of Viticulture and Enology,
                        University of California at Davis
                    Co-author: *Principles and Practices of Winemaking*

Melba Brajkovich   Managing director
                    Kumeu River Wines
                    Kumeu, New Zealand

Laura Catena   Vice-president
                    Bodega Catena Zapata
                    Mendoza, Argentina

Cathy Corison   Winemaker/owner
                    Corison Winery
                    St. Helena, California

Eileen Crane   President/winemaker
                    Domaine Carneros
                    Napa, California

Debra Crestoni   Proprietor
                    Connoisseur Wines
                    Chicago, Illinois

Vanya Cullen   Managing director/winemaker
                    Cullen Wines
                    Wilyabrup (Margaret River), Australia

Merry Edwards   Owner/winemaker
                    Meredith Vineyard Estate Inc.
                    Windsor, California

Catherine Faller   Owner/marketing director
                    Domaine Weinbach
                    Kaysersberg (Alsace), France

Laurence Faller   Owner/winemaker
                    Domaine Weinbach
                    Kaysersberg (Alsace), France

Elisabetta Foradori	Owner/winemaker Foradori Trentino, Italy
Gina Gallo*	Winemaker Gallo of Sonoma Healdsburg, California
Annegret Reh-Gartner	Managing director Weingut Reichgraf von Kesselstatt Trier, Germany
Paola Gloder	Managing director Poggio Antico Montalcino (Tuscany), Italy
MaryAnn Graf	Founder and co-owner (retired) Vinquiry Windsor, California
Anne Gros	Winemaker/proprietor Domaine Anne Gros Vosne-Romanée, France
Nadine Gublin	Head winemaker Antonin Rodet Burgundy, France
Mireille Guiliano	President and CEO Cliquot Inc. New York, New York Author: *French Women Don't Get Fat*
Prue Henschke	Co-owner and viticulturist C. A. Henschke & Company Eden Valley, Australia

Ursula Hermacinski	Senior adviser and auctioneer
	Zachys Wine Auctions
	Scarsdale, New York
	Former executive vice-president, Winebid.com;
	    former head wine auctioneer, Christie's,
	    Los Angeles

Tricia Horgan	Managing director Leeuwin Estate Margaret River, Australia
Jane Hunter, OBE	Managing director/ viticulturist Hunter's Blenheim, New Zealand
Eloise Jarvis	Winemaker Cape Mentelle Margaret River, Australia
Sarah Kemp	Publisher *Decanter* magazine London, England
Mia Klein**	Winemaker/consultant/ owner Selene Napa, California
Alexandra Marnier-Lapostolle (de Bournet)	Proprietor Casa Lapostolle Santiago, Chile
Anne-Claude Leflaive	General manager Domaine Leflaive Puligny-Montrachet, France
May-Eliane de Lencquesaing	Owner Château Pichon Longueville Comtesse de Lalande Pauillac, France
Lalou Bize-Leroy	Winemaker/owner Domaine Leroy Vosne-Romanée, France

Zelma Long	Co-owner/winemaker/
	  consultant
	Long Vineyards, Zelphi Wines
	Healdsburg, California
	Former president and CEO,
	  Simi

Kathy Lynskey

Managing director
Kathy Lynskey Wines Ltd.
Marlborough, New Zealand

Sandra MacIver

Founder and former owner
Matanzas Creek Winery
Santa Rosa, California

Karen MacNeil

Chairman
Rudd Center for Professional Wine Studies
Culinary Institute of America (CIA),
    Greystone
St. Helena, California
Author: *The Wine Bible*

Cristina Mariani-May

Vice-president of marketing
Castello Banfi
New York, New York

Sarah Marquis

Director/winemaker
Grapes Consulting
Adelaide, Australia

Corinne Mentzelopoulos

Owner
Château Margaux
Margaux, France

Carole Meredith, PhD

Professor emerita
Department of Viticulture and Enology
University of California at Davis
Davis, California
Co-owner: Lagier Meredith
Napa, California

Beth Novak Milliken

President
Spottswoode Winery
St. Helena, California

Marie-Christine Mugneret

Co-winemaker/proprietor
Domaine Georges Mugneret
Vosne-Romanée, France

Mary Ewing-Mulligan, MW   President
International Wine Center
New York, New York
Co-author: *Wine for Dummies*

Hazel Murphy   Consultant
London, United Kingdom
Former director, Australian Wine Bureau

Su Hua Newton   Winemaker/owner
Newton Vineyards
Napa, California

Ann Noble, PhD   Professor emerita
Department of Viticulture and Enology
University of California at Davis
Davis, California

Mary Novak   Owner
Spottswoode Winery
St. Helena, California

Robert M. Parker Jr.*   Wine critic
Author and publisher: *The Wine Advocate*
Author: *Bordeaux*

Susan Reed   Former winemaker
Matanzas Creek Winery
Santa Rosa, California

Michelle Richardson**   Winemaker
Peregrine Wines
Gibbston, New Zealand
Former chief winemaker, Villa Maria,
     Marlborough, New Zealand

Andrea (Immer) Robinson, MS   Dean of wine studies
French Culinary Institute
New York, New York
Former beverage director, Starwood;
     former sommelier, Windows on the
     World, New York
Author: *Great Tastes Made Simple*

Jancis Robinson, MW, OBE

Wine critic
Author: *The Oxford Companion to Wine*
Sponsor: www.jancisrobinson.com
London, England

Michaela Rodeno

CEO/executive vice-president
St. Supéry Winery
Rutherford (Napa), California

Louisa Rose

Senior winemaker
Yalumba Wine Company
Barossa Valley, Australia

Anne Rosenzweig

Former chef/proprietor
Arcadia; The Lobster Club
New York, New York
Founding member, Association of
   Women Chefs and Restaurateurs

Baroness Philippine de Rothschild

Owner
Château Mouton Rothschild
Pauillac, France

Heidi Schröck

Winemaker/proprietor
Heidi Schröck Vineyards
Rust, Austria

Lorenza Sebasti

CEO
Castello di Ama
Lecchi in Chianti (Tuscany), Italy

Teresa Severini

Winemaker/director
Cantine Lungarotti
Torgiano (Umbria), Italy

Alpana Singh, MS

Director of wine and spirits
Lettuce Entertain You Enterprises
Former sommelier, Everest, Chicago,
   Illinois

Sylvie Spielmann

Owner/winemaker
Domaine Spielmann
Bergheim (Alsace), France

Pamela Starr   Winemaker/partner
Crocker & Starr
Napa, California

Wendy Stuckey   Senior winemaker
Beringer Blass Wine Estates
Nuriootpa (Barossa Valley), Australia

Serena Sutcliffe, MW   Head of international wine sales
Sotheby's
London, England
Author: *Wines of Burgundy*

Madeline Triffon, MS   Wine director
Unique Restaurant Corporation
Detroit, Michigan

Delia Viader   Winemaker/owner
Viader Vineyards
St. Helena, California

Becky Wasserman-Hone   Owner
SARL Le Serbet
Beaune, France

WOMEN MASTERS OF WINE

2005

Barbara Abraham (United Kingdom)
Nicola Arcedeckne-Butler (United Kingdom)
Maureen Ashley (United Kingdom and Italy)
Laura Baker (United Kingdom)
Fiona Barlow (United Kingdom)
Liz Berry (France)
Dee Blackstock (United Kingdom)
Beverly Blanning (United Kingdom)
Jane Boyce (United Kingdom)
Jane Brocket (United Kingdom)
Meg Brodtmann (Chile)
Rose Murray Brown (United Kingdom)
Juliet Bruce-Jones (United Kingdom)
Philippa Carr (United Kingdom)
Minette Constant (France)
Sally Easton (United Kingdom)
Alison Flemming (Germany)
Elizabeth Gabay (France)
Marina Gayan (United Kingdom)
Rosemary George (United Kingdom)
Caroline Gilby (United Kingdom)

Nancy Gilchrist (United Kingdom)
Claire Gordon-Brown (United Kingdom)
Julia Harding (United Kingdom)
Andrea Hargrave (United Kingdom)
Margaret Harvey (United Kingdom)
Rebecca Hull (United Kingdom)
Jane Hunt (United Kingdom)
Xenia Irwin (United Kingdom)
Laura Jewell (United Kingdom)
Linda Jothman (United Kingdom)
Carmel Kilcline (United Kingdom)
Jo Locke (United Kingdom)
Penelope Mansell-Jones (United Kingdom)
Sarah Marsh (United Kingdom)
Jane Masters (United Kingdom)
Susan McCraith (United Kingdom)
Maggie McNie (United Kingdom)
Liz Morcom (United Kingdom)
Fiona Morrison (Belgium and France)
Angela Muir (United Kingdom)
Mary Ewing-Mulligan (United States)
Toni Paterson (Australia)
Liz Robertson (United Kingdom)
Jancis Robinson (United Kingdom)
Sheryl Sauter (United States)
Gabrielle Shaw (France)
Lynne Sherriff (United Kingdom)
Jane Skilton (New Zealand)
Patricia Stefanowicz (United Kingdom)
Serena Sutcliffe (United Kingdom)
Sabrina Sykes (United Kingdom)
Beverly Tabbron (United Kingdom)
Anne Tupker (United Kingdom)
Jean Wareing (United Kingdom)
Marcia Waters (United Kingdom)
Arabella Woodrow (United Kingdom)

Source: Institute of Masters of Wine, "IMW Members: Who Are Members?" www.masters-of-wine.org/MembersWhoAre.aspx.

WOMEN MASTER SOMMELIERS

2005

Laura De Pasquale (United States)
Catherine Fallis (United States)
Sarah Floyd (United States)
Claudia Harris (United States)
Sally Mohr (United States)
Virginia Philip (United States)
Andrea (Immer) Robinson (United States)
Elizabeth Schweitzer (United States)
Alpana Singh (United States)
Cameron Sisk (United States)
Madeline Triffon (United States)
Claudia Tyagi (United States)
Barbara Werley (United States)
Vera Wessel
Laura Williamson (United States)

*Sources: Court of Master Sommeliers, "Master Sommeliers 1969–2005," www.gs-design
.co.uk/court/ms.html; Court of Master Sommeliers, Membership: American Chapter,
"Master Sommelier Directory" www.mastersommeliers.org/membership_list.html; phone
conversation with Kathleen Lewis of the U.S. chapter of the Court of Master Sommeliers,
July 14, 2004.*

GLOSSARY

11 Women and Their Wines: An informal group of Austrian women winemakers and proprietors.

Aging: The process of "holding wines for a period of time in barrels, tanks or bottles to affect the character of the finished wine."[A]

American or (Approved) Viticultural Area (AVA): "The term given in the United States to an officially designated winegrape growing region." Historically, AVAs were "defined officially by the Bureau of Alcohol, Tobacco and Firearms (BATF) based on geographic, climatic and historical criteria."[A] To-day, the AVA designations are regulated by the Alcohol and Tobacco Tax and Trade Bureau within the U.S. Department of the Treasury.

Appellation d'Origine Contrôlée (AOC): The French classification system for guar-anteeing the origin of wines and other food products such as cheese. "AOC rules establish specific areas of production, grape varieties, minimum levels of sugar in the must and of alcohol in the wine, maximum yield per hectare, pruning practices, and cultivation and vinification methods."[B] Wines desig-nated AOC are regulated by the Institut National des Appellations d'Ori-gine des Vins et Eaux-de-Vie (INAO).

Aroma: A "tasting term used to indicate the smells of a wine, particularly those deriving from the grape and fermentation."[C] Some distinguish aroma (the smells derived from the grape) from bouquet (the smells associated with the winemaking process), particularly in the bottle.

Aroma Wheel: A graphical representation of tasting terms for aroma, which helps to standardize terminology used in wine tasting. It was created by Dr. Ann Noble.

Assemblage: "The blending of wine from different grape varieties, fermentation vats, and/or vineyard plots."[B]

AVA: See American (Approved) Viticultural Area

Azienda Agricola: An Italian wine estate that produces wine from grapes grown in its own vineyards.

Bacchus: The Roman god of fertility and wine.

Barrel: A "vessel used for ageing, and sometimes fermenting."[C] Barrels are usually made from wood such as American or French oak and come in different sizes and shapes.

Barrique: A French barrel that contains 225 liters (twenty-four cases of twelve bottles). Often associated with Bordeaux, it is used for aging wine.[B]

Biodynamics: A philosophical approach to natural agricultural practices originally developed by Rudolf Steiner, which links farming activities to the seasons and planetary movements in a global ecosystem.

Blending: See Assemblage

Blind tasting: An event in which tasters judge various wines whose identity is masked.

Bodega: "The Spanish term for a winery, or the building where wine is stored."[A]

Bouquet: "The odors of wine attributed to the winemaking process: fermentation, processing, and aging, particularly those that develop after bottling."[A] Some distinguish bouquet from aroma, the odors derived from the grape itself.

Boutique winery: A "term used in the USA and Australia to describe a small winery making quality wines."[B]

Brut: The driest form of champagne or other sparkling wine.

Bureau of Alcohol, Tobacco, and Firearms (BATF): A U.S. government agency that regulated the American wine industry until 2003. Historically, it was associated either with the Internal Revenue Service as part of the Department of the Treasury (DOT) or with the Department of Justice (DOJ). The Homeland Security Act of 2002 transferred BATF's tax collection and regulatory functions to a new Alcohol and Tobacco Tax and Trade Bureau within DOT. BATF's law enforcement functions were shifted to the DOJ.[E] BATF has been renamed the Bureau of Alcohol, Tobacco, Firearms, and Explosives.

Canopy management: "The viticultural techniques used to balance shoot growth and fruit development to maximize the varietal character of the grapes."[A]

Cantina: An Italian term for a winery or a winemaking cellar.

Castello: An Italian term for a castle or a wine-producing estate.

Cellar: A location where "grapes are processed and wines are stored and aged." The term can also refer to a wine collection. At one time, wine cellars were all below ground, but that is no longer true.[C]

Château: A French term for a castle or a wine-producing estate.

Climat: A French term from Burgundy describing a legally defined geographic area or vineyard site.[B, C]

Clone: "A subvariety of a wine grape variety that exhibits specific enological characteristics."[A] Clones are developed for various reasons—for example, to suit local conditions, to meet yield requirements, or to resist disease.[C] A clone is the genetic progeny of a single (mother) vine.

Clos: A French term for a walled vineyard.

Cluster thinning: See Green harvesting

Complex: A tasting term for a "wine that exhibits many different odors and flavors."[A] "Complexity is one of the hallmarks of a great wine."[C]

Confrère: Member of a confrérie.

Confrérie: A French wine brotherhood.

Convivium: A Roman gathering place and fellowship center originally restricted to men. Women were eventually admitted.

Cooper: A maker of wine barrels.

Cooperage: The business of making wine barrels.

Cooperative: A "union of grape-growers who jointly own winemaking facilities and sometimes bottle and market wines."[B]

Corked (corky): "A moldy odor or flavor from a fungus-infested cork attributable to the presence of small amounts of tyrene in the wine."[D]

Cru: The French term for growth. It also indicates "a particular vineyard site, particularly in Bordeaux."[C]

Crush: The process of splitting grapes open before fermentation in order to release their juice. The term also applies to the seasonal harvest during the year when this occurs.[A]

Cult wine: A highly sought-after wine, often from a boutique winery. These wines are ordinarily in short supply and command extremely high prices because they are difficult to obtain. Cult wines from Australia are referred to as "iconic wines."

Denominazione di Origine Controllata (DOC): The Italian system for designating quality wines from a specific region.

Denominazione di Origine Controllata e Garantita (DOCG): Italy's highest quality wine designation.

Dionysus: The Greek god of fertility and wine.

Disgorging: The process of "using the pressure of gas in the wine to remove the collected sediment from bottle-fermented sparkling wine."[A]

DOC: See Denominazione di Origine Controllata

DOCG: See Denominazione di Origine Controllata e Garantita

Domaine: A French wine estate.

Drip irrigation: A method for controlling and rationing the irrigation of grapevines using droplets of water.

Enologist (oenologist): A practitioner of the science of winemaking.

Enology (oenology): The study of wine and winemaking.

Enophile (oenophile): A wine lover.

En primeur: A French term referring to "wine sold before it has been bottled. Common in Bordeaux when classed growths are sold in the year after they are made."[B]

Estate bottled: This is mainly a New World term, "used to indicate that the wine was bottled on the property where the grapes were grown."[C]

Eucharist: The Catholic sacrament of Holy Communion using consecrated bread and wine.

Fattoria: An Italian wine estate.

Fermentation—alcoholic: "The process by which sugar in grape juice is transformed into alcohol and carbon dioxide, and the juice to wine, through the action of yeast organisms."[A]

Fermentation—malolactic: A second fermentation stage intended to make wines softer and less acidic by converting the malic acid of young wines into lactic acid and carbon dioxide.[B]

Filtering: The process of clarifying wine before bottling by separating and removing unwanted elements.[B]

Fining: A procedure in which a winemaker adds a substance such as egg whites to the wine, which gathers and removes unwanted materials that may be suspended in the wine.[C]

Flying winemaker: A wine consultant who takes advantage of reversed seasonality to work harvests in both the Northern and Southern hemispheres. The original flying winemakers were Australians who worked in the Old World during the off-season. Today, flying winemakers come from all the major winemaking nations.

Generic wines: Wines named after general categories, such as red or white table wines.

Grafting: A technique for "joining fruit-bearing vines (usually *Vitis vinifera*) to rootstocks, usually of other *Vitis* species," often those that are resistant to phylloxera.[C]

Grand cru: A French term for a top-quality wine. The exact meaning varies by region.[B]

Grande marque: "A champagne-producing firm belonging to the Institut de Grandes Marques de Champagne."[B]

Green harvesting: A viticultural process for reducing yields by pruning green or unripened grapes from a vine in order to enhance the ripening and quality of the remaining grapes. Also known as cluster thinning.

Hybridization: The process of crossing two vines of different species to produce a third that is superior to either of the parents. The hybrid may, for example, ripen earlier, or it may be more disease resistant. Hybridization is not the same process as a cross in which the two vines used are of the same species.[C]

Iconic wine: A term used for cult wines in Australia. *See* Cult wines

Indicazione Geographica Tipica (IGT): Upscale Italian wines that do not qualify for DOC or DOCG.

Institut National des Appellations d'Origine (INAO): A French regulatory authority that controls AOC wines.

Jug wine: Inexpensive generic wines sold in large containers. The phrase is often used as a derogatory term for cheap wines of inferior quality.

Jurade: A French term for a wine brotherhood.

Jurat: A French masculine term for a member of a jurade.

Kiddush: A Hebrew prayer (blessing) said before consuming wine.

Kosher wine: Wine made according to Jewish tradition and Jewish law under rabbinical supervision.

Le Donne del Vino: An Italian organization of women wine proprietors, vintners, journalists, restaurateurs, and sommeliers.

Les Aliénor du Vin: A network of French women winemakers from Bordeaux.

Limoncello: A sweet, lemon-based Italian liqueur.

Malolactic fermentation: See Fermentation—malolactic

Mashgiach: A rabbi who supervises the making of kosher wine.

Maturation: "The aging period at the winery during which the wine evolves to a state of readiness for bottling. Also, the ongoing development of fine wines during a period of bottle aging."[A]

Méthode Champenoise: "The bottle-fermentation method of making Champagne and other sparkling wines that are released for sale in the same bottle in which the secondary fermentation took place."[A] This term is no longer used because of a ban by the European Union.[B] *See* Méthode traditionnelle

Méthode traditionnelle: The method of making sparkling wine that originated in Champagne. By directive of the European Union, this designation has replaced the term "méthode Champenoise" and can be used only for wines made in the Champagne region.[B]

Mevushal: Kosher wines that have been pasteurized or heat-flashed, a practice dating from Biblical prohibitions regarding idolatry. These wines remain kosher even if handled by non-Jews.

Must: "Unfermented grape juice obtained by crushing or pressing."[B]

Négociant: A French wine merchant "who buys grapes or wine from growers to mature it and/or sell it to wholesalers and foreign importers."[B]

New World: Winegrowing areas originally colonized by Europeans: the United States, Australia, New Zealand, South Africa, Argentina, and Chile.

Old World: European winegrowing nations.

Organic: Viticultural techniques that do not use chemicals.

Palate: A "tasting term used to indicate the range of sensations detected in the mouth (rather than on the nose)."[C]

Phylloxera: A "vine disease caused by an aphid which attacks the root system."[C]

Prohibition: In the United States, the period during which the production, sale, and consumption of alcoholic beverages were largely forbidden. Prohibition was established by the Eighteenth Amendment and the passage of the Volstead Act in 1919 and later repealed by the Twenty-first Amendment in 1933.

Quinta: A Portuguese farm, wine estate, or vineyard.

Rav Hamachshir: The rabbinical authority that determines whether a wine qualifies as kosher.

Riddling: "The process of gradually turning and shaking bottle-fermented sparkling wine (such as Champagne) so that the sediment of dead yeast cells moves to the neck, for subsequent removal by disgorgement."[C]

Sommelier: A wine steward.

Sparkling wine: Wine made by the méthode traditionnelle outside the region of Champagne.

Still wine: All nonsparkling or noneffervescent wines.

Supertaster: An individual with a heightened sensitivity to differences in flavor.

Symposium: A Greek gathering and fellowship center for men.

Tasting: The process of discovering the sensory qualities of a wine, such as appearance, palate, complexity, aroma, and bouquet.

Tenuta: An Italian wine estate.

Terroir: "A French word for the particular growing conditions of a vineyard, including soil, drainage, slope, climate, altitude, etc., that give the grapes grown there unique characteristics."[A]

Varietal: A term that "describes the aromas and/or flavors characteristic of a particular grape variety";[A] "wine made from a single grape variety."[B]

Viniculture: A word combining the terms "vinification" and "viticulture," used to signify that winemaking really begins in the vineyard.

Vinification: "The process of making grape juice into wine."[A]

Vinissima: A German organization of women wine estate proprietors, winemakers, journalists, and sommeliers.

Vino da Tavola (VdT): Italian table wine.

Vintage: "The year in which a wine's grapes grew and were harvested. The term is often used as a synonym for the grape harvest."[A]

Vintner: "A person who makes or sells wine."[D]

Viticultrice: A woman winemaker (French).

Viticulture: "The science or activity of growing grapes."[A]

Vitis vinifera: The grape species from which most of the world's wines are made.

Weingut: A German wine estate.

Women for Winesense: An American women's organization seeking to increase the American public's acceptance of wine.

Yield: The "quantity of grapes harvested from a given area of vineyard."[C]

Sources:

A. Clos du Bois, *"About Wine: Wine Glossary,"* www.closdubois.com/about_wine_glossary .html.

B. *"Glossary," Larousse Encyclopedia of Wine (New York: Larousse/VUEF, 2001), pp. 594–599.*

C. *David Rowe, comp., "The Glossary,"* www.decanter.com/learningroute/glossary.asp.

D. *Marian W. Baldy, PhD, The University Wine Course, 3rd ed. (South San Francisco: Wine Appreciation Guild, 1998).*

E. *"History of TTB,"* www.ttb.gov/about/history/htm.

BIBLIOGRAPHY

AAUW Educational Foundation and AAUW Legal Advocacy Fund. *Tenure Denied: Cases of Sex Discrimination in Academia.* Washington, D.C.: AAUW, 2004.

Adams, Leon. *The Wines of America.* 4th ed. New York: McGraw-Hill, 1990.

"All of a Ferment." *Massey,* November 2001. http://masseynews.massey.ac.nz/magazine/2001_Nov/stories/cover_story.html.

American Association of Medical Colleges. "Table 1: Women Applicants, Enrollees and Graduates, Selected Years, 1949–1950 through 2002–2003." www.aamc.org/members/wim/statistics/stats03/table1.pdf.

"American Charity Wine Auctions: Everyone a Winner." www.jancisrobinson.com/winenews/jr413.

Ante, Spencer E. "Heavyweights behind the Great Wines." *Business Week,* March 19, 2001, pp. 102–103.

Apple, R. W., Jr. "From a Granite Coast, Velvet Wines." *New York Times,* January 2, 2002, p. B13.

———. "Mile-High Vineyards Reach the Stars." *The Age,* July 16, 2002. www.theage.com.au/articles/2002/07/16/1026185175197.html.

"Arrival in Australia." www.nicks.com.au/index.aspx?link_id=67.701.

Atkin, Tim. "Critical Juncture." *Harpers Supplement: Australia,* January 2002, pp. 2–3.

Austin, Christine. "A Woman's Touch." *Hilton Guest,* no. 1, 2000, pp. 64–65.

Australian Wine and Brandy Corporation. "Australian Wine Industry at a Glance." www.awbc.com.au/winefacts/data/free.asp?subcatid=93.

Barker, Tracey. "Women-Only Wine Group Launches in New Zealand." *Decanter,* October 9, 2002. www.decanter.com/news/46278.html.

Barrett, Jean T. "Climbing the Vine." *Market Watch,* November 1991, pp. 16–18, 20, 22, 24, 26, 28–29.

Barron, Cheryll Aimee. *Dreamers of the Valley of Plenty.* New York: Scribners, 1995.

Bastianich, Joseph, and David Lynch. *Vino Italiano: The Regional Wines of Italy.* New York: Clarkson Potter, 2002.

Beeston, Fiona. *The Wine Men.* London: Sinclair-Stevenson, 1991.

Beeston, John. *A Concise History of Australian Wine.* St. Leonards, New South Wales: Allen and Unwin, 1994.

Berberoglu, Hrayr. *New World Wine Producing Countries.* Toronto: Food and Beverage Consultants, 2001.

Berger, Dan. "Drink, Wine, Brothers, and Song." *Los Angeles Times,* August 19, 1998, p. 9.

"Biography: Andrea (Immer) Robinson." www.andreaimmer.com/biography .cfm.

Boyd, Gerald D. "Duval-Leroy Returns to the U.S." *Decanter,* March 2004, pp. 94–95.

Bradford, Sarah. *The Story of Port: The Englishman's Wine.* Rev. ed. London: Christie's Wine Publications, 1978.

Brenner, Leslie. "The Grape Communicator." *Avenue,* January 1995, p. 55.

Brook, Stephen, ed. *A Century of Wine: The Story of a Wine Revolution.* San Francisco: Wine Appreciation Guild, 2000.

Brooks, Cynthia. *Marlborough Wines and Vines,* vol. 1. Wellington: Graham and Cynthia Brooks, 1992.

Broom, Dave. "Heads in the Stars." *Decanter,* September 1999, pp. 66–69.

Brown, Eryn. "Breaking the Wineglass Ceiling." *Fortune,* August 14, 2000, pp. 222–224, 226, 228, 230, 232.

Browne, Kingsley R. "Sex and Temperament in Modern Society: A Darwinian View of the Glass Ceiling and the Gender Gap." *Arizona Law Review* 37 (Winter 1995): 971–1106.

California Wine Pioneers. 1995 ed. San Francisco: M. Shanken Communications, 1994.

Camp, Craig. "Wine Camp: The Food (Wine) Chain." *The Daily Gullet,* February 13, 2004. www.vinocibo.com/winecamp/winechain.htm (no longer available).

Carmen. "Winemakers." www.carmen.com/OpenDocs/asp/pagDefault.asp?
boton=Doc86&argInstanciaId=86&argCarpetaId=&argTreeNodoSel=.

Catalyst. "Bit by Bit: Catalyst's Guide to Advancing Women in High Tech Companies." www.catalystwomen.org/knowledge/titles/title.php?page=lead
_bitbybit_03.

———. "Catalyst Charts Growth of Women on America's Corporate Boards."
December 4, 2001. www.charitywire.com/charity34/02605.html.

Center for Women's Business Research. "Top Facts about Women-Owned
Businesses." www.womensbusinessresearch.org/topfacts.html.

Cernilli, Daniele. "A Chianti Life." *Gambero Rosso,* no. 33, 2002, pp. 18–21.

Cernilli, Daniele, Fabbio Rizzari, and Marco Sabellico. "The Lords of the
Vines." *Gambero Rosso,* no. 14, 1998, pp. 58–66, 68–69.

Champagne Pommery. Reims: Champagne Pommery, n.d.

"Château Haut-Brion: Joan Dillon, Duchesse de Mouchy." www.haut-brion
.com/chb/history/jdem.htm.

Chimay, Princess Jean de Caraman. *Madame Veuve Clicquot Ponsardin: Her Life
and Time.* Reims, 1961.

Clark, Emma. "Mixing Wine with Medicine." BBC News Online, October 3,
2002. http://news.bbc.co.uk/1/hi/business/2261885.stm.

Coates, Clive. "Ferreira." *The Vine,* December 1989, pp. 14–22.

Coelho, Alfredo Manual, and Jean-Louis Rastoin. "Globalization of the Wine
Industry and the Restructuring of Multinational Enterprises." Paper presented at Oenometrie XI, Université de Bourgogne, Dijon, France, May
21–22, 2004.

"The Committee of 200: Membership Requirements." www.c200.org/external/
committee/requirements.asp.

Conaway, James. *Napa: The Story of an American Eden.* New York: Avon Books,
1990.

Cooper, Michael. "In the Wake of Ernie Hunter." *North & South,* September
1988, pp. 117, 158.

Courtney, Caroline. *Wine in New Zealand.* Auckland: Random House New
Zealand, 2003.

Court of Master Sommeliers. "Board of Directors." www.mastersommeliers
.org/board_of_dir.html.

———. "Master Sommeliers 1969–2005." www.gs-design.co.uk/court/ms.html.

Crestin-Billet, Frédérique. *Veuve Clicquot: La Grande Dame de la Champagne.*
Translated by Carole Fahy. Grenoble: Glenát, 1992.

Cullen Wines. "Qantas/*The Wine Magazine* Winemaker of the Year Award 2000." www.cullenwines.com.au/pages/qwoty.htm.

"Curnonsky (Maurice Edmund Sailland)." www.foodreference.com/html/w-curnonsky.html.

Dayagi-Mendels, Michal. *Drink and Be Merry: Wine and Beer in Ancient Times.* Jerusalem: The Israel Museum, 1999.

"Di Cullen: A Life of Passion." *Scoop: The Essential Western Australian Lifestyle Magazine,* no. 4, Winter 2003.

Doty, Richard L., et al. "Sex Differences in Odor Identification Ability: A Cross-Cultural Analysis." *Neuropsychologia* 23, no. 5 (1985): 667–672.

Downes, John. "The Fab Four: Argentine Producers." *Decanter,* February 2004. www.decanter.com/archive/article.php?id=47623.

"Dr. Ann C. Noble: She's a 'First.'" *Wines & Vines,* April 1974, p. 24.

"Dr. Hildegard Heymann." http://wineserver.ucdavis.edu/people/faculty.php?id=9.

Duecy, Erica. "Wine Connoisseur Builds Reputation on Honesty, Ethics." *Daily Herald* (Arlington Heights, Ill.), October 15, 2003, pp. B6–B7.

Duijker, Hubrecht. *The Wines of Chile.* Utrecht: Uitgeverij Het Spectrum B.V./Segrave Foulkes, 1999.

Edelman, Renée. "When Little Sister Means Business." *Working Woman,* February 1990, pp. 82–86, 88.

Elia, Richard L. "Concho y Toro's Bonne Femme." *Quarterly Review of Wines,* Winter 1995, pp. 26, 28–29.

"Erste Diplom-Ingenieurin für Weinbau." *Der Deutsche Weinbau,* no. 4, February 28, 2003, pp. 34–35.

Essex, Andrew. "The Golden Grape Awards." *Food & Wine,* October 1998, pp. 73–74, 76, 79, 80, 82.

"Ewing-Mulligan to Head Prestigious Wine Programs in U.S." *Wine & Spirits,* December 2003, p. 14.

"Expansion and Reputation." www.nicks.com.au/index.aspx?link_id=67.702.

Feinstein, Rabbi Moshe. *Igros Moshe Yoreh Deah II.* Brooklyn: Moriah Offset, 1973.

"Ferreirinha 'A. Ferreira.'" *ABC,* May 1988, pp. 18–19.

Ferretti, Fred. "A Gourmet at Large: Master of Wine—Mary Ewing-Mulligan." *Gourmet,* August 1998, pp. 54, 57.

Fielden, Christopher. *The Wines of Argentina, Chile, and Latin America.* London: Mitchell Beazley, 2003.

Fife Vineyards. "Karen MacNeil." www.fifevineyards.com/fife/kfbio.html.

Fincas Patagónicas Bodega Tapiz. "Argentina: History of Winemaking." www .tapiz.com/argentina.

Flagship Wines. "Weingut: Morgenhof Estate." www.flagshipwines.ch/d/John_ Platter/JP_Morgenhof.htm.

Fletcher, Wyndham. *Port: An Introduction to Its History and Delights*. San Francisco: Wine Appreciation Guild, 1981.

Forbes, Patrick. *Champagne: The Wine, the Land, and the People*. New York: Reynal, 1967.

Fowler, Kathie. "Linda Rieff and the NVVA: A Perfect Fit to Lead Vintners on Critical Issues." *Spring Valley Times,* Joseph Phelps Vineyards seasonal newsletter, Fall-Winter 2002, pp. 2, 6.

Fox, Kate. "The Smell Report: Sex Differences." Social Issues Research Centre. www.sirc.org/publik/smell_diffs.html.

Franson, Paul. "Wine, Women, and Strong." *San Francisco Examiner,* July 5, 1998, pp. D1, D4.

Friedrich, Jacqueline. *A Wine and Food Guide to the Loire*. New York: Henry Holt, 1996.

Fuhrman, Jane. "Women Winemakers Barreling to the Top." *San Francisco Chronicle,* October 6, 2000, p. 3.

Fuller, Martin. "News from the Cape Winelands." www.wineloverspage.com/ martinfuller/martin032500.shtml.

Fuller, Robert C. *Religion and Wine: A Cultural History of Wine Drinking in the United States*. Knoxville: University of Tennessee Press, 1996.

Garrett, Peter. "Phyllis Hands and Her Influence on the South African Wine Industry." *International Journal of Wine Marketing* 5, no. 4 (1993): 27–34.

Geraci, Victor W. "Grape Growing to Vintibusiness: A History of the Santa Barbara, California, Regional Wine Industry, 1965–1995." PhD diss., University of California, Santa Barbara, 1997.

Goldfarb, Alan. "Di Vine." *Guest West,* October 1993, pp. 8–9.

Goodman, Joshua. "Don't Cry for These Argentine Wines." *Business Week,* October 14, 2002, p. 162.

Green, Blake. "The Women behind Those Vineyards." *San Francisco Chronicle,* June 24, 1976.

Guiliano, Mireille, with Alice Feiring. "No Hiccups in Risk Taking." *New York Times,* November 8, 2000, p. C8.

Guy, Kolleen M. "Drowning Her Sorrows: Widowhood and Entrepreneurship in the Champagne Industry." *Business and Economic History* 26, no. 2 (Winter 1997): 505–514.

————. "Wine, Work, and Wealth: Class Relations and Modernization in the Champagne Wine Industry, 1870–1914." PhD diss., Indiana University, 1996.

Halliday, James. *A History of the Australian Wine Industry, 1949–1994.* Adelaide: Winetitles, 1994.

Hawkes, Ellen. *Blood and Wine: The Unauthorized Story of the Gallo Wine Empire.* New York: Simon and Schuster, 1993.

Hazan, Victor. *Italian Wine.* New York: Alfred A. Knopf, 1982.

"Hazel Murphy: Our Lady in London." Jim McMahon's Wineworld 2000. www.wine2000.com.au/writing01.html.

Hedden, Jenny. "These Women of the Vine Have Mastered the Wine Industry." www.thewineman.com/women.htm.

Hennig, Margaret, and Anne Jardim. *The Managerial Woman.* Garden City, N.Y.: Anchor Press, 1976.

Hinkle, Richard Paul. "From Gunslinger to 'Winegrower Counselor.'" *Wines & Vines,* August 1994), pp. 13, 32–34.

Hooke, Huon. "Pioneers of the West." *Australian Gourmet Traveller,* October/November 2003, pp. 89–93.

Hutchinson, Ralph Burton. "The California Wine Industry." PhD diss., University of California at Los Angeles, 1969.

Institute of Masters of Wine. "About the IMW." www.masters-of-wine.org/about.aspx.

————. "IMW Members: Who Are Members?" www.masters-of-wine.org/MembersWhoAre.aspx.

International Wine Center. "About International Wine Center." www.learnwine.com/aboutus2.asp.

"In Vino Veritas." *The Economist,* February 24–March 2, 2001, pp. 82–83.

Italian Wines 2003. New York: Gambero Rosso, 2003.

"Jancis Robinson." *Financial Times* (London), January 21, 2004. http://news.ft.com/cms/s/a69472e2-b72d-11d9-9f22-00000e2511c8.html.

"Janet Holmes à Court." www.abc.net.au/btn/australians/acourt.htm.

Jefford, Andrew. "Jancis Robinson, MW." *Decanter,* March 1999, pp. 26–30.

————. "Wine, Geography, and Transport." In *A Century of Wine: The Story of a Wine Revolution,* edited by Stephen Brook. San Francisco: Wine Appreciation Guild, 2000.

Jenster, Per V., Lars V. Jenster, and Neville Watchurst. *The Business of Wine: An Analysis of the Global Wine Industry.* Lausanne: SMC Publishing, CIMID SA, 1993.

Johnson, Hugh. *The World Atlas of Wine.* 4th ed. New York: Simon and Schuster, 1994.

Jones, Andrew. *Wine Talk: A Vintage Collection of Facts and Legends for Wine Lovers.* London: Judy Piatkus, 1997.

Jordan, Ray. "Best Western." *Decanter,* February 2004, p. 35.

"Kashrut." www.abarbanel.com/kashrut.shtml.

Kassel, Chris. "WINE: Detroit's Best Is Madeline Triffon." *Detroit Free Press,* August 19, 2003. www.freep.com/features/food/eps19_20030919.htm.

Kipling, Kay. "Wine Bid-ness." *Sarasota Magazine,* April 1998, p. 21.

Kitty, Graham. "Vin Superieur." *International Business,* October 1993, p. 22.

Kladstrup, Don, and Petie Kladstrup. *Wine and War: The French, the Nazis, and the Battle for France's Greatest Treasure.* New York: Broadway Books, 2001.

Knox, Graham. *Wines of South Africa.* Vlaeberg: Fernwood Press, 2002.

Koerner, Brendan. "Leading Ladies." *Food & Wine,* October 2003, pp. 116, 118–119.

"Kosher Wine . . . A Little History." www.abarbanel.com/history.shtml.

"Krispy Kreme Restructures Board to Establish an Independent Majority; Announces Board of Directors Appointment." Press release, April 27, 2003. http://phx.corporate-ir.net/phoenix.zhtml?c=120929&p=irol-newsArticle&ID=609912&highlight=.

Kueny, Kathryn. *The Rhetoric of Sobriety: Wine in Early Islam.* Albany: State University of New York Press, 2001.

Lapsley, James T. *Bottled Poetry: Napa Winemaking from Prohibition to the Modern Era.* Berkeley: University of California Press, 1996.

Lawther, James. "Women in a Man's World." *Decanter,* September 1999, pp. 40–42, 44.

Layton, T. A. *Wines and People of Alsace.* London: Cassell and Cassell, 1970.

Lechmere, Adam. "Mentzelopoulos Is Sole Owner of Margaux." *Decanter,* March 10, 2003. www.decanter.com/news/46155.html.

Levere, Jane L. "Mireille Guiliano: The Bubbly Biz's Bon Vivant." *BIZBash,* March 5, 2001. http://bizbash.com/content/editorial/e236.asp.

Levy, Paul. "Wine Women." William F. Heintz Archives, Napa Valley Wine Library, St. Helena, Calif.

Liddell, Alex. *Port Wine Quintas of the Douro.* London: Sotheby's, 1992.

"Linda Bartoshuk." http://info.med.yale.edu/bbs/faculty/bar_li.html.

Littlewood, Joan. *Milady Vine: The Autobiography of Philippe de Rothschild.* London: Jonathan Cape, 1984.

Long, Zelma. "The Past Is the Beginning of the Future: Simi Winery in Its Second Century." Interview by Carole Hicks. Introduction by Ann Noble. Oral history transcript, 1992. Regional Oral History Office, Bancroft Library, University of California at Berkeley.

Loubère, Leo A. *The Red and the White*. Albany: State University of New York Press, 1978.

Low, Susan. "New Breed of South African Winemakers." *Wines & Vines,* November 2001. www.findarticles.com/cf_dls/m3488/11_82/80234972/print.jhtml.

"LVMH Announces Appointment of Cécile Bonnefond as President and CEO of Veuve Clicquot." www.findarticles.com/p/articles/mi_m0EIN/is_2000_Dec_7/ai_67685778.

MacDonogh, Giles. "They're Back." *Decanter,* December 1998, pp. 110–111, 113–114.

MacNeil, Karen. "Veuve Clicquot in Russia." *Quarterly Review of Wines,* August 1992, pp. 29–30.

————. *The Wine Bible*. New York: Workman, 2001.

MacQuitty, Jane. "Woman Who Built a Portuguese Empire." *The Times* (London), January 11, 1986.

Mann, Julia, and James Suckling. "Grand Dame of Bordeaux Dies." *Wine Spectator,* March 31, 2000, pp. 130, 133.

Mansson, Per-Henrik. "Americans in Burgundy." *Wine Spectator Online,* November 15, 1998. www.winespectator.com/Wine/Archives/Show_Article/0,1275,1966,00.html.

————. "Behind the Breakup." *Wine Spectator,* February 15, 1993, pp. 20–27.

————. "The Billionaires." *Wine Spectator,* November 30, 1995, pp. 60–80, 83–84, 86, 89–90, 92.

————. "Bize-Leroy Loses Suit in Bitter Burgundy Feud." *Wine Spectator,* November 15, 1992, p. 9.

Mansson, Per-Henrik, and Kim Marcus. "Château Margaux Sold to Former Owner." *Wine Spectator,* May 15, 2003. www.winespectator.com/Wine/Archives/Show_Article/0,1275,4113,00.html.

Mansson, Per-Henrik, and Thomas Matthews. "*Wine Spectator*'s Distinguished Service Award Winners." *Wine Spectator,* November 15, 1995, pp. 20–21.

Marcus, Kim. "Château Margaux Sold." *Wine Spectator,* March 10, 2003. www.winespectator.com/wine/Daily/News/0,1145,2003,00.html.

"Margaret Shahenian: A Woman of Many 'Firsts.'" *Wines & Vines,* July 1975, p. 24.

Marques, A. H. de Oliveira. *History of Portugal*. Vol. 2, *From Empire to Corporate State*. 2nd ed. New York: Columbia University Press, 1976.

Marriner, Cosima. "Part-Time Workplace: Labor's Bid for Women." *Sydney Morning Herald,* January 26, 2004, p. 4.

Matthews, Patrick. "Grape Britain." *Food & Wine,* April 19, 2004. www.foodand wine.com/articles/invoke.cfm?label=grape-britain.

Matthews, Thomas. "Chile's Two Worlds of Wine." *Wine Spectator,* June 15, 1995. www.winespectator.com/Wine/Archives/Show_Article/0,1275,457,00 .html.

—————. "New Directions in Chile." *Wine Spectator,* June 30, 1997. www.wine spectator.com/Wine/Archives/Show_Article/0,1275,1276,00.html.

—————. "Where Are the Women?" *Wine Spectator,* November 30, 1999. www .winespectator.com/Wine/Archives/Show_Article/10,1275,2431.00.html.

Mayer, Caroline E. "Women Break Barriers at Wineries." *St. Louis Post-Dispatch,* July 2, 1994, p. D4.

Mayson, Richard. "Port's Home Side." *Decanter,* May 1998, pp. 56–57, 59–60, 62.

McCarthy, Ed, and Mary Ewing-Mulligan. *Wine for Dummies.* Foster City: IDG Books, 1997.

McLean, Bethany. "Growing Up Gallo." *Fortune,* August 14, 2000, pp. 211–214, 216, 218, 220.

McWilliam's Wine. "Maurice O'Shea Award." www.mcwilliams.com.au/ Awards/Oshea.asp.

Meltzer, Peter D. "Sotheby's Serena Sutcliffe." *Wine Spectator,* May 15, 1995. www.winespectator.com/Wine/Archives/Show_Article/0,,414,00.html.

Minnaar, Melvyn. "A Trio of Firsts Signals Shift in South Africa's Wine Industry." *Wine Spectator,* December 31, 1999. www.winespectator.com/Wine/ Archives/Show_Article/0,1275,2530,00.html.

Mintz, Susannah B. "Poised for the Future." *Quarterly Review of Wines,* Summer 1999, pp. 91–93.

Molesworth, James. "Catena and Rothschild Release Their First Joint Wine." *Wine Spectator,* October 25, 2002. www.winespectator.com/Wine/Daily/ News/0,1145,1868,00.html.

Morgan, Jeff. "Lady in Red." *Wine Spectator,* November 30, 1997. www.wine spectator.com/Wine/Archives/Show_Article/0,1275,1479,00.html.

—————. "Mad Rush to Chile by California and French Vintners." *Wine Spectator,* May 31, 1996. www.winespectator.com/Wine/Archives/Show_Article/ 0,1275,831,00.html.

Mueller, Tom. "Grape Expectations." *Hemisphere Magazine,* January 2001, pp. 35–39.

Murphy, Linda. "Ten Leading Ladies." *Decanter,* October 2001. www.decanter
  .com/archive/4445.html.
————. "Winemaker of the Year." December 9, 2004. www-news.ucdavis.edu/
  in_the_news/full_text/view_clip.lasso?id=9927.
National Library of South Africa. "Fruits of the Vine: Empowerment." www
  .nlsa.ac.za/vine/empowerment.html.
New Zealand Wines Online. "Overview." www.nzwine.com/statistics/overview
  .php3.
————. "Wine Exports." www.nzwine.com/statistics/exports1.php3.
Nigro, Dana, and staff. "LVMH Takes Controlling Stake in Napa and Aussie
  Wineries." *Wine Spectator,* March 31, 2001. www.winespectator.com/Wine/
  Archive/Show_Article/0,1275,3140,00.html.
Norman, Remington. *The Great Domaines of Burgundy.* 2nd ed. London: Kyle
  Cathie, 1996.
Norrie, Dr. Philip. "The Wine Doctor: Wine and Health." *Winestate Magazine,*
  May/June 2000. www.winestate.com.au/magazine/article.asp?articleno=
  131.
"OBE for Jancis Robinson." *Asia Cuisine: Weekly Ezine* 5, no. 26, June 21, 2003.
  http://asiacuisine.com.sg/ezine/ezine5–26.html.
Olney, Richard. *Romanée-Conti: The World's Most Fabled Wine.* New York: Riz-
  zoli, 1991.
O'Neill, Anne-Marie. "Andrea Immer." *People,* May 4, 1998, pp. 87–88, 90.
Parker, Robert M., Jr. "25 Years in Wine: The Critic Robert M. Parker, Jr." *Food
  & Wine,* September 2003, pp. 132–135, 164.
Parnell, Colin. "Madame May-Eliane de Lencquesaing." *Decanter,* March 1994,
  pp. 31–35.
Parry, Melanie, ed. *Larousse Dictionary of Women.* New York: Larousse King-
  fisher Chambers, 1996.
Perkins, Sam. "Noses Seek Wine Geekdom's Biggest Prize." *New York Times,*
  April 7, 2004, pp. D1, D4.
Phillips, Rod. *A Short History of Wine.* New York: Ecco, 2002.
Pitcher, Steve. "Napa Valley's Most Coveted Cabs (and the People Who Make
  Them)." *The Wine News,* June/July 1997. www.thewinenews.com/junjul97/
  napacabs.htm.
Pohl, Otto. "New Zealand Stokes Its Wine Ambitions." *New York Times,* March
  3, 2004, pp. W1, W7.
Pommery. Reims: Champagne Pommery, n.d.

Poo, Mu-Chou. *Wine and Wine Offerings in the Religion of Ancient Egypt.* London: Kegan Paul, 1995.

Port, Jeni. *Crushed by Women: Women and Wine.* Melbourne: Arcadia, 2000.

Prchal, Dolly. "Josephine Marlin Tychson: The First Woman Winemaker in California." *Napa County Historical Society Gleanings* 3, no. 4 (December 1986): 1–20.

Prial, Frank J. "'Making Sense' Still Making Sense." *New York Times,* October 8, 2003, p. D6.

Price, Pamela Vandyke. *Woman of Taste: Memoirs from the Wine World.* London: John Murray, 1990.

Priewe, Jens. *Wine: From Grape to Glass.* Rev. ed. New York: Abbeville Press, 2001.

Rachman, Gideon. "The Globe in a Glass." *The Economist* 323, December 18–30, 1999, pp. 91–105.

Ray, Cyril. *Bollinger: Tradition of a Champagne Family.* Updated, with a new chapter, "Bollinger Today," by Serena Sutcliffe. London: William Heinemann, 1994.

Read, Jan. *The Wines of Portugal.* London: Faber and Faber, 1982.

Renaud, S., and M. de Lorgeril. "Wine, Alcohol, Platelets, and the French Paradox for Coronary Heart Disease." *The Lancet* 339 (June 20, 1992): 1523–1526.

Rhodes, Anthony. *Princes of the Grape.* London: Weidenfeld and Nicolson, 1975.

Roberto, Michael A. "The Changing Structure of the Global Wine Industry." *International Business and Economic Research Journal* 2, no. 9 (September 2003): 1–14.

Robinson, Jancis, ed. *The Oxford Companion to Wine.* New York: Oxford University Press, 1994.

———. "Stars of Burgundy." *Food & Wine,* October 1999, pp. 136–139, 174.

———. *Tasting Pleasure: Confessions of a Wine Lover.* New York: Viking Penguin, 1997.

Roby, Norm. "A New Breed of Winemaker." *Wine News,* June/July 1995, pp. 17–23.

"Ronell Wiid." www.wine.co.za/Directory/Contact.aspx?CONTACTID= 230&PRODUCERID=1102.

Saratoga Wine Exchange. "Chilean Wine History." www.saratogawinex.com/ chilean-wine.htm#his.

Sax, David, with James Molesworth. "Argentina's Wine Industry Rises above Country's Economic Crisis." *Wine Spectator,* January 30, 2004. www.wine spectator.com/Wine/Daily/News/0,1145,2330,00.html.

Sax, Irene. "Master Mind." *New York Newsday,* August 11, 1993, p. 69.

Schachner, Michael. "A Giant Awakens in South America." *Wine Enthusiast,* October 2001. www.winemag.com/ME2/dirmod.asp?sid=&nm=&type= Publishing&mod=Publications%3A%3AArticle&mid=8F3A7027421841978 F18BE895F87F791&tier=4&id=D04244EC39584E319BFB99B387150415.

Schmid, Doreen. "Italy's Women of Wine." *Quarterly Review of Wines,* Autumn 1989, pp. 34–36.

Schultz, Stanley K. "The Politics of Prohibition: The 1920s." http://us.history .wisc.edu/hist102/lectures/lecture17.html.

Scientific American Frontiers. "Ask the Scientists: Linda Bartoshuk." www.pbs .org/safarchive/3_ask/archive/bio/94_bartoshuk_bio.html.

Seely, James. *Great Bordeaux Wines.* Boston: Little, Brown, 1986.

————. *The Wines of South Africa.* London: Faber and Faber, 1997.

Shah, Michèlle. "Prima Donna." *Decanter,* May 2002, pp. 26–27, 29–30, 33.

Shaw, John. "Constellation Brands Agrees to Buy Australian Winery." *New York Times,* January 18, 2003, p. B3.

Sheahan, Randy. "Zelma Long and the New Simi." *Quarterly Review of Wines,* Autumn 1987, pp. 29–31, 33.

Shriver, Jerry. "Coaxing Greatness from Grapes: Turley's Fine Wines Put Taste over Technology." *USA Today,* July 8, 1997, p. D1.

Simon, Andre L. *The History of Champagne.* London: Octopus Books, 1971.

————. *The Wines, Vineyards, and Vignerons of Australia.* Melbourne: Lansdown Press, 1967.

Solsten, Eric, ed. *Portugal: A Country Study.* 2nd ed. Washington, D.C.: Federal Research Division, Library of Congress, 1994.

"Sonador Wines: History." www.sonadorwines.com/default.asp?V_DOC_ID =834.

Southern Starz. "Morgenhof." www.southernstarz.com/vineyard.cfm?preview =500.

Spahni, Pierre. *The International Wine Trade.* 2nd ed. Cambridge: Woodhead, 2000.

Spencer, Alan. "Saint-Emilion Women Enfranchised after 800 Years." *Decanter,* April 12, 2001. www.decanter.com/news/46862.html.

Stevenson, Tom. *The New Sotheby's Wine Encyclopedia: A Comprehensive Reference Guide to the Wines of the World.* New York: DK Publishing, 1997.

Stimpfig, John. "Still Waters Run Deep." *Decanter,* September 2000, pp. 56–59.

————. "Wine, Women, Misconceptions." *Decanter,* December 1999, pp. 54–55, 57–58.

Stimpfig, John, and Susan Keevil. "The Woman Who Outsold Bordeaux." *Decanter,* August 2000, pp. 28–33.

Stuller, Jay, and Glen Martin. *Through the Grapevine: The Real Story Behind America's $8 Billion Wine Industry.* New York: HarperCollins West, 1994.

Suckling, James. *Vintage Port.* San Francisco: Wine Spectator Press, 1990.

Sullivan, Charles L. *Zinfandel: A History of a Grape and Its Wine.* Berkeley: University of California Press, 2003.

Sutcliffe, Serena. "Bollinger Today." In *Bollinger: Tradition of a Champagne Family,* by Cyril Ray. London: Heinemann, 1994.

———. *Champagne: The History and the Character of the World's Most Celebrated Wine.* New York: Simon and Schuster, 1988.

———. *The Simon and Schuster Guide to the Wines of Burgundy.* New York: Simon and Schuster, 1992.

———. "Women in Wine: A Personal View." www.sothebys.com/connoisseur/espert/ei_wiw_0900.html (accessed October 8, 2001; no longer available).

Székely, Ágata. "Red Wine: The Healthiest Drink." *Vuelo,* February 2003, pp. 40–42.

Tanzer, Stephen. *International Wine Cellar.* November/December 2004.

Tesconi, Tim. "Vintners' Daughters." *Santa Rosa Press Democrat,* September 20, 1998, pp. A1, A6–A7.

Toerien, Wendy. *Wines and Vineyards of South Africa.* Cape Town: Struik, 2000.

"Top International Award for Jane." *Hunter's Club Newsletter,* Summer 2003.

"Treasured Hunter." *Harpers Supplement: Treasured Trophies,* October 2003, p. 19–20.

Unwin, Tim. *Wine and the Vine: An Historical Geography of Viticulture and the Wine Trade.* London: Routledge, 1991.

"Veuve Clicquot in the U.S." *Messages: Management Review LVMH/FA,* no. 16 (January 1997), pp. 20–21.

Viña Errazuriz. "Chilean Wine History." www.errazurizwines.com/Chilean%20Wine%20History.htm.

Viña Santa Carolina. "Chilean Wine History." www.vscwine.com/aboutchile/history.htm.

———. "Consuelo Marín Gamé, Winemaker." www.vscwine.com/about/winemaker.htm.

———. "The Land," www.vscwine.com/aboutchile/land.htm

Viña Santa Rita. "Winemakers." www.santarita.com/tour7.asp.

Vine, Richard P., et al. *Winemaking: From Grape Growing to Marketplace.* New York: Chapman and Hall, 1997.

Vintage Cellars. "Winemaker of the Year." *Cellar News,* September 2000. www
.vintagecellars.com.au/shared/html/sec/cellar/archive/winemaker.htm.
"Visit Chile." www.visitchile.com/detalle_noticia.asp?codigo_noticia=8&idioma
=ing.
"Volstead Act." http://college.hmco.com/history/readerscomp/rcah/html/ah_
089600_volsteadact.htm.
"Volstead Act: 1920." www.multied.com/documents/volstead.html.
Wade, Nicholas. "DNA Testing Digs Up Lowly Roots of an Aristocratic Wine
Grape." *International Herald Tribune,* September 4–5, 1999, pp. 1, 6.
———. "Vintage Genetics Turns Out to Be Ordinaire." *New York Times,* No-
vember 23, 1999, Science Times, pp. 1–2.
Walker, Larry. "Larry Walker Talks with Karen Ross." *Wines & Vines,* June 1998,
pp. 16–18, 20–22.
———. "Women for Winesense." *Wines & Vines,* November 2001. www.find
articles.com/cf_dls/m3488/11_82/80234987.
Wasserman, Sheldon, and Pauline Wasserman. *Italy's Noble Red Wines.* 2nd ed.
New York: Macmillan, 1991.
Weston, Lilyane. "How South Africa Has Developed into a Major Wine
Maker." *Bucks Free Press,* January 3, 2002. www.bucksfreepress.co.uk/search/
display.var.33205.0.how_south_africa_has_developed_into_a_major_wine_
maker.php.
Williams, Andrew. *Flying Winemakers: The New World of Wine.* Adelaide: Wine-
titles, 1995.
"Wine, Women, and Song." *Sunday Times* (Cape Town), November 21, 1999.
www.sundaytimes.co.za/1999/11/21/lifestyle/life03.htm.
"Wine Expert Marian Baldy Tastes National Success." *Inside Chico State* 3, no. 8,
December 12, 2002. www.csuchico.edu/pub/inside/archive/02_12_12/03_
wine.html.
Wine Institute. "Economic Importance of California Wine Is $33 Billion to State."
News release, January 20, 2000. www.wineinstitute.org/communications/
statistics/economicimportance.htm.
———. "Key Facts: California Wine Industry Statistical Highlights." www
.wineinstitute.org/communications/statistics/stathio1.htm.
———. "Key Facts: Wine Consumption in the U.S., 1934 to 2002." www.wine
institute.org/communications/statistics/consumption1934_99.html.
———. "Key Facts: World Vineyard Acreage by Country." www.wineinstitute
.org/communications/statistics/keyfacts_worldacreage4.htm.

———. "Key Facts: World Wine Production by Country." www.wineinstitute .org/communications/statistics/keyfacts_worldwineproduction02.htm.

"Winemaker of the Year: Mia Klein." *Food & Wine,* October 2003, p. 139.

WinePros. "Barons of Barossa: The Winds of Change Dinner." March 21, 2003. www.winepros.com.au/jsp/cda/authors/article.jsp?ID=5018.

"Winery Locator by State within the USA." www.allamericanwineries.com/ AAWMain/locate.htm.

"Wines of South Africa: Transformation of the Wine Industry." www.wosa .co.za/sa/industry_plan.htm.

Winik, Marion. "The Women of Champagne." *American Way,* March 1, 1997, pp. 40–41, 43–45, 110, 112–113, 116.

Wippel, Teresa. "President's Message." Association for Women in Communications, Seattle branch, newsletter, September 2001. www.seattleawc.org/prez_ msg_sept01.html.

Women for Winesense. www.womenforwinesense.org.

"Women Winemakers Make a Stand at Nederburg Auction." March 30, 2001. http://iafrica.com/highlife/herlife/news/250851.htm.

Woodham, Richard. "Di Cullen Dies." *Decanter,* March 4, 2003. www.decanter .com/news/46162.html.

"Yalumba: Winemakers." www.yalumba.com/content.asp?p=209.

INDEX

Italicized page numbers refer to illustrations and captions.

Text:	11/15 Granjon
Display:	Granjon
Compositor:	Integrated Composition Systems
Indexer:	Sharon Sweeney
Printer and binder:	Thomson-Shore. Inc.